## A Guide to Biblical Hebrew Syntax

*A Guide to Biblical Hebrew Syntax* introduces and abridges the syntactical features of the original language of the Hebrew Bible or Old Testament. Scholars have made significant progress in recent decades in understanding Biblical Hebrew syntax. Yet intermediate readers seldom have access to this progress because of the technical jargon and sometimes-obscure locations of the scholarly publications. This guide is an intermediate-level reference grammar for Biblical Hebrew. As such, it assumes an understanding of elementary phonology and morphology, and it defines and illustrates the fundamental syntactical features of Biblical Hebrew that most intermediate-level readers struggle to master. The volume divides Biblical Hebrew syntax, and to a lesser extent morphology, into four parts. The first three cover the individual words (nouns, verbs, and particles) with the goal of helping the reader move from morphological and syntactical observations to meaning and significance. The fourth section moves beyond phrase-level phenomena and considers the larger relationships of clauses and sentences.

Bill T. Arnold is Director of Hebrew Studies and Professor of Old Testament and Semitic Languages at Asbury Theological Seminary. He is the coauthor of *Encountering the Old Testament: A Christian Survey* and author of the forthcoming volume on Genesis in the New Cambridge Bible Commentary Series.

John H. Choi is a Hebrew Teaching Fellow at Asbury Theological Seminary.

# A Guide to Biblical
# Hebrew Syntax

BILL T. ARNOLD
*Asbury Theological Seminary*

JOHN H. CHOI
*Asbury Theological Seminary*

CAMBRIDGE
UNIVERSITY PRESS

CAMBRIDGE UNIVERSITY PRESS
Cambridge, New York, Melbourne, Madrid, Cape Town, Singapore,
São Paulo, Delhi, Dubai, Tokyo

Cambridge University Press
32 Avenue of the Americas, New York, NY 10013-2473, USA

www.cambridge.org
Information on this title: www.cambridge.org/9780521533485

© Cambridge University Press 2003

First published 2003
8th printing 2009

Printed in the United States of America

*A catalog record for this publication is available from the British Library.*

*Library of Congress Cataloging in Publication Data*

Arnold, B. T.
A guide to biblical Hebrew syntax / Bill T. Arnold, John H. Choi.
p.  cm.
Includes bibliographical references and index.
ISBN 0-521-82609-8 – ISBN 0-521-53348-1 (pb.)
1. Hebrew language – Syntax.  I. Choi, John H.  II. Title.
PJ4701 .A76  2003
492.4'5 – dc21    2002041025

ISBN 978-0-521-82609-9 Hardback
ISBN 978-0-521-53348-5 Paperback

# Contents

113098

# Preface

This book is intended to introduce basic and critical issues of Hebrew syntax to beginning and intermediate students. It grows out of eighteen collective years of experience in teaching Biblical Hebrew to seminarians. Each year, we teach or supervise the instruction for approximately 180 students in preparation for ordained ministry or other religious professions. Our experiences led us to conclude that a significant gap exists between, on the one hand, the current scholarly understanding of Hebrew syntax, based on significant progress in the discipline in recent decades, and on the other hand, the understanding of Hebrew syntax among our students. The problem seemed compounded by the lack of an intermediate-level grammar, holding a position between beginning grammars and advanced reference grammars. In addition, the ever-growing demands on theological education today have resulted in less time to master Biblical Hebrew. Often the first thing omitted in a beginning Hebrew course is an overview of syntactical features. Our purpose, then, has been simply to bridge the gap, as best we can, between our students and the best of current research on Biblical Hebrew syntax.

This book, then, is not intended to replace the standard reference grammars, which we have consulted constantly in the process, but to present to beginning and intermediate students a means of entry into the latest scholarship on Biblical Hebrew. To this end, we have included extensive references in the footnotes where appropriate. In particular, we have been most influenced by the unity brought to bear on the Hebrew verbal system by Bruce K. Waltke and Michael O'Connor. We have also consulted frequently the grammars by Joüon-Muraoka and Gesenius-Kautzsch-Cowley, and to some degree those by van der Merwe-Naudé-Kroeze and Meyer. Through interaction with these and other sources of scholarship, we feel that we have, at several points, introduced innovations in our explanations of Biblical Hebrew syntax in an attempt to refine the way we read and interpret the Bible today.

We express appreciation to our colleagues Joseph R. Dongell, David L. Thompson, Lawson G. Stone, and Brent A. Strawn for helpful suggestions on several points, and especially Dr. Stone for permission to use his chart in Appendix 2. We also benefited greatly from the comments and suggestions of the anonymous external reviewers hired by Cambridge University Press. The editors of the Press have been exemplary in every way, and we note especially Andrew Beck, who has been a source of encouragement from the beginning. In addition, Phyllis Berk and Janis Bolster made many improvements during the production process.

# 1 *Introduction*

At the heart of biblical interpretation is the need to read the Bible's *syntax*, that is, to study the way words, phrases, clauses, and sentences relate to one another in order to create meaning. Biblical Hebrew is a language far removed from us in time and culture. Mastering it is a noble but daunting task. Students often learn to discern the elementary phonology and morphology in order to "read" the biblical text. But we believe exegesis (or the extraction of a text's meaning) requires more than phonology and verb parsing. Achieving a deep-level reading requires a grasp of a text's syntactical relationships, a topic that most beginning grammars do not present in detail. Thus, our task has been to help the reader grasp the building blocks of Biblical Hebrew, that is, the syntactical specifics that constitute meaning. These are the linguistic details through which the most profound of all statements can be made, and have been made – those of Israel's monotheism and the nation's covenant relationship with YHWH.

We have defined and illustrated the fundamental morphosyntactical features of Biblical Hebrew. The volume divides Hebrew syntax, and to a lesser extent morphology ("the way words are patterned or inflected"), into four parts. The first three cover individual words (nouns, verbs, and particles) with the goal of helping the reader move from morphological and syntactical observations to meaning and significance. The fourth section moves beyond phrase-level

1

phenomena and considers the larger relationships of clauses and sentences. Each syntactical category begins with at least one paragraph, giving definition to that grammatical category. This is followed by a list of the most common exegetical possibilities for that particular grammatical phenomenon. We have provided at least one example (and in most cases more than one) for each syntactical function. Each example is followed by a translation, in which the syntactical feature in question is italicized and underlined where possible. The translations are often related to the NRSV, although we have frequently taken the liberty of altering the translations at points in order to illustrate better the particular syntactical feature under discussion. This is followed by the biblical reference. All examples are taken directly from the Hebrew Bible; on occasion, certain prefixed or conjoined particles, which have no bearing on the syntactical principle being illustrated, have been omitted for the sake of clarity in the English translation.

The categories for classification presented here are by no means exhaustive, which would have required a book many times this size. We have made frequent reference to the leading reference grammars for additional information. We have also omitted discussions of elementary phonology and morphology, including difficult forms or spellings that may be unique or exceptional in some way, all of which are covered sufficiently by numerous beginning grammars. In our footnotes we have frequently included references to the elementary grammars so as to encourage the reader to consult a familiar source in order to review an elementary detail of phonology or morphology, which may have been forgotten. For example, our discussion of "determination" (section 2.6) reminds the reader that one of the ways a noun may be marked as definite is with the prefixed definite article. Since all beginning grammars explain the morphological details of the definite article, with examples of the various forms it takes depending on the noun it marks, we have not repeated that information here. Instead, we direct the reader to review the beginning grammars where needed.[1] We have also omitted entirely, or in some cases briefly summarized, certain theoretical and complex grammatical issues that regularly make the standard reference grammars unintelligible to the intermediate student. We have, however, included many discussion footnotes dealing with these issues in order to provide additional background information that we believe will be of particular interest to advanced students and scholars. In this way, we have attempted to create a user-friendly volume of modest size.

For the most part, the features defined and illustrated here pertain to the language used in the extended narratives of the Pentateuch and the Historical Books, along with prose sections of the Prophets and Writings. This language is sometimes known as Classical Biblical Hebrew, although we refer to it simply as Biblical Hebrew (BH).[2] At times, we make further observations on Late Biblical Hebrew (LBH), by which we mean the language of most of the biblical books written after the exile (1–2 Chronicles, Ezra-Nehemiah, Esther, Daniel, selected Psalms, Song of Songs, Ecclesiastes, and portions of others).[3] Although LBH has features that are often unique, it also shares many features with BH. Thus, in some cases, we have used examples from both BH and LBH to illustrate the continuity of certain grammatical features of the Hebrew language.

---

[1] For more on morphology, students may now consult the convenient "How Hebrew Words Are Formed" in Landes 2001, 7–39.

[2] "BH" will be used throughout for "Biblical Hebrew." All other abbreviations may be found in Patrick H. Alexander et al., eds., *The SBL Handbook of Style for Ancient Near Eastern, Biblical, and Early Christian Studies* (Peabody, Mass.: Hendrickson, 1999), 121–52.

[3] This list is only partial, since it depends to a large degree on interpretive issues about which scholars are not agreed. For more on the distinction between BH and LBH, see Polzin 1976, 1–2; Rooker 1990; and Sáenz-Badillos 1993, 50–75 and 112–29.

## 2 *Nouns*

B y comparing evidence from early Semitic languages, scholars have concluded that pre-biblical Hebrew, and most likely all the Semitic languages of the second millennium B.C.E., had a declension system for the nouns (i.e., inflections), using cases parallel to those of Indo-European languages.[1] Thus, endings were used to mark a subject case (the nominative, ending in singular -*u*, plural -*ū*, and dual -*ā*), an adjectival case, which was used also with all the prepositions (genitive in -*i*, -*ī*, and -*ay*), and an object case that also had many adverbial uses (accusative in -*a*, -*ī*, and -*ay*). However, the case endings were almost completely lost in all first-millennium Northwest Semitic languages, and they were certainly lost throughout all attested Hebrew.[2]

[1] Akkadian retains the cases in most dialects, as does Classical Arabic. Among the Northwest Semitic languages, Amorite, Ugaritic, and the Canaanite glosses in the Tell Amarna texts – all from the second millennium B.C.E. – retain the case endings. On the preservation of cases in Amarna letters written by Canaanite scribes, see the important discussion of Rainey (1996, 1:161–70), although note his preference for "dependent" case over "genitive."

[2] Garr 1985, 61–63; Sáenz-Badillos 1993, 23; Moscati 1980, 94–96; Bergsträsser 1983, 16–17; Harris 1939, 59–60; Joüon and Muraoka 1993, 277–78; Bauer and Leander 1991, 522–23. Earlier grammarians believed the unaccented Hebrew ending הָ ־, used on certain nouns denoting direction, was a vestige of the old accusative case ending (so אַרְצָה, the

Biblical Hebrew compensates for the lack of case endings through a variety of means, primarily word order (as in modern English) and syntactical relationships, as well as through the use of prepositions. So the nominative case is most frequently discerned by word order and the lack of other markers. The genitive is marked by the construct relationship (section 2.2), and the accusative primarily by the definite direct object marker אֵת/אֶת and other syntactical relationships (section 2.3). Although we are able to trace the history of the three case *functions* in ancient Hebrew by comparing other Semitic languages, some authorities believe we should abandon the traditional case terms (especially "nominative") when describing BH syntax because the language does not mark the cases morphologically.[3] While we admit BH does not mark the cases with specific noun inflections, our objective is to identify and describe the functions of the noun.[4] Since the nouns in BH function syntactically in the same distinct "cases" as its parent language, it is still helpful to distinguish three case functions in BH using the traditional terminology: nominative, genitive, and accusative.[5]

so-called directive הָ ָ, or *he locale*). However, Ugaritic has a separate adverbial suffix -*h* in addition to an accusative case ending -*a*, proving beyond doubt that the *he locale* in Hebrew is not a remnant of the accusative (Waltke and O'Connor 1990, 185; Seow 1995, 152–53; and for the older – now outdated view – cf. Kautzsch 1910, 249). The closest BH comes to having cases is in the declension of the personal pronoun (cf. van der Merwe, Naudé, and Kroeze 1999, 191).

[3] Kroeze 2001, 33–50.

[4] Regarding the nominative, Kroeze accepts "subject" as a designation for category 2.1.1, but proposes the following alternative designations for the others: "copula-complement" for *predicate nominative*, "addressee" for *vocative*, and "dislocative" for *nominative absolute* (2001, 47). If the reader remembers that we are describing the *syntactical* functions of these nouns rather than their grammatical morphemes, we believe the traditional terminology is more helpful.

[5] It should be remembered that pronouns may serve in all these functions as well.

## 2.1 Nominative

Since a noun's case function is not marked morphologically, the nominative can be detected only by the noun's or pronoun's word order, by its agreement in gender and number with a verb (although with many exceptions), or by the sense of the context. Generally, the nominative may be categorized as follows.[6]

### 2.1.1 *Subject*

The noun or pronoun serves as the subject of an action: בָּרָא אֱלֹהִים, "*God* created" (Gen 1:1), וַיֹּאמֶר אֱלֹהִים, "And *God* said" (Gen 1:3). In the same way, when used with stative verbs the noun or pronoun may serve as the subject of a state: מָלְאָה הָאָרֶץ חָמָס, "*the earth* is filled with violence" (Gen 6:13).

### 2.1.2 *Predicate Nominative*

The noun or pronoun is equated with the subject by a "to be" verb (stated or implied): יְהוָה מֶלֶךְ, "YHWH *is king*" (Ps 10:16). In this example, the *subject* noun (section 2.1.1) is YHWH, and the *predicate nominative* is "king." The predicate nominative is often a clause of *identification,* in which case the word order is likely subject-predicate: אֲנִי יְהוָה, "I *am YHWH*" (Exod 6:2), אַתָּה הָאִישׁ, "You *are the man*" (2 Sam 12:7).[7] However, the word order is flexible, as this clause of *description* illustrates, also with subject-predicate order: מִשְׁפְּטֵי־יְהוָה אֱמֶת, "the ordinances of YHWH *are true*" (Ps 19:9 [Eng 19:10]). The predicate nominative is one

---

[6] Van der Merwe, Naudé, and Kroeze 1999, 247–49; Kautzsch 1910, 451–55; Waltke and O'Connor 1990, 128–30; Lambdin 1971a, 55; Chisholm 1998, 61; Williams 1976, 10.

[7] Andersen 1970, 31–34.

of several ways nominal clauses are constructed (see section 5.1.1,a).

### 2.1.3 *Vocative*

The noun designates a specific addressee and normally has the definite article (see section 2.6.2): הִנֵּה חֲנִית הַמֶּלֶךְ, "here is the spear, *O king*" (1 Sam 26:22 *Qere*). The vocative noun stands separate from the clause's syntax and is often juxtaposed to a second-person pronoun (or pronominal suffix) reflecting the direct speech: חֵי־נַפְשְׁךָ הַמֶּלֶךְ, "as your soul lives, *O King*" (1 Sam 17:55), דְּבַר־סֵתֶר לִי אֵלֶיךָ הַמֶּלֶךְ, "I have a secret message for you, *O King*" (Judg 3:19). The second person may be expressed by the imperative: הוֹשִׁיעֵנוּ אֱלֹהֵי יִשְׁעֵנוּ, "Save us, *O God* of our salvation" (1 Chr 16:35), הוֹשִׁיעָה יְהוָה, "Save now, *O Yhwh*" (Ps 12:2 [Eng 12:1]).

### 2.1.4 *Nominative Absolute*

The noun is isolated from the following sentence (sometimes by an intervening subordinate clause or series of appositional terms) and then resumed by a pronoun serving as the subject of the sentence: יְהוָה הוּא הָאֱלֹהִים, "*Yhwh, he* is God" (1 Kgs 18:39), הָאִשָּׁה אֲשֶׁר נָתַתָּה עִמָּדִי הִוא נָתְנָה־לִּי מִן־הָעֵץ וָאֹכֵל, "The *woman*, whom you gave to be with me, *she* gave me fruit from the tree, and I ate" (Gen 3:12).

The nominative absolute is also known as *casus pendens* (Latin "hanging case") or as *focus marker*.[8] These are general designations for a grammatical element isolated outside a clause, usually at the start of the clause.

---

[8] Other designations include *dislocated construction* and *pendens construction*. The sentence constituent taking up the noun or pronoun again may be called the *resumptive*. Joüon and Muraoka 1993, 586–88; Waltke and O'Connor 1990, 692; and for a distinction from so-called *fronting*, see van der Merwe, Naudé, and Kroeze 1999, 336–39.

## 2.2 Genitive

Most relationships that exist between two nouns are expressed
in BH by means of the genitive construction. English usually expresses this genitive relationship between two nouns
with the word "of." For example, in the phrase "the daughter of the king," the noun "king" acts as a genitive modi-
fier of "daughter." Thus, the genitive relationship often denotes a possessive sense: "the king's daughter." However, the
genitive relationship is used in BH to denote a wide variety
of other uses besides possessive. For example, "the word of
truth" does not mean "truth's word," but rather "the true
word."[9]

The genitive relationship is marked grammatically in
Hebrew by means of the construct state, in which two (or
more) nouns are bound together to form a construct phrase
or chain. In the structure *construct plus genitive,* the genitive
modifies the construct in some way, frequently as some sort
of attributive adjective.[10] This list includes the most common
ways in which a genitive modifies the preceding noun(s) or
adjective(s).[11]

### 2.2.1 *Possessive*

The genitive has ownership of the construct: בֵּית־יְהוָה,
"the temple *of YHWH*" or "*YHWH*'s temple" (1 Kgs 6:37),
צְבָאוֹת יְהוָה, "the hosts *of YHWH*" or "the hosts *possessed*

---

9 English also uses noun-noun compounds (as in "notebook" and "airport")
   and apostrophe-*s* (Jeremiah's confession) in ways similar to the Hebrew
   construct phrase (Waltke and O'Connor 1990, 141).
10 Joüon and Muraoka 1993, 463–77; Waltke and O'Connor 1990, 136–
   60; Kautzsch 1910, 410–23, esp. 416–19; Williams 1976, 10–12; Chisholm
   1998, 62–64; van der Merwe, Naudé, and Kroeze 1999, 197–200. The
   *genitive* may also be called the *postconstructus* (van der Merwe, Naudé,
   and Kroeze 1999, 192). On the genitive in epigraphic Hebrew, see Gogel
   1998, 240–45.
11 The genitive function may also be expressed by the object of a preposition
   or a pronominal suffix on a noun (Waltke and O'Connor 1990, 138). The
   genitive categories listed here also apply to these.

*by YHWH*" (Exod 12:41). That which is possessed may be body parts:[12] שִׂפְתֵי־מֶלֶךְ, "lips of *a king*" or "a *king's* lips" (Prov 16:10), or a characteristic (הֲדְרַת־מֶלֶךְ, "the glory of *a king*" or "a *king's* glory" (Prov 14:28).

The direction of ownership may be reversed resulting in a *possessed* genitive, in which case the genitive is owned by the construct: בַּעַל־הַבַּיִת, "the owner *of the house*" or "*the house's* owner" (Exod 22:7 [Eng 22:8]), יְהוָה צְבָאוֹת, "YHWH *of hosts*" or "YHWH *who possesses hosts*" (1 Sam 1:11).

### 2.2.2 *Relationship*

The genitive marks someone standing in association with the construct: בְּנֵי הַמֶּלֶךְ, "the *king's* sons" (2 Sam 13:23), בֶּן־דָּוִיד, "the son of *David*" or "*David's* son" (1 Chr 29:22). This genitive is common with pronominal suffixes: אָחִי, "*my* brother" (Gen 20:13). The genitive of human relationship normally refers to kinship, although other social structures are possible.[13]

### 2.2.3 *Subjective*

The genitive is the subject of a verbal notion expressed by the construct noun: יֵשַׁע אֱלֹהִים, "the salvation of *God*" (Ps 50:23), דְּבַר־יְהוָה "*YHWH's* word," (Gen 15:1), חָכְמַת שְׁלֹמֹה, "*Solomon's* wisdom" (1 Kgs 5:10).

### 2.2.4 *Objective*

The genitive is the object of a verbal notion expressed by the construct noun: יִרְאַת יְהוָה, "the fear of *YHWH*" (Ps 19:8 [Eng 19:9]), שֹׁד עֲנִיִּים, "the violence of the *oppressed*" or "the violence done *to the oppressed*" (Ps 12:6). Sometimes the genitive identifies the recipient of the action implied in the construct: מְטַר־אַרְצְךָ, "rain *for your land*" (Deut 28:12).

---

[12] Waltke and O'Connor's "genitive of inalienable possession" (145).
[13] Waltke and O'Connor 1990, 145.

The direction is reversed in the *action* genitive, in which the genitive expresses a verbal notion denoting action directed toward the construct: עַם עֶבְרָתִי, "the people of *my wrath*" or "the people who are the *objects of my wrath*" (Isa 10:6).

### 2.2.5 *Attributive*

The genitive denotes a quality or attribute of the construct. In translation, the genitive often becomes an adjective: גִּבּוֹר חַיִל, "a man of *worth*" or "a *valorous* man" (Judg 11:1), אֵשֶׁת חַיִל, "a woman of *worth*" or "a *valorous* woman" (Ruth 3:11), הַר־קָדְשׁוֹ, "the mountain of *his holiness*" or "*his holy* mountain" (Ps 48:2 [Eng 48:1]), מֶלֶךְ הַכָּבוֹד, "the king *of glory*" or "*the glorious king*" (Ps 24:7), שִׂמְחַת עוֹלָם, "joy *of perpetuity*" or "*everlasting* joy" (Isa 61:7).

The nouns אִישׁ־, בַּעַל־, and בֶּן often occur with genitives to express the possessor of a quality, which is one way BH compensates for the lack of genuine adjectives:[14] אִישׁ הַדָּמִים, "a man *of blood*" or "a *bloodthirsty* man" (2 Sam 16:7), אִישׁ דְּבָרִים, "a man *of words*" or "an *eloquent* man" (Exod 4:10), בֶּן־מָוֶת, "the son *of death*" or "one *who deserves death*" (1 Sam 20:31), בֶּן־חֲמֵשׁ מֵאוֹת שָׁנָה, "a son *of five hundred years*" or "*five hundred years old*" (Gen 5:32), בַּעַל כָּנָף, "master *of wings*" or "*winged creature*" (Prov 1:17).

### 2.2.6 *Specification*

The reverse of the *attributive* genitive, the *specification* genitive is characterized by a quality or attribute of an adjectival construct: קְשֵׁה־עֹרֶף, "stiff *of neck*" or "stiff-*necked*" (Exod 32:9), יְפֵה־תֹאַר, "attractive *of shape*" or "*good-looking*" (Gen 39:6), טְמֵא שְׂפָתַיִם, "unclean *of lips*" or "unclean *with regard to the lips*" (Isa 6:5), אֶרֶךְ אַפַּיִם, "long *of nostrils* [as source of anger]" or "patient *with regard to anger*"

---

[14] Joüon and Muraoka 1993, 468–69.

(Exod 34:6). The specification genitive may also be called the *epexegetical genitive*.[15]

### 2.2.7 *Cause*

The genitive may be caused by the construct: רוּחַ חָכְמָה, "the spirit of *wisdom*" or "the spirit *that causes wisdom*" (Exod 28:3). The causal relationship may move in the opposite direction, so that the genitive is perceived as causing the construct: חוֹלַת אַהֲבָה, "sick *of love*" or "sick *because of love*" (Song 2:5), מְזֵי רָעָב, "those exhausted *of hunger*" or "exhausted people *because of hunger*" (Deut 32:24).[16]

### 2.2.8 *Purpose*

The genitive denotes the intended use of the referent of the construct: צֹאן טִבְחָה, "sheep *of slaughter*," or "sheep *intended for slaughter*" (Ps 44:23 [Eng 44:22]), אַבְנֵי־קֶלַע, "slingstones" or "stones *intended for the sling*" (Zech 9:15).

Closely related to the idea of *purpose* is the *genitive of result*, which denotes the result of an action implied in the construct: מוּסַר שְׁלוֹמֵנוּ, "the chastisement *of our welfare*" or "the chastisement *that resulted in our peace*" (Isa 53:5), כּוֹס הַתַּרְעֵלָה, "the cup *of staggering*" or "the cup *which results in staggering*" (Isa 51:17).

### 2.2.9 *Means*

The genitive is the instrument by means of which the action implied in the construct is performed: חַלְלֵי־חֶרֶב, "wounded *of the sword*" or "those wounded *by the sword*" (Isa 22:2), שְׂרֻפוֹת אֵשׁ, "burned *of fire*" or "burned *with fire*"

---

[15] Waltke and O'Connor 1990, 151.
[16] In which case the *causational genitive* is very close in meaning to 2.2.9, the *genitive of means* (Joüon and Muraoka 1993, 468; Waltke and O'Connor 1990, 146, and cf. note 22).

(Isa 1:7), טְמֵא־נֶפֶשׁ, "impure *of a corpse*" or "impure *by reason of contact with a corpse*" (Lev 22:4).

When the genitive is personal, this becomes a *genitive of agency*, which is similar to the *subjective genitive*: מֻכֵּה אֱלֹהִים, "stricken *by God*" (Isa 53:4).[17]

### 2.2.10 *Material*

The genitive denotes the material from which the construct is made: אֲרוֹן עֵץ, "an ark *of wood*" or "a *wooden* ark" (Deut 10:1), כְּלִי־כֶסֶף, "vessels *of silver*" or "*silver* vessels" (Gen 24:53), שֵׁבֶט בַּרְזֶל, "a rod *of iron*" or "an *iron* rod" (Ps 2:9).

### 2.2.11 *Measure*

The genitive marks the thing measured by a numeral in the construct: שְׁנֵי בָנִים, "two *sons*" (Gen 10:25), שִׁבְעַת יָמִים, "seven *days*" (Gen 8:10). The construct may be a non-numeric quantifier, such as רֹב/רוֹב, "multitude" or כָּל־/כֹּל/כוֹל, "all": רֹב דָּגָן, "plenty of *grain*" (Gen 27:28), בְּכָל־לְבַבְכֶם, "all your *heart*" (1 Sam 7:3).[18]

### 2.2.12 *Explicative*

The genitive is a specific member of a general category or class denoted by the construct, and typically specifies the proper noun for the construct: נְהַר־פְּרָת, "the river *Euphrates*" (Gen 15:18), אֶרֶץ מִצְרַיִם, "the land *of Egypt*" (Gen 41:19), גַּן־עֵדֶן, "the garden *Eden*" (Gen 2:15), בְּתוּלַת יִשְׂרָאֵל, "Virgin *Israel*" (Amos 5:2), בַּת־צִיּוֹן, "Daughter *Zion*"

---

[17] On the *genitive of agency* as a variation of subjective genitives, cf. Waltke and O'Connor 1990, 143.

[18] On the special connotations of כָּל־/כֹּל/כוֹל depending on the determination or indetermination of its genitive, see Kautzsch 1910, 411, and Joüon and Muraoka 1993, 518–19.

(2 Kgs 19:21). Note that "of" is often unnecessary in English translations of the *explicative genitive*.

### 2.2.13 *Superlative*

The genitive can be divided into parts, of which the construct is the best, most, or the greatest form or expression of the whole: מִבְחַר קְבָרֵינוּ, "the choice *of our graves*" or "the choicest *of our graves*" (Gen 23:6). Frequently a plural genitive will occur with the singular construct of the same noun to express the superlative: קֹדֶשׁ קָדָשִׁים, "holy *of holies*" or "*most* holy" (Exod 29:37), מֶלֶךְ מְלָכִים, "king *of kings*" or "*the greatest* king of all" (Ezek 26:7), שִׁיר הַשִּׁירִים, "the song *of songs*" or "*the choicest* song" (Song 1:1).[19]

## 2.3 Accusative

As we have said, the accusative function of the noun is not indicated morphologically as in Greek or Latin, but similar functions are expressed through other grammatical features. The use of the definite direct object (DDO) marker אֵת/אֶת־ is one such grammatical tag, although it hardly exhausts the forms taken by the accusative. In later biblical texts, the preposition לְ is used as the DDO, probably due to Aramaic influence.[20] So, for example, in the Hebrew examples that follow, some accusatives are marked as pronominal suffixes on the verb. In others, the accusative will appear as the object of a prepositional phrase, since some Hebrew verbs mark objects with specific prepositions (e.g., לְ plus עָזַר, "to help," בְּ plus דָּבַק, "to

---

[19] A similar meaning is possible (although not universally accepted) when a divine name occurs as the genitive: כְּגַן־יְהוָה, "like a *splendid* garden (literally: a garden *of YHWH*)" (Isa 51:3), תַּרְדֵּמַת יְהוָה, "a *very deep* sleep (literally: a deep sleep *of YHWH*)" (1 Sam 26:12). For more on the use of divine references to express a superlative, see Thomas 1954, 209–24.

[20] Joüon and Muraoka 1993, 447–48; Kautzsch 1910, 366. Cf. Lam 4:5; Ps 145:14; Ezra 8:24; 2 Chr 25:10.

cling to," בְּ plus בָּקַע, "to prevail," בְּ plus נִלְחַם, "to fight").[21]
The English translations of the examples may look simplistic,
while the Hebrew illustrates the variety of ways for marking
the accusative function.

As we have seen, nouns in the genitive modify other nouns
by means of the bound construction with those nouns (or by
means of prepositions). Nouns in the accusative modify verbs,
denoting either the direct object of a verb or serving as adverbial modifiers. Although BH lacks explicit indicators of the
accusative beyond the DDO, its functions can be identified
by comparison with other Semitic languages where the accusative case is marked by an ending (sg. -*a*, pl. -*ī*, du. -*ay*).[22]
This list includes the most common ways in which the accusative is used.[23] We have divided the uses into two groups,
the first listing examples of verbal objects in which the accusative is the recipient of a verb's action. The second group
lists adverbial accusatives, in which the accusative modifies the
circumstances surrounding the action of the verb.

### 2.3.1 *Object*

The simplest form of the accusative is the direct object of
a transitive verb: בָּרָא אֱלֹהִים אֵת הַשָּׁמַיִם וְאֵת הָאָרֶץ, "God created *the heavens* and *the earth*" (Gen 1:1), צִוָּה יְהוָה אֶת־מֹשֶׁה,
"Yнwн commanded *Moses*" (Exod 40:32).[24] However, the

---

[21] See Joüon and Muraoka 1993, 440–43, and Waltke and O'Connor 1990,
166.

[22] Since Hebrew no longer marks accusatives morphologically, some grammarians prefer to avoid such designations as "direct object" and "adverbial accusative," referring instead to a verb's "nominal complements" and
"nominal adjuncts" (van der Merwe, Naudé, and Kroeze 1999, 241–45,
and see the discussion in Waltke and O'Connor 1990, 162–63).

[23] Joüon and Muraoka 1993, 440–63; Meyer 1992, 412–20; Waltke and
O'Connor 1990, 161–86; Kautzsch 1910, 362–76; Williams 1976, 12–14;
Chisholm 1998, 64–66; van der Merwe, Naudé, and Kroeze 1999, 241–47.

[24] The DDO is primarily a marker of this *accusative of object*, although it
occasionally also appears with certain adverbial accusatives (Joüon and
Muraoka 1993, 444).

simplicity of the direct *object accusative* changes depending
on the nature of the verb itself. The following variations
are possible.

*(a) Affected* – The object, which exists before and apart
from the action of the verb, is reached by the action: וַיַּרְא אֱלֹהִים אֶת־הָאוֹר, "and God saw *the light*" (Gen
1:4), וַיַּעְזָר־לוֹ, "and he helped *him*" (2 Sam 21:17),
יְבָרֶכְךָ יְהוָה וְיִשְׁמְרֶךָ, "May YHWH bless *you* and keep *you*"
(Num 6:24).

*(b) Effected* – The object did not exist prior to the verbal
action, but is brought about by the action and is therefore
the product or result of the action: נִלְבְּנָה לְבֵנִים, "let us make
*bricks*" (Gen 11:3), זֶרַע זָרַע, "yielding *seed*" (Gen 1:29).[25]
The *effected accusative* is rare except with a denominative
verb of the same root. It is also concrete and external to
the verbal action, and therefore distinct from the *internal
accusative* (see the following).

*(c) Internal* – The object is an abstract noun of action,
and implies an action in most cases identical with that
of the verb:[26] פָּחֲדוּ פָחַד, "they were overcome *with fear*
[literally: they feared a *fear*]" (Ps 14:5). The object itself may precede the verb: חֵטְא חָטְאָה יְרוּשָׁלַם, "Jerusalem
sinned *grievously* [literally: sinned a *sin*]" (Lam 1:8).
As these two examples illustrate, the object is a noun
formed from the same root as the verb (so technically
also *cognate accusative*), is generally indefinite, and as
the following examples show, is frequently modified by

---

[25] This same idiom elsewhere (תִזְרַע אֶת־זַרְעֶךָ, Deut 11:10, and compare
22:9) is not an *effected accusative* because as the context makes clear and
as all the grammars recognize, the seed existed prior to the sowing and
is not brought about by the action. Thus, not every *cognate accusative* is
an effected accusative (Joüon and Muraoka 1993, 449–50; Waltke and
O'Connor 1990, 166).

[26] For the following, see Joüon and Muraoka 1993, 450–51; Kautzsch 1910,
366–67; and Waltke and O'Connor 1990, 167.

an attributive adjective: וַיֶּחֱרַד יִצְחָק חֲרָדָה גְּדֹלָה, "and Isaac trembled *violently* [literally: trembled a great *trembling*]" (Gen 27:33), וַיַּךְ יְהוָה בָּעָם מַכָּה רַבָּה מְאֹד, "and YHWH struck the people with a very great plague [literally: struck . . . with a very great *striking*]" (Num 11:33).

The concrete noun קוֹל, "voice," takes special uses of the *internal accusative*. Although it has no corresponding verb, קוֹל appears to be used in a way similar to the internal accusative with verbs expressing an emission of voice (Joüon and Muraoka 1993, 451; Kautzsch 1910, 367–68). Thus, we find it as an internal accusative noun of action with קָרָא, בָּכָה, זָעַק, and עָנָה, and usually modified as well: וְעָנוּ הַלְוִיִּם וְאָמְרוּ אֶל־כָּל־אִישׁ יִשְׂרָאֵל קוֹל רָם, "Then the Levites shall declare *in a loud voice* to all the Israelites" (Deut 27:14), וַיְבָרֶךְ אֵת כָּל־קְהַל יִשְׂרָאֵל קוֹל גָּדוֹל, "and he [Solomon] blessed all the assembly of Israel *with a loud voice*" (1 Kgs 8:55).

*(d) Complement* – The object is a noun used with certain intransitive verbs, which take on new transitive meanings through a modification of their original meanings (Kautzsch 1910, 368–70; Waltke and O'Connor 1990, 168). Verbs often taking the *complement accusative* include רִיב, רָצָה, חָפֵץ, יָכֹל, and שָׁכַב. So, for example: רִיבוּ אַלְמָנָה, "plead for *the widow*" (Isa 1:17), פֶּן־יֹאמַר אֹיְבִי יְכָלְתִּיו, "lest my enemy say, 'I have prevailed *against him*'" (Ps 13:5), חָפֵץ בְּךָ הַמֶּלֶךְ, "the king is delighted *with you*" (1 Sam 18:22).

Most of these occur in the Qal stem, but occasionally even the reflexive stems (Niphal and Hithpael) may take such an accusative:

וַיִּתְפָּרְקוּ כָּל־הָעָם אֶת־נִזְמֵי הַזָּהָב אֲשֶׁר בְּאָזְנֵיהֶם

"and all the people took off *the rings of gold* from their ears" (Exod 32:3). Other verbs sometimes taking the *complement accusative* are verbs of robing and disrobing (פָּשַׁט, לָבַשׁ, and עָדָה), verbs of fullness and emptiness (מָלֵא, נִזְרַע, שָׁרַץ, שָׂבַע,

גְּבֵר , פָּרַץ, גָּזַל , and others), as well as verbs of dwelling (יָשַׁב, שָׁכַב, גּוּר).[27]

*(e) Double* – The causative derived stems (Piel and Hiphil) and certain other verbs sometimes have more than one object.[28] Both of the accusatives are often direct objects, meaning we may speak of a *double object accusative*, although occasionally the second of two objects is a *complement accusative* or an *adverbial accusative*. In the case of the latter, we may speak rather of a *complex accusative*.

(e.1) In causative sentences, the Piel or Hiphil of verbs that are Qal transitives frequently require two accusatives. Typically, the subject of the causation (often a person) is used as a second accusative: לִמַּדְתִּי אֶתְכֶם חֻקִּים וּמִשְׁפָּטִים, "I have taught *you statutes and ordinances* [literally: I have caused *you* (subject of causation/accusative #2) to learn *statutes and ordinances* (accusative #1)]" (Deut 4:5), וַיַּאֲכִלֵנִי אֵת הַמְּגִלָּה הַזֹּאת, "and he [Yʜwʜ] fed me this scroll [literally: and he caused *me* (subject of causation/accusative #2) to eat *this scroll* (accusative #1)]" (Ezek 3:2). This *double accusative* is common with verbs of fullness and emptiness, robing and disrobing, and other causative constructions. In some, however, the first object is not a direct *object accusative*, but rather an *adverbial accusative* (see section 2.3.2): מִלֵּא אֹתָם חָכְמַת־לֵב, "He [Yʜwʜ] filled *them with skill* [literally: he caused *them* (subject of causation/accusative #2) to be full *of skill* (accusative #1)]" (Exod 35:35).

(e.2) The *double accusative* is also required by the nature of certain verbs that are not necessarily verbs of causation. So verbs of making, forming, naming, or counting often require two accusatives, the second

---

[27] See Kautzsch 1910 (369–70) for details.
[28] For details, see Kautzsch 1910, 370–72; Joüon and Muraoka 1993, 451–54; Waltke and O'Connor 1990, 173–77; and van der Merwe, Naudé, and Kroeze 1999, 243–44.

of which is frequently *adverbial*:[29] וַיִּבְנֶה אֶת־הָאֲבָנִים מִזְבֵּחַ,
"and he built *the stones* [object #1] *into an altar* [ob-
ject #2]" (1 Kgs 18:32), וַיִּיצֶר יְהוָה אֱלֹהִים אֶת־הָאָדָם עָפָר,
"Then Yhwh God formed *man* [object #1] *of dust* [ob-
ject #2]" (Gen 2:7), קָרְאָה שְׁמוֹ דָּן, "she called *his name*
[object #1] *Dan* [object #2]" (Gen 30:6). Likewise,
verbs of speaking and giving often require two accusatives: וַיִּתֶּן־לָנוּ אֶת־הָאָרֶץ הַזֹּאת, "and he [Yhwh] gave
*us* [object #1] *this land* [object #2]" (Deut 26:9),
וָאֲצַוֶּה אֶתְכֶם בָּעֵת הַהִוא אֵת כָּל־הַדְּבָרִים אֲשֶׁר תַּעֲשׂוּן, "And
I commanded *you* at that time *all the things* that you should
do" (Deut 1:18).

### 2.3.2 *Adverbial*

In addition to the simple direct object of a verb, some
accusative nouns are indirectly subordinated to the verb.
Rather than specifying the person or thing directly affected
by the verb, such accusatives modify more precisely the circumstances under which an action or situation occurs. In
other words, they serve as *adverbial* accusatives.[30]

*(a) Place* – The accusative signifies location with verbs
of motion or dwelling: צֵא הַשָּׂדֶה, "go out (into)
*the field*" (Gen 27:3), יָצָא אַשּׁוּר, "he went (into)
*Assyria*" (Gen 10:11), וַיֵּרְדוּ כָל־יִשְׂרָאֵל הַפְּלִשְׁתִּים, "and all
Israel went down (to) *the Philistines*" (1 Sam 13:20),
וַתֻּקַּח הָאִשָּׁה בֵּית פַּרְעֹה, "and the woman [Sarai] was taken

---

[29] See the accusatives of *material* and *product* in 2.3.2,f, and 2.3.2,g.

[30] Often such syntactical relationships are designated by prepositional
phrases, especially taking the place of accusatives of time or place
(Kautzsch 1910, 377–84). Instead of the *accusative of place*, the *he locale*
(Lambdin 1971a, 51–52; Seow 1995, 152–53) is often used. On the *adverbial accusatives* in general, see Joüon and Muraoka 1993, 455–59; Kautzsch
1910, 372–76; Waltke and O'Connor 1990, 169–73; Williams 1976, 12–14;
van der Merwe, Naudé, and Kroeze 1999, 244–45; and Chisholm 1998,
64–65.

(into) *Pharaoh's house*" (Gen 12:15), וַיַּעֲמֹד פֶּתַח הָאֹהֶל, "and he [YHWH] stood (at) *the doorway of the tent*" (Num 12:5). The location may specify the spacial extent of the verbal action: וַיִּרְדֹּף אַחֲרָיו דֶּרֶךְ שִׁבְעַת יָמִים, "and he pursued after him *a seven-day journey*" (Gen 31:23), וַנֵּלֶךְ אֵת כָּל־הַמִּדְבָּר הַגָּדוֹל וְהַנּוֹרָא הַהוּא, "and we went (through) all that great and terrible wilderness" (Deut 1:19). Sometimes the *accusative of place* is used with verbs that have no specific locational quality: וְאַתָּה תִּשְׁמַע הַשָּׁמַיִם, "and you yourself will hear (in) *heaven*" (1 Kgs 8:32).

*(b) Time* – The accusative locates an action in time or states its duration: וָאָבֹא הַיּוֹם אֶל־הָעָיִן, "and I came *today* to the spring" (Gen 24:42), יְהוָה בֹּקֶר תִּשְׁמַע קוֹלִי בֹּקֶר אֶעֱרָךְ־לְךָ, "O YHWH, *in the morning* you hear my voice; *in the morning* I plead my case to you" (Ps 5:4), אָנֹכִי מַמְטִיר עַל־הָאָרֶץ אַרְבָּעִים יוֹם וְאַרְבָּעִים לָיְלָה, "I will send rain on the earth *forty days and forty nights*" (Gen 7:4), אָגוּרָה בְאָהָלְךָ עוֹלָמִים, "Let me abide in your tent *forever*" (Ps 61:5).

*(c) Manner* – The accusative is an indefinite noun describing the way in which an action or situation is performed: וַיִּשְׁכֹּן יִשְׂרָאֵל בֶּטַח, "and Israel will swell *in safety*" (Deut 33:28), דִּבְרֵי הַנְּבִיאִים פֶּה־אֶחָד טוֹב אֶל־הַמֶּלֶךְ, "the words of the prophets *with one accord* are favorable to the king" (1 Kgs 22:13), וַיַּעַן כָּל־הָעָם קוֹל אֶחָד, "and all the people answered *with one voice*" (Exod 24:3). Adjectives and participles may also serve as *accusatives of manner*. וַיָּבֹא יַעֲקֹב שָׁלֵם עִיר שְׁכֶם, "and Jacob came *safely* into the city of Shechem" (Gen 33:18),[31] וְאָנֹכִי הוֹלֵךְ עֲרִירִי, "and I go *childless*" (Gen 15:2), קוֹל דּוֹדִי הִנֵּה־זֶה בָּא מְדַלֵּג עַל־הֶהָרִים, "the voice of my beloved; behold he comes *leaping* upon the mountains" (Song 2:8).

---

[31] Notice that this example also has a second accusative, which is an *accusative of place*: "into the city of Shechem."

*(d) State* – The accusative is an indefinite noun describing a feature, state, or quality of the *subject* at the time of the verbal action:[32] וַיֵּצֵא הַמַּשְׁחִית מִמַּחֲנֵה פְלִשְׁתִּים שְׁלֹשָׁה רָאשִׁים, "And raiders came out of the camp of the Philistines *in three companies*" (1 Sam 13:17), וַאֲרָם יָצְאוּ גְדוּדִים, "and the Arameans went forth *as maurading bands*" (2 Kgs 5:2), שְׁבִי אַלְמָנָה בֵית־אָבִיךְ, "remain *as a widow* in your father's house" (Gen 38:11).[33]

The accusative may also describe a feature, state, or quality of the *object* at the time of the verbal action: וַאֲנִי הִנְנִי מֵבִיא אֶת־הַמַּבּוּל מַיִם, "and I myself [Yhwh] am bringing a flood *of waters*" (Gen 6:17), תִּדְרְכִי נַפְשִׁי עֹז, "march on, my soul, *in strength*" (Judg 5:21), הִרְאַנִי יְהוָה אֹתְךָ מֶלֶךְ עַל־אֲרָם, "Yhwh has shown me that you will be *king* over Aram" (2 Kgs 8:13).

Like the *accusative of manner*, the *accusative of state* may be expressed by adjectives or participles: אֵרֵד אֶל־בְּנִי אָבֵל שְׁאֹלָה, "I will go down to the grave to my son *mourning*" (Gen 37:35), אֲנִי מְלֵאָה הָלַכְתִּי, "I went away *full*" (Ruth 1:21), וַיִּשְׁמַע מֹשֶׁה אֶת־הָעָם בֹּכֶה, "and Moses heard the people *weeping*" (Num 11:10).

*(e) Specification* – The accusative clarifies or explains further the verbal action, which would otherwise be generally or ambiguously stated:[34] חָלָה אֶת־רַגְלָיו, "he was diseased *in his feet*" (1 Kgs 15:23), לֹא נַכֶּנּוּ נָפֶשׁ, "we must not strike him *to death* [literally: *with respect to life*]" (Gen 37:21), רַק הַכִּסֵּא אֶגְדַּל מִמֶּךָּ, "it is only (with respect to) *the throne* that I shall be greater than you" (Gen 41:40), וּנְמַלְתֶּם אֵת בְּשַׂר עָרְלַתְכֶם, "and you shall be circumcised (with respect to) *the flesh of your foreskins*" (Gen 17:11).

---

[32] This use of the accusative is similar to the *accusative of manner,* and some grammars combine the treatment of the two (cf. Kautzsch 1910, 374–75).

[33] Note that this example contains two accusatives, the first an *accusative of state* (widow) and the second an *accusative of place* (father's house).

[34] May also be called the *epexegetical accusative* or the *accusative of limitation.*

*(f) Material* – The accusative denotes the matter used in the verbal action.[35] This use of the accusative is common with verbs for making, forming, or building, which typically take two accusatives; the first an *object accusative*, the second an *accusative of material:* וַיִּרְגְּמוּ אֹתוֹ כָל־יִשְׂרָאֵל אֶבֶן, "and all Israel stoned him *with stones*" (Josh 7:25), וַיִּיצֶר יְהוָה אֱלֹהִים אֶת־הָאָדָם עָפָר, "and YHWH God formed man *from dust*" (Gen 2:7), וְעָשִׂיתָ שְׁנַיִם כְּרֻבִים זָהָב, "and you shall make two cherubim *of gold*" (Exod 25:18), וַיַּעַשׂ אֶת־הַמְּכֹנוֹת עֶשֶׂר נְחֹשֶׁת, "and he made ten stands *of bronze*" (1 Kgs 7:27).

At times, it is impossible to determine by morphology alone whether the relationship between two nouns is genitival, accusatival, or appositional (compare sections 2.2.10, 2.3.2,f and 2.4.3).[36]

*(g) Product* – The accusative denotes the result of the verbal action. This use of the accusative is common with verbs for making, preparing, or shaping, which typically take two accusatives; the first an *object accusative*, the second an *accusative of product:* וַיָּשֶׂם אֶת־בָּנָיו שֹׁפְטִים לְיִשְׂרָאֵל, "and he [Samuel] made his sons *judges* over Israel" (1 Sam 8:1), וַיִּבְנֶה אֶת־הָאֲבָנִים מִזְבֵּחַ, "and he built the stones *into an altar*" (1 Kgs 18:32), וְלָקַחְתָּ סֹלֶת וְאָפִיתָ אֹתָהּ שְׁתֵּים עֶשְׂרֵה חַלּוֹת, "and you shall take choice flour, and bake it *into twelve cakes*" (Lev 24:5).

## 2.4 Apposition

In addition to the three main case functions (nominative, genitive, and accusative), BH also uses nouns in apposition, that is, in simple juxtaposition in order for the second noun (the *apposition*) to modify or elucidate the first

---

[35] For more on this and the next (*accusative of product*), see Kautzsch 1910, 371–72 and Waltke and O'Connor 1990, 174–75.

[36] Joüon and Muraoka 1993, 460–61; Waltke and O'Connor 1990, 173.

(the *leadword*).[37] Such nouns generally agree in gender, number, and definiteness, have the same function in the syntax, and refer to the same person, place, or thing in the external world. The apposition may often be translated by an adjective or prepositional phrase.[38] This list includes the most common ways in which apposition is used.[39]

### 2.4.1 *Species*

The apposition denotes the species or subclass to which the leadword belongs: זְבָחִים שְׁלָמִים, "peace-offerings [literally: sacrifices, *peace-offerings*]" (Exod 24:5). This usage is common when the leadword is a common noun for a person: אִישׁ כֹּהֵן, "a priest [literally: a man, *a priest*]" (Lev 21:9), אִישׁ מִצְרִי, "an Egyptian [literally: a man, *an Egyptian*]" (Exod 2:11), הַנַּעַר הַנָּבִיא, "the young prophet [literally: the young man, *the prophet*]" (2 Kgs 9:4), אֲנָשִׁים אַחִים, "brothers [literally: men, *brothers*]" (Gen 13:8).

### 2.4.2 *Attributive*

The apposition denotes a quality or attribute of the leadword. In translation, the apposition often becomes an adjective: אֲמָרִים אֱמֶת, "*true* words [literally: words, *truth*]" (Prov 22:21), אֱלֹהִים אֱמֶת, "the *true* God" (Jer 10:10), דְּבָרִים נִחֻמִים, "*comforting* words" (Zech 1:13), מִלְּשׁוֹן רְמִיָּה, "from a *deceitful* tongue" (Ps 120:2).

---

[37] Pronouns may also occur as the leadword (Waltke and O'Connor 1990, 232–33; Williams 1976, 15–16; and van der Merwe, Naudé, and Kroeze 1999, 230).

[38] Kautzsch 1910, 423–27; Waltke and O'Connor 1990, 226–34; Joüon and Muraoka 1993, 477–81; van der Merwe, Naudé, and Kroeze 1999, 228–30; Williams 1976, 15–16.

[39] On the emphatic and distributive uses of *repetitive apposition*, see Waltke and O'Connor 1990, 233–34, and van der Merwe, Naudé, and Kroeze 1999, 230. On apposition in epigraphic Hebrew, see Gogel 1998, 237–40.

### 2.4.3 *Material*

The apposition denotes the material from which the lead-word is made. Similar to the *attributive apposition,* this often becomes an adjective in translation: הָעֲבֹתֹת הַזָּהָב, "*gold* cords [literally: the cords, *the gold*]" (Exod 39:17), הַבָּקָר הַנְּחֹשֶׁת, "the *bronze* oxen" (2 Kgs 16:17), הָאֶבֶן הַבְּדִיל, "the *alloy* stone (i.e., plummet)" (Zech 4:10), מְצִלְתַּיִם נְחֹשֶׁת, "*brass* cymbals" (1 Chr 15:19). Occasionally the apposition may omit the definite article: הַמַּבּוּל מַיִם, "the flood (of) *waters*" (Gen 6:17), אֲשֵׁרָה כָּל־עֵץ, "Asherah made of *every kind of wood*" (Deut 16:21).

### 2.4.4 *Measure*

The apposition specifies the thing measured or weighed, in which case the leadword is a measuring unit: סְאָה־סֹלֶת, "a seah [unit of dry measurement] of *flour*" (2 Kgs 7:1), כִּכְּרַיִם כָּסֶף, "two *silver* talents" (1 Kgs 16:24).

Although the *apposition of measure* is not particularly common, a variation of it using numerals is. The apposition thus specifies the thing numbered, while the leadword is a numeral: שִׁבְעָה בָנִים וְשָׁלוֹשׁ בָּנוֹת, "seven *sons* and three *daughters*" (Job 1:2), חֲמִשָּׁה אֲנָשִׁים, "five *men*" (2 Kgs 25:19), שִׁבְעִים בָּנִים, "seventy *sons*" (Judg 8:30), שְׁנֵים הֶעָשָׂר אִישׁ, "the twelve *men*" (Josh 4:4).[40] Sometimes, however, the order is reversed, in which case the apposition is the numeral and the leadword specifies the thing numbered. This is often the case in inventories or enumerated lists: עִזִּים מָאתַיִם וּתְיָשִׁים עֶשְׂרִים רְחֵלִים מָאתַיִם וְאֵילִים עֶשְׂרִים, "*two hundred* female goats and *twenty* male goats, *two hundred* ewes and *twenty* rams" (Gen 32:15), בָּקָר שְׁנַיִם אֵילִם חֲמִשָּׁה עַתּוּדִים חֲמִשָּׁה כְּבָשִׂים בְּנֵי־שָׁנָה חֲמִשָּׁה, "*two* oxen, *five* rams, *five* male goats, and *five* male lambs a year old" (Num 7:17, and compare Num 28:19).

---

[40] Compare the *genitive of measure* in 2.2.11.

### 2.4.5 *Explicative*[41]

The apposition is a particular member of a general category denoted by the leadword, and typically gives the proper noun for the leadword: הַמֶּלֶךְ שְׁלֹמֹה, "King *Solomon*" (1 Kgs 1:34), הַנָּהָר פְּרָת, "the River *Euphrates*" (1 Chr 5:9), הָאָרֶץ כְּנַעַן, "Canaan [literally: the land, i.e., *Canaan*]" (Num 34:2). Occasionally the order is reversed, in which case the apposition specifies the category and the proper noun is the leadword: שְׁלֹמֹה הַמֶּלֶךְ, "*King* Solomon" (1 Chr 29:24).[42]

This becomes an *apposition of relationship* when the leadword is a noun of kinship: אֶת־אָחִיו אֶת־הֶבֶל, "his brother *Abel*" (Gen 4:2). The order here may likewise be reversed: הֶבֶל אָחִיו, "Abel *his brother*" (Gen 4:8).[43]

## 2.5 Adjectives

As might be expected, nouns may also be modified by adjectives. BH makes no morphological distinction between nouns and adjectives (although the adjective has no dual form).[44] The distinction between a noun and an adjective is left to the inherent lexical meanings of the terms and to their syntactical functions. Since most beginning grammars detail the uses of the adjective quite clearly, their syntactical features will only be summarized here.[45]

---

[41] The *explicative genitive* is more common than this *explicative apposition* (see 2.2.12 and Joüon and Muraoka 1993, 479).

[42] When the apposition is a proper noun requiring a preposition or DDO (אֵת/אֶת־), the particle is generally repeated on both words. If the leadword has the proper noun, the particle is not repeated. See Waltke and O'Connor 1990 (232), Joüon and Muraoka 1993 (479–80), Kautzsch 1910 (425), and Williams 1976 (15).

[43] Compare the *genitive of relationship* (2.2.3).

[44] Plural adjectives are thus used when modifying dual nouns (van der Merwe, Naudé, and Kroeze 1999, 231). Occasionally, adjectives can carry a vowel pattern distinct from the nouns.

[45] Lambdin 1971a, 13–15; Seow 1995, 72; Pratico and Van Pelt 2001, 61–64; Kittel, Hoffer, and Wright 1989, 251; Kelly 1992, 45–47; Weingreen 1959, 32–33.

Adjectives modify nouns by describing their state or condition. This list includes the most common ways in which the adjective is used. For more of what follows, the reference grammars may be consulted.[46]

### 2.5.1 *Attributive*

The adjective ascribes a quality to a noun. The *attributive adjective* forms a phrase with the noun it modifies, having a single function in the sentence. The adjective stands in apposition to the noun it modifies, normally following it and agreeing in gender, number, and definiteness: גָּדוֹל אִישׁ, "a *great* man" (2 Kgs 5:1), אִשָּׁה חֲכָמָה, "a *wise* woman" (2 Sam 14:2), הָעִיר הַגְּדֹלָה, "the *great* city" (Gen 10:12).

If the noun occurs in construct state with another noun, the attributive adjective follows the entire genitive construction: אִישׁ אֱלֹהִים קָדוֹשׁ, "a *holy* man of God" (2 Kgs 4:9). Wherever both nouns and the adjective are of the same gender, ambiguity may occur, and it can only be made clear by broader context. A series of attributive adjectives may occur after the noun modified, usually with a demonstrative adjective occurring in the final position: הָהָר הַטּוֹב הַזֶּה, "*this good* hill country" (Deut 3:25), הַגּוֹי הַגָּדוֹל הַזֶּה, "*this great* nation" (Deut 4:6).[47]

Rarely, the adjective precedes the noun it modifies, most often with numerals and רַבּוֹת/רַבִּים, probably because "many" was thought to be similar to numerals in function: רַבִּים צַיָּדִים, "*many* hunters" (Jer 16:16).

The definite article of the attributive adjective is sometimes omitted, perhaps because certain adjectives were thought inherently definite (such as רַבִּים and אַחֵר, as

---

[46] Kautzsch 1910, 427–32; Waltke and O'Connor 1990, 255–71; Joüon and Muraoka 1993, 521–25; Meyer 1992, 371–76; Horsnell 1999, 193–201; Chisholm 1998, 66–67; van der Merwe, Naudé, and Kroeze 1999, 230–37; Williams 1976, 16–18. On the adjectives in epigraphic Hebrew, see Gogel 1998 (202).

[47] For more details of the syntactical peculiarities of two or three adjectives following a noun, see Kautzsch 1910 (428).

well as the numeral אֶחָד, "one"): אֲחִיכֶם אַחֵר, "your *other* brother" (Gen 43:14), הָרֹאשׁ אֶחָד, "*one* company" (1 Sam 13:17), הַגּוֹיִם רַבִּים, "*many* nations" (Ezek 39:27). At other times, the noun being modified is inherently definite and therefore anarthrous, even while the adjective retains the article: יוֹם הַשִּׁשִּׁי, "the *sixth* day" (Gen 1:31).

### 2.5.2 *Predicate*

The adjective expresses an assertion about a noun requiring a form of the verb "to be" in translation. The *predicate adjective* often precedes the noun it modifies and agrees in gender and number, but is always indefinite:[48] גָּדוֹל עֲוֹנִי, "my punishment *is great*" (Gen 4:13), טוֹב הָעֵץ, "the tree *was good*" (Gen 3:6), צַדִּיק יְהוָה, "righteous *is Yhwh*" (Ps 145:17), יָשָׁר דְּבַר־יְהוָה, "the word of Yhwh *is upright*" (Ps 33:4). The predicate adjective is often used in nominal clauses of description (see section 5.1.1,b).

### 2.5.3 *Substantive*

The adjective functions as a noun, most often occurring with the definite article: הַחֲכָמִים, "the *skillful men* [literally: *the wise men*]" (Exod 36:4), though also without the definite article, as in חֲכָמִים, "*wise men*" (Job 5:13).

The *substantive adjective* may serve in any of the normal functions of a regular noun: as nominative (הַקָּטֹן, "the *young one*" [Gen 42:13]), as either noun of the genitive relationship (בֵּית גָּדוֹל, "*great* house [literally: house of a *great one*]" [2 Kgs 25:9]),[49] as accusative (אֶת־הַצַּדִּיק, "*the righteous*" [Eccl 3:17]), as apposition (צַדִּיק עַבְדִּי, "the *righteous one*, my servant" [Isa 53:11]), or as object of a preposition (וְעַל־קַל נִרְכָּב, "we will ride upon *swift horses* [literally: upon a *quick one*]" [Isa 30:16]).

---

[48] The tense of the translation must be determined from the Hebrew context.

[49] And see the *genitive of specification* in 2.2.13.

## 2.5.4 *Comparative and Superlative*

Hebrew has no inflected forms of the adjectives to express degrees of the adjectival quality, such as in English: big–bigger–biggest, great–greater–greatest, and so on. Instead, BH uses the adjectives in a number of syntactical variations to express the comparative and superlative degrees.

*(a) Comparative* – A higher degree of the adjectival quality is expressed when the preposition מִן is used with the noun being surpassed (see section 4.1.13,h). The preposition identifies the standard against which the noun is being compared, and typically the adjective has no definite article: חָכָם אַתָּה מִדָּנִיֵּאל, "you are *wiser than* Daniel" (Ezek 28:3 *Qere*), גָּבֹהַּ מִכָּל־הָעָם, "*taller than* all the people" (1 Sam 9:2), עַז מֵאֲרִי, "*stronger than* a lion" (Judg 14:18), גָּדוֹל יְהוָה מִכָּל־הָאֱלֹהִים, "YHWH is *greater than* all gods" (Exod 18:11).[50]

Sometimes the *comparative* denotes a condition that is too little or too much in force for attainment:[51] כִּי־כָבֵד מִמְּךָ הַדָּבָר, "for the task is *too heavy* for you" (Exod 18:18), הַמְעַט מִכֶּם, "*too slight a thing* for you" (Isa 7:13). In such uses, the preposition מִן may be attached to an infinitive construct rather than a noun: גָּדוֹל עֲוֹנִי מִנְּשֹׂא, "my punishment is *too great* to bear" (Gen 4:13), הָיָה רְכוּשָׁם רָב מִשֶּׁבֶת יַחְדָּו, "Their property had become *too great* for them to live together" (Gen 36:7), כִּי־מִזְבַּח הַנְּחֹשֶׁת אֲשֶׁר לִפְנֵי יְהוָה קָטֹן מֵהָכִיל אֶת־הָעֹלָה, "For the bronze altar which was before YHWH was *too small* to hold the burnt offering" (1 Kgs 8:64).

---

[50] At times the comparative is required even without the preposition מִן, and at other times the adjective is replaced by stative verbs. In some cases, the context must determine when the comparative is intended (see Kautzsch 1910, 430–31).

[51] See Waltke and O'Connor's *comparison of capability* (1990, 266) and Joüon's *elliptical comparison* (1991, 523–24); also see Kautzsch (1910, 430).

*(b) Superlative* – The highest degree of the adjectival quality is expressed when the adjective is made definite, whether by a definite article, a genitive construction,[52] or a pronominal suffix: הַקָּטָן, "the *youngest* [of eight sons]" (1 Sam 16:11), קְטֹן בָּנָיו, "the *youngest* of his sons" (2 Chr 21:17), מִגְּדוֹלָם וְעַד־קְטַנָּם, "from *the greatest* of them to *the least* of them" (Jonah 3:5).

The *superlative adjective* may rarely take the preposition בְּ with a noun: הַיָּפָה בַּנָּשִׁים, "the *most beautiful* among women" (Song 1:8), הָאִישׁ הָרַךְ בְּךָ, "*The most refined person* among you" (Deut 28:54).[53]

## 2.6 Determination

Nouns in BH are indeterminate (i.e., indefinite) unless marked otherwise. They may be marked as determinate/definite in three ways: a) by a prefixed definite article, b) by a pronominal suffix, or c) by occurring in the construct state bound to a definite noun.[54] Proper nouns and other appellatives are also definite by nature and do not require other determination, since they name a specific person or thing.

In general, indefinite nouns tend to focus on the class or quality of the person, place, or thing, while definite nouns focus on a unique or particular identity. Although BH has no *indefinite* article, the numeral "one" (אֶחָד/אַחַת) is used to

---

[52] That is, a *substantive* adjective serving as a construct in bound relationship with a noun, as in גְּדֹלֵי הָעִיר, "*the greatest men* of the city" (2 Kgs 10:6).

[53] The superlative may be expressed in a number of other ways, including the *superlative* genitive (2.2.13), repetition, the use of מְאֹד or עַד־מְאֹד after an adjective, or מִכָּל/־מִכֹּל after an adjective. See Joüon and Muraoka 1993, 524–25; Horsnell 1999, 198–201; Kautzsch 1910, 431–32; Waltke and O'Connor 1990, 267–71; van der Merwe, Naudé, and Kroeze 1999, 236–37; and Williams 1976, 17–18. On the distinction between the *absolute superlative* (excels all others in its class) and the *comparative superlative* (excels in some particular quality or condition), see Ben Zvi, Hancock, and Beinert 1993, 192, and Waltke and O'Connor 1990, 267–71.

[54] In all three cases, the mark of determination causes morphological changes, for which, see the beginning grammars.

denote indetermination, especially in the books of Judges, Samuel, and Kings (see section 2.7.1,b).[55] This often requires the translation "certain": וַיְהִי אִישׁ אֶחָד מִן־הָרָמָתַיִם, "There was a *certain* man from Ramathaim" (1 Sam 1:1).

The use of the definite article in BH is similar to the use of the article in English. However, there are also several uses of the article in BH that are dissimilar to use in English. In these cases, definiteness in the English translation will often not correspond to the definiteness of Hebrew. It is important, therefore, not to expect a literal, word-for-word translation of the definiteness of nouns, which may lead to awkward, or even incorrect English phrasings. Additionally, since the definite article developed late in the history of Classical Hebrew,[56] its sparse use in poetry is a key distinction between prose and poetry in general. Compare, for instance: זָכַר לְעוֹלָם בְּרִיתוֹ דָּבָר צִוָּה לְאֶלֶף דּוֹר, "He has remembered his covenant to eternity, *the word* which he commanded to a thousand generations" (Ps 105:8), הַדָּבָר אֲשֶׁר דִּבַּרְתָּ עַל־עַבְדְּךָ וְעַל־בֵּיתוֹ הָקֵם עַד־עוֹלָם, "*The word* which you spoke concerning your servant and his house, confirm it forever" (2 Sam 7:25).

The following categories are useful when considering the uses of the definite article in BH.[57]

## 2.6.1 *Referential*

A noun with the definite article can refer to a person or thing already introduced into the context: וַיֹּאמֶר אֱלֹהִים יְהִי אוֹר וַיְהִי־אוֹר וַיַּרְא אֱלֹהִים אֶת־הָאוֹר כִּי־טוֹב,

55 Joüon and Muraoka 1993, 513; see also Waltke and O'Connor 1990, 251–52; Pratico and Van Pelt 2001, 49; and van der Merwe, Naudé, and Kroeze 1999, 187.

56 Garr 1985, 89; Joüon and Muraoka 1993, 507; Seow 1995, 157; Andersen and Forbes 1983, 165–69.

57 Meyer 1992, 367–70; Joüon and Muraoka 1993, 505–21; Waltke and O'Connor 1990, 235–52; Kautzsch 1910, 401–13; Chisholm 1998, 72–75; van der Merwe, Naudé, and Kroeze 1999, 187–91; and for comparison with epigraphic Hebrew, see Gogel 1998, 235–37.

"God said, 'Let there be light,' and there was light.
And God saw that *the light* was good" (Gen 1:3–4);
וַיִּקַּח בֶּן־בָּקָר...וַיִּקַּח חֶמְאָה וְחָלָב וּבֶן־הַבָּקָר, "And he
(Abraham) took a calf ... then he took curds and milk,
and *the calf*" (Gen 18:7–8). If the person or thing is
particularly well known, it need not have been mentioned
previously: וַיִּטְמֹן אֹתָם יַעֲקֹב תַּחַת הָאֵלָה אֲשֶׁר עִם־שְׁכֶם, "and
Jacob hid them [the foreign gods] under *the oak* that was
near Shechem" (Gen 35:4).

### 2.6.2 *Vocative*

A noun with the definite article can denote a specific addressee (see section 2.1.3): בֶּן־מִי אַתָּה הַנָּעַר, "Whose son
are you, *young man*?" (1 Sam 17:58), הוֹשִׁיעָה הַמֶּלֶךְ, "Help,
*O King*!" (2 Sam 14:4).[58]

### 2.6.3 *Naming*

The definite article can mark a common noun as a proper
noun. Since proper nouns themselves denote particular
persons, places, or things, they do not normally take the
definite article: מֹשֶׁה, "Moses" (Exod 2:10), דָּוִד, "David"
(Ruth 4:22), יְהוָה, "YHWH" (Gen 2:4). However, some
nouns (or primitive appellatives) are still in the process
of becoming proper names:[59] הַגִּבְעָה, "Gibeah [literally: *the*
hill]" (Judg 19:14), הַיְאֹר, "*the* Nile [literally: *the* stream]"
(Gen 41:1), הַיַּרְדֵּן, "*the* Jordan [literally: *the* river]" (Gen
13:10), הַלְּבָנוֹן, "Lebanon [literally: "*the* white (mountains?)]" (Josh 9:1).
  Related to this category is the *solitary* use of the definite
article (see next section), in which appellatives referring

---

[58] However, the vocative frequently omits the definite article. See Meyer
      1992, 27; Kautzsch 1910, 405; Joüon and Muraoka 1993, 508.
[59] Joüon and Muraoka 1993, 505; Meyer 1992, 370.

to unique persons, places, or things are on their way to becoming a name: הָאֱלֹהִים, "God [literally: *the* God]" (Gen 5:22).

Also related to this category is the *gentilic* use of the definite article, often used collectively (i.e., in the singular): הַכְּנַעֲנִי, "*the* Canaanites" (Gen 10:18), but occasionally in the plural: הָעִבְרִים, "*the* Hebrews" (Gen 40:15).

### 2.6.4 *Solitary*

The definite article marks a unique person, place, or thing: הַכֹּהֵן הַגָּדוֹל, "*the* high priest" (Josh 20:6), הַשֶּׁמֶשׁ, "*the* sun" (Gen 15:12), הַיָּרֵחַ, "*the* moon" (Deut 4:19), אֵת הַשָּׁמַיִם וְאֵת הָאָרֶץ, "*the* heavens and *the* earth" (Gen 1:1).

Certain titles may take the definite article because they are understood by everyone to designate someone unique: הַמֶּלֶךְ דָּוִד, "King David [literally: *the* King David]" (2 Sam 5:3), יְחִי הַמֶּלֶךְ שְׁלֹמֹה, "Long live King Solomon [literally: *the* King Solomon]" (1 Kgs 1:34), הַשַּׂר, "*the* chief" (1 Chr 15:5).[60]

### 2.6.5 *Generic*

A noun with the definite article denotes a class of persons or things: הַגָּמָל, "*the* camel" (Lev 11:4), בָּאֵשׁ, "with *the* fire" (Josh 11:9), הָרָעֵב, "a hungry person [literally: *the* hungry]" (Isa 29:8), כַּאֲרִי, "like *the* lion" (Num 24:9).

When used with a plural noun, the *generic* use may indicate that all the individuals of the class are included: הָרְשָׁעִים, "*the* wicked" (Ps 1:4), הַכּוֹכָבִים, "*the* stars" (Gen 1:16), הַגּוֹיִם, "*the* nations" (Gen 10:32).

---

[60] The noun הַשַּׂר could be used in various constructions for titles, military and royal, although in LBH, it appears to have become a title standing alone with the article (*HALOT* 3:1351–52).

Use of the definite article to mark *abstract* nouns is related to this category: הַמְּלוּכָה, "*the* kingship" (1 Sam 11:14),

וַיִּמָּלֵא אֶת־הַחָכְמָה וְאֶת־הַתְּבוּנָה וְאֶת־הַדַּעַת לַעֲשׂוֹת
כָּל־מְלָאכָה בַּנְּחֹשֶׁת

"he [Hiram] was full of *skill, intelligence,* and *knowledge* in working bronze" (1 Kgs 7:14).

### 2.6.6 *Demonstrative*

The definite article has a "pointing out" (i.e., deictic) force when used with nouns referring to present time.[61] Such *demonstrative* uses of the article typically take on adverbial force: פֹּה עִמָּנוּ עֹמֵד הַיּוֹם לִפְנֵי יְהוָה אֱלֹהֵינוּ, "standing here with us *today* before YHWH our God" (Deut 29:14 [Eng 29:15]), לִינוּ פֹה הַלַּיְלָה, "stay here *tonight*" (Num 22:8), הַשָּׁנָה אַתָּה מֵת, "*this year* you will die" (Jer 28:16), חָטָאתִי הַפָּעַם, "*this time* I have sinned" (Exod 9:27).

### 2.6.7 *Possessive*

The definite article occasionally denotes ownership of the noun, and requires a possessive pronoun in translation: וְהַחֲנִית בְּיַד־שָׁאוּל, "Saul had *his spear* in his hand" (1 Sam 18:10), וַיִּשְׁתַּחוּ יִשְׂרָאֵל עַל־רֹאשׁ הַמִּטָּה, "Israel bowed himself on the head of *his bed*" (Gen 47:31), וַיָּקָם מֵעַל הַכִּסֵּא, "He [King Eglon] rose from *his seat*" (Judg 3:20).

### 2.7 Numerals

Numbers in BH are written as words, rather than represented graphically as with the Arabic digits used in English

---

[61] It is often assumed that Hebrew's definite article originated from a prefixed pronominal with demonstrative force, explaining its occasional demonstrative use in BH as a vestige of its history. See Blau 1976, 43; Kautzsch 1910, 404; Joüon and Muraoka 1993, 506; Bergsträsser 1983, 23–24; Garr 1985, 87–89; but see the challenging discussion in Lambdin 1971b, 315–33.

(so "thirty-two" rather than "32").[62] Most are derived from substantives, but unfortunately their syntax is varied. Thus, the numeral "one" most frequently functions as an adjective, following the noun it modifies and agreeing in gender. But the numerals from "two" to "ten" function as nouns that may stand either before or after the noun they modify when appositional (for which, see section 2.4.4), or may stand before the noun in the construct state (see section 2.2.11). While the numeral "two" exhibits gender agreement with the noun it modifies, those from "three" to "ten" take feminine forms with masculine nouns, but masculine forms when modifying feminine nouns.[63] All beginning grammars of BH explain and illustrate these syntactical peculiarities of the numerals, and as a result we include here only a few additional categories useful when considering the uses of the numerals.[64]

Numerals are morphologically divided into the cardinal and ordinal variations.

### 2.7.1 *Cardinal Numbers*

*(a) Measure* – Indicating the amount or quantity of something denoted by the noun being modified: שְׁלֹשָׁה בָנִים, "*three* sons" (Gen 6:10), שְׁלֹשָׁה אֲנָשִׁים, "*three* men" (Gen 18:2), עָרִים שְׁתַּיִם, "*two* cities" (Josh 15:60).

*(b) Indetermination* – The numeral "one" (אֶחָד or אַחַת) may follow an indefinite noun to mark an unnamed individual: וַיְהִי אִישׁ אֶחָד מִן־הָרָמָתַיִם, "There was *a certain*

---

[62] Most languages of biblical times used number signs, although Ugaritic preferred to spell numbers out completely as in BH (Segert 1984, 52–54).

[63] This inexplicable feature of Hebrew numerals is limited to the cardinals. With double-figure numerals (11 to 19), the lowest number includes this reverse gender, while the tens take the gender of the noun being modified.

[64] Kautzsch 1910, 286–92 and 432–37; Meyer 1992, 204–11; Joüon and Muraoka 1993, 525–30; Waltke and O'Connor 1990, 272–89; van der Merwe, Naudé, and Kroeze 1999, 263–70.

man of Ramathaim" (1 Sam 1:1), אִשָּׁה אַחַת, "*a certain* woman" (Judg 9:53), נָבִיא אֶחָד, "*a certain* prophet" (1 Kgs 20:13). Occasionally this use takes on an emphatic nuance, often reflected in English by "single" or "same": שְׁנֵים עָשָׂר עֲבָדֶיךָ אַחִים אֲנַחְנוּ בְּנֵי אִישׁ־אֶחָד, "We, your servants, are twelve brothers, the sons of *the same* man" (Gen 42:13), בְּיוֹם אֶחָד, "on *the same* day" (1 Sam 2:34), בְּבַיִת אֶחָד, "in *the same* house" (1 Kgs 3:17).

*(c) Multiplication* – The cardinals may express multiples of the noun being modified. Multiplicatives of "four" and "seven" are attested in the feminine duals of the cardinals:[65] וְאֶת־הַכִּבְשָׂה יְשַׁלֵּם אַרְבַּעְתָּיִם, "and he shall restore the lamb *four times over*" (2 Sam 12:6), שִׁבְעָתָיִם, "*sevenfold*" (Gen 4:15).[66] Occasionally the feminine dual of "two" may be used for "twice": אַחַת דִּבַּרְתִּי וְלֹא אֶעֱנֶה וּשְׁתַּיִם וְלֹא אוֹסִיף, "I have spoken once, and I will not answer; *twice*, but I will not again" (Job 40:5), פַּעַם וּשְׁתָּיִם, "once or *twice*" (Neh 13:20).

The singular also may be used for *multiplication*, often with פַּעַם or פְּעָמִים for "occurrence, times":[67] שָׁלֹשׁ פְּעָמִים בַּשָּׁנָה, "*three times* a year" (Exod 23:17), פְּעָמִים שֶׁבַע, "*seven times*" (Gen 33:3),

וְיָסַפְתִּי לְיַסְּרָה אֶתְכֶם שֶׁבַע עַל־חַטֹּאתֵיכֶם

"and I will continue to punish you *sevenfold* for your sins" (Lev 26:18), מֵאָה פְעָמִים, "*one hundredfold*" (2 Sam 24:3).

*(d) Distribution* – Repetition of a cardinal number will often express a distributive sense: שְׁנַיִם שְׁנַיִם בָּאוּ אֶל־נֹחַ אֶל־הַתֵּבָה,

---

[65] The ending may in fact be an adverbial ending rather than a dual proper (Joüon and Muraoka 1993, 327).

[66] The forms are feminine possibly because of the omission of פַּעַם or פְּעָמִים, "times" (Kautzsch 1910, 436).

[67] *HALOT* 3:952; see also רֶגֶל (*HALOT* 3:1185) and יָד (*HALOT* 2:388, *DCH* 4:82). A variation occurs when פַּעַם occurs in the dual (פַּעֲמַיִם) without the numeral (Num 20:11).

"*Two by two*, they came to Noah into the ark" (Gen 7:9). The repeated numerals may be joined with the conjunction *waw* : וְאֶצְבְּעֹת יָדָיו וְאֶצְבְּעֹת רַגְלָיו שֵׁשׁ וָשֵׁשׁ, "*Six* fingers on his hands, and *six* fingers on his feet (2 Sam 21:20). The distributive concept may also be expressed by the repetition of the numeral with its object: שְׂרָפִים עֹמְדִים מִמַּעַל לוֹ שֵׁשׁ כְּנָפַיִם שֵׁשׁ כְּנָפַיִם לְאֶחָד, "Seraphim stood above him, each one having *six wings*" (Isa 6:2). A numeral prefixed with the preposition *lamed* may also mark the distributive: וְסַרְנֵי פְלִשְׁתִּים עֹבְרִים לְמֵאוֹת וְלַאֲלָפִים, "And the lords of the Philistines were marching *by the hundreds* and *by the thousands*" (1 Sam 29:2).

*(e) Succession* – The cardinal "one" (אֶחָד or אַחַת) may function as an ordinal when denoting the first of a small list of items: וַיְהִי־עֶרֶב וַיְהִי־בֹקֶר יוֹם אֶחָד, "And there was evening, and there was morning; the *first* day" (Gen 1:5), הַטּוּר הָאֶחָד, "the *first* row" (Exod 39:10).

## 2.7.2 *Ordinal Numbers*[68]

*Succession* indicates consecution or sequence, especially in formulae expressing dates:[69] בַּיּוֹם הָרִאשׁוֹן, "on the *first* day" (Exod 12:15), בִּשְׁנַת הַתְּשִׁיעִית לְהוֹשֵׁעַ, "in the *ninth* year of Hoshea" (2 Kgs 17:6), וּבִשְׁנַת אַחַת עֶשְׂרֵה שָׁנָה לְיוֹרָם, "In the *eleventh* year of Joram" (2 Kgs 9:29), בֵּן שֵׁנִי, "a *second* son" (Gen 30:7).

---

[68] The ordinals function as attributive adjectives, following the noun and agreeing in gender and definiteness (see 2.5.1). There are no separate forms for ordinals above the number 10 (review the beginning grammars for more on the forms).

[69] However, the cardinals are frequently used instead of the ordinals in the expressions of date (Kautzsch 1910, 435; Waltke and O'Connor 1990, 284–86).

# 3  *Verbs*

Biblical Hebrew has no *tenses* in the strict sense of the term. By this statement, we mean that Hebrew does not locate an action or state in time by means of specific morphology. Of course, this does not mean that Hebrew fails to express time relations entirely, only that it does so through a variety of syntactical and contextual features, rather than through verbal inflections or grammatically realized tenses.[1]

Rather than a morphologically precise tense system, Hebrew uses an *aspect* system to indicate first, the contour of a situation in time, and second, the type of action. The

---

[1] Caution is in order in such statements as "BH has no tenses." We have expressed the majority opinion in this paragraph on the general nature of the Hebrew verbal system, but scholars are not unanimous. Older grammarians believed that the *perfect* denoted past time and the *imperfect* the present-future, and that therefore Hebrew did, in fact, employ a tense system. But during the past century, this view gave way to the current understanding of *aspect* rather than *tense*. See Kautzsch 1910, 117; Bauer and Leander 1991, 268–78; Bergsträsser 1962, 2.9–10; Endo 1996; Sáenz-Badillos 1993, 73; Waltke and O'Connor 1990, 346–47; Chisholm 1998, 85–86; Emerton 2000b, 191–93; and van der Merwe, Naudé, and Kroeze 1999, 141–43. Some prefer to say that Hebrew does, in fact, express tense, though in a less complete way (Bauer 1910; Joüon and Muraoka 1993, 354–58; and more emphatically, Rainey 1986, 7, and 1988; and Zevit 1988 and 1998, 39–48). It is likely that such arguments have overstated the case against aspect and in favor of tense in the prefixed form (Huehnergard 1988, 20–21).

first grammatical category (*Aspekt*) identifies the action as either undefined or progressive ("perfect" or "imperfect"). The second category (*Aktionsart*) refers to the type of action with regard to voice, fientivity, transitivity, causation, and various reflexive actions.[2] The latter (*Aktionsart*) is marked by verbal stems, the former (*Aspekt*) by verbal conjugations.

## 3.1 Stem

In general, the Qal and Niphal have no element of causation in their predication, in distinction to the other stems.[3] The Piel, Pual, and Hithpael have "causation with a patiency nuance," and the Hiphil and Hophal represent "causation notion with an agency nuance."[4]

### 3.1.1 *Qal (the G stem)*

The Qal[5] is the "simple active" stem. The voice of the primary subject is active (see vertical axis of the appendixes). Since there is no element of causation, the Qal has no secondary subject (first column of the horizontal axis of Appendix II). Hence, the stem is "simple."

---

[2] This aspectual explanation (i.e., speaking of *Aspekt*, "contour of action," and *Aktionsart*, "type of action") follows modern linguistic theory (e.g., Comrie 1976), and has become the consensus of scholars working on BH (Waltke and O'Connor 1990, 346–50; and for a different view, Zevit 1998, 41–48).

[3] Variously known as *derived stems, patterns, themes,* or better, the Hebrew designation, *binyanim,* "structures."

[4] Waltke and O'Connor 1990, 355.

[5] The Qal is also known as the "G stem" (for German *Grundstamm,* "basic stem"). The verbal stems in other Semitic languages have different names, making it difficult to study them together. Scholars use a standardized list of sigla for the verbal stems, thus facilitating comparisons across the various languages. We will include the siglum for each stem in parenthesis after its name. The advanced student would do well to learn the designations in addition to the traditional stem name.

*(a) Fientive* – describes action, motion, or change of state.[6] Fientive verbs may be transitive (לְקַח אֹתוֹ אֱלֹהִים, "God *took* him" [Gen 5:24], וַיִּיצֶר יְהוָה אֱלֹהִים אֶת־הָאָדָם, "YHWH God *formed* humanity" [Gen 2:7]), or intransitive (וְגַם־הַרְבֵּה נָפַל מִן־הָעָם וַיָּמֻתוּ, "but also many of the people *fell* and died" [2 Sam 1:4], וְאָבַד כָּל־בֵּית אַחְאָב, "the whole house of Ahab shall *perish*" [2 Kgs 9:8]). Several fientive verbs may be both, as these examples of מלא demonstrate: וְהֶעָנָן מָלֵא אֶת־בֵּית יְהוָה, "the cloud *filled* the house of YHWH" (1 Kgs 8:10), כִּי יִמְלְאוּ יָמֶיךָ, "when your days are *complete*" (2 Sam 7:12).[7]

*(b) Stative* – describes a state or quality of the subject. English translations often make no distinction between stative verbs and predicate adjectives: וַיִּכְבַּד לֵב פַּרְעֹה, "and Pharaoh's heart *was heavy*" (Exod 9:7), וַתִּקְטַן עוֹד זֹאת בְּעֵינֶיךָ, "And yet, this *was insignificant* in your eyes" (2 Sam 7:19), אֲנִי זָקַנְתִּי, "I *am old*" (Josh 23:2).

### 3.1.2 *Niphal (the N stem)*

The "simple middle-passive" and "simple reflexive" stem. The voice of the primary subject is middle-passive or reflexive (see vertical axis of the appendixes). Since there is no element of causation, the Niphal has no secondary subject (first column of the horizontal axis of Appendix II). Hence, the stem is "simple."

Niphal was originally the simple reflexive, that is, the reflexive of the Qal. It gradually acquired the passive meaning of the Qal as well when the Qal passive fell from

---

[6] Since the term "active" is regularly used to denote voice, the term "fientive" is used to describe this type of action (Waltke and O'Connor 1990, 363).

[7] The question of transitivity or intransitivity is a less important distinction for the verb than that of fientive versus stative, because stative verbs may be transitive as well as the expected intransitive. Thus, stative verbs such as "to dress," "to don" (לבש) and "be full," "to fill" (מלא) may be transitive (Joüon and Muraoka 1993, 357).

use.[8] Grammarians sometimes use the expression "medio-passive" for the Niphal, although Waltke and O'Connor refer to a "medio-reflexive notion," from which they derive four specific meanings (1990, 380): a) middle, b) passive, c) adjectival (simple adjectival, ingressive, gerundive), and d) double-status (reflexive, benefactive, reciprocal, tolerative, causative-reflexive). They state further, "In all the specific uses of the Niphal, we find the common notion(s) that the action or state expressed by the verb affects the subject (as in the middle voice) or its interests (as in the reflexive). Species 1, 2, and 3 can plausibly be associated with the middle notion, and the others with the reflexive. Even in the double-status uses, where the subject is both actor and patient of the action, the primary option is that the subject is affected by the action."[9] The following semantic categories are helpful in classifying verbs in the Niphal.

*(a) Passive* – frequently the passive of the Qal. This is its simplest meaning, though not necessarily its primary one. So קבר ("bury") and אכל ("eat") may become "be buried" and "be eaten" in the Niphal: שָׁם אֶקָּבֵר, "there I will *be buried*" (Ruth 1:17), and בְּבַיִת אֶחָד יֵאָכֵל, "in one house *it shall be eaten*" (Exod 12:46).

Hebrew's use of the Niphal is an "incomplete passive" (Lambdin 1971a, 176). The passive in English is a construction, not a category of verbal meaning. Thus, "the students read the lesson" has a passive construction, "the lesson was read by the students." By the incomplete passive we mean this same transformation minus the agent: "the lesson was read." The speaker is not concerned with specifying the agent of the action. All Hebrew passives belong to this category; constructions with a specified agent are virtually nonexistent.[10]

---

[8] Joüon and Muraoka 1993, 149.

[9] Waltke and O'Connor 1990, 380.

[10] Examples of the infrequent complete passive include Deut 33:29; Gen 9:6, 11; Exod 12:16; 1 Sam 25:7.

*(b) Middle* – Verbs that are normally used in passive constructions may be used in a quasi-active sense, but with
the object as the subject of the verb. Unlike the incomplete passives, middle verbs are active in form, but the
meaning (i.e., voice) is, in a sense, reversed. The object
of the active verb has become the subject of the middle verb: נִפְתְּחוּ הַשָּׁמַיִם, "the heavens *opened*" (Ezek 1:1),
וַתִּבָּקַע הָאָרֶץ בְּקוֹלָם, "the earth *split* with their sound"
(1 Kgs 1:40).

*(c) Reflexive* – action for, or concerning, oneself. The subject is at the same time object (recipient) of the action, so
that this use of the Niphal may be called the double-status
use.[11] In many languages a reflexive pronoun is added
to clarify the object, but in the Hebrew Niphal verb, no
reflexive pronoun is needed.[12]

In most reflexive uses, the subject and object
refer to the same person or thing: וְאִנָּקְמָה מֵאוֹיְבַי,
"and *I will avenge myself* on my enemies" (Isa 1:24),
וְנִמְכַּר־לְךָ לֹא־תַעֲבֹד בּוֹ עֲבֹדַת עָבֶד, "[If] they *sell themselves* to
you, you shall not make them serve as slaves" (Lev 25:39).
The reflexive may also occur in conjunction with a prepositional phrase, as in the frequent Niphal imperative
הִשָּׁמֶר לְךָ, "guard yourself for yourself," or "*take great care*"
(Exod 34:12), בִּי נִשְׁבַּעְתִּי נְאֻם־יְהוָה, " '*I have sworn by myself,*'
declares Yʜᴡʜ" (Gen 22:16).

Additionally, the reflexive may denote permission (*tolerative*): אִדָּרֵשׁ, "I will *allow myself to be enquired*" (Ezek 36:37),
וְנֶעְתַּר לָהֶם וּרְפָאָם, "He will respond to them (literally:
he will *allow himself to be entreated*) and heal them"
(Isa 19:22), נִדְרַשְׁתִּי לְלוֹא שָׁאָלוּ נִמְצֵאתִי לְלֹא בִקְשֻׁנִי,
"*I permitted myself to be sought* by those who did not inqure,

[11] The subject is both agent and patient (or undergoer) of the action in
Waltke and O'Connor's terminology (1990, 387–91).
[12] Cf. the "tolerative," Williams 1976, 138; Waltke and O'Connor 1990,
389–90.

I permitted myself to be found by those who did not seek"
(Isa 65:1). The *reciprocal* construction may be seen as a plural variation of the reflexive: וַיֵּאָסְפוּ אֵלָיו כָּל־בְּנֵי לֵוִי, "and
all the children of Levi gathered (themselves) around him"
(Exod 32:26). In one root particularly (ידע), the Niphal denotes a *causative-reflexive* meaning, similar to the Hithpael:
וְנוֹדַע יְהוָה לְמִצְרַיִם, "and YHWH will make himself known to
the Egyptians" (Isa 19:21), וּשְׁמִי יְהוָה לֹא נוֹדַעְתִּי לָהֶם, "but
by my name YHWH, I did not make myself known to them"
(Exod 6:3).

*(d) Stative* – describes the state of the subject produced
by the verbal action:[13] וּבְיוֹם הַשַּׁבָּת יִפָּתֵחַ "on the sabbath
day [the gate] shall be opened" (Ezek 46:1), וְאַל־תֵּעָצֵבוּ,
"do not be grieved" (Neh 8:11). The stative Niphal is often equivalent to a simple adjectival state, and is also
often the same as the passive in translation. So for example, the verb נִשְׁבָּר may be "to be broken," or "to be
in pieces": כִּי־נִשְׁבְּרוּ לִפְנֵי־יְהוָה, "for they were broken before
YHWH" (2 Chr 14:12[Eng 2 Chr 14:13]).[14]

### 3.1.3 *Piel (the D stem)*

The Piel is the "causative (with patiency nuance) active"
stem and is the most elusive of the Hebrew stems.[15]
One leading scholar recently signaled a warning about
the futility of searching for a unifying central understanding of the stem's use: "[I]t is pointless to try to
find a single . . . explanation to account for all of the

---

[13] Lambdin's *resultative* (1971, 177).

[14] Some verbs in the Niphal have little or no Qal counterpart (ex., נִלְחַם
and נִסְתַּר). Others may have an "ingressive-stative" connotation, describing "coming" into a certain state, rather than "being" in such a state
(ex., certain occurrences of נִבָּא; see Ben Zvi, Hancock, and Beinert
1993, 120).

[15] Joüon and Muraoka 1993, 151.

transformative power of the D stem. It is simply a form."[16]

Traditionally the Piel had been considered *intensive* in meaning. Older grammars defined the idea as "to busy one-self eagerly with the action indicated," and even associated the doubling of the second radical of verbs in Piel as an out-ward expression of this intensification.[17] However, in light of today's deeper understanding of the Semitic languages generally, we can no longer refer to the Piel as bascially and primarily intensive.[18] Furthermore, it has long been assumed that as the *derived* stems are built morphologically upon the base form of the Qal, so the semantic use and function of those stems may be defined primarily by means of association with the Qal (as *intensive* of the Qal, *causative* of the Qal, *passive* of the Qal, etc.). We now recognize that although such semantic associations may be present in many verbs in the Qal and Piel, this is not always the case, and each stem should be regarded as independent.[19] Many Piel verbs simply cannot be placed in one of the cate-gories that follow. In some cases, the verb may occur in both Qal and Piel with no discernible difference in meaning.

The Piel frequently expresses the bringing about of a state. Thus, the Piel focuses on causation and the outcome

---

[16] Kaufman 1996, 282. See also Joosten's conclusion that the various func-tions of the Piel cannot be reduced to one underlying basic function (Joosten 1998, 227).

[17] Kautzsch 1910, 141; and see Blau 1976, 52; Bauer and Leander 1991, 323–29; Martin-Davidson 1993, 136–37. The view that the doubling of the middle consonant is unassociated with intensification may need to be reconsidered in light of recent linguistic work on iconicity, that is, the iconic nature of language (cf. Kouwenberg 1997).

[18] The Piel in recent decades has been recognized as the key to the Hebrew verbal system. Albrecht Goetze opened the discussion to new approaches with his famous survey of the Akkadian D-stem (1942, 1–8), and subse-quently the significance of his work for the West Semitic languages was investigated by Ernst Jenni (1968). For useful surveys of these develop-ments, see Waltke and O'Connor 1990, 354–59; Fassberg 2001, 243–44. For caveats on Goetze's arguments, see Kaufman 1996, 281–82.

[19] Richter 1978, 73.

of the action, though with a patiency nuance rather than an agency nuance (as in Hiphil). The foregrounded interest is not the event that happens to the subject, but rather the condition attained by it. It is for all practical purposes an adjectival causation predicate. Jenni's important study proposed a basic distinction between the Piel and Hiphil as the difference between the imposition of a state (adjectival) and the imposition of process (verbal).[20] So using as an example the verb חָיָה ("live" in the Qal), the Piel is "to cause to be alive," whereas the Hiphil is "to cause to live." The distinction is between causing to *be* something or to *do* something. Specifically with Qal intransitive verbs, we use the term *factitive* to denote a cause producing a state (as distinct from a cause producing an event, or *causative*).[21] This factitive use of the Piel designates, without regard to the process, the bringing about of the state depicted by an adjective. The object experiences this action as an "accident" (signifying that a quality or situation is not essential to the person or thing in question). With some Qal transitive verbs the Piel is *resultative*, meaning that it denotes the bringing about of the outcome of the action designated by the base root, which action can be expressed in terms of an adjective, and without regard to the actual process of the event.[22] In our analysis, we follow Waltke and O'Connor's practice of reserving causative for the Hiphil, which causes an action rather than a state. In the Piel, the object of causation is in a state of suffering the effects of an action and is inherently passive in part (see the second column of the horizontal axis of Appendix II).

The following semantic categories are helpful in classifying verbs in the Piel.

---

[20] Jenni (1968), and see also Lambdin 1969, 388–89. For dissenting voices, see Joosten 1998 and Fassberg 2001, 243–44.

[21] "Factitive," from Latin *factitare*, "to do often," "to practice," "to declare (someone) to be."

[22] Waltke and O'Connor 1990, 400.

*(a) Factitive* – makes transitive many verbs that are intransitive in the Qal (mostly stative, although a few fientive verbs are intransitive). By transitivizing verbs that are Qal intransitives, the Piel factitive denotes a cause producing a state (rather than a cause producing an action; see Hiphil *causative* in section 3.1.6,a). So typically, Qal intransitives become factitive Piels:[23] וּבְיָדְךָ לְגַדֵּל, "and it is in your hand *to make great*" (1 Chr 29:12), וַאֲגַדְּלָה שְׁמֶךָ, "and I will *make* your name *great*" (Gen 12:2), אֲנִי יְהוָה מְקַדִּשְׁכֶם, "I YHWH *sanctify* you" (Exod 31:13), יְהוָה מֵמִית וּמְחַיֶּה, "YHWH kills and *brings to life*" (1 Sam 2:6), וַיְאַבְּדֵם יְהוָה, "YHWH *destroyed* them" (Deut 11:4).

Such a use is frequently *resultative,* meaning that the Piel can bring about a state (or "result") corresponding to the verbal notion of a Qal transitive:[24] שִׁבַּר אֶת־הַמַּצֵּבֹת, "*he broke down* the pillars" (2 Kgs 18:4), לִמַּדְתִּי אֶתְכֶם חֻקִּים וּמִשְׁפָּטִים, "*I have taught* you statutes and ordinances" (Deut 4:5).

*(b) Denominative* – indicates a derived verbal idea related to a noun or substantive. The nominal form is primary and the verb secondarily derived from it. Piel is the stem most commonly used to form denominatives (though see also the Hithpael and Hiphil denominatives): לֹא־נָפַל דָּבָר אֶחָד מִכֹּל דְּבָרוֹ הַטּוֹב אֲשֶׁר דִּבֶּר בְּיַד מֹשֶׁה עַבְדּוֹ, "not one *word* has failed of all his good promise [literally: word], which *he spoke* through his servant

---

[23] Waltke and O'Connor 1990, 400–04; Joüon and Muraoka 1993, 154–56; Seow 1995, 173–75; Lambdin 1972, 193–95. These roots typically become causative Hiphils, a relationship that may be illustrated as follows: Qal intransitive::Piel factitive::Hiphil causative (cf. Waltke and O'Connor 1990, 400).

[24] Waltke and O'Connor 1990, 404–10; Lambdin 1972, 193; van der Merwe, Naudé, and Kroeze 1999, 80–81. Thus, the profile would be as follows: Qal transitive::Piel resultative::Hiphil causative (cf. Waltke and O'Connor 1990, 404). For similar uses of the Piel in the Canaanite dialect of the Amarna letters, Rainey 1996, 2:138–68.

Moses" (1 Kgs 8:56); זַמְּרוּ לַיהוָה בְּכִנּוֹר בְּכִנּוֹר וְקוֹל זִמְרָה,
"*Sing praises* to YHWH with the lyre, with the lyre and the
sound of <u>melody</u> [literally: <u>praise song</u>]" (Ps 98:5).

*(c) Frequentative* – pluralizes the action denoted by the Qal.
Many verbs in the Piel reflect multiple, repeated, or busy
action. This use of the Piel may be *iterative* over time, or *pluralic* through space, and often takes on the nuance of an
*intensive*, although the intensive force is difficult to identify
in most occurrences:[25] כָּל־הַיּוֹם קֹדֵר הִלָּכְתִּי, "all day long
*I go around* mourning" (Ps 38:7), בְּחֻקּוֹתַי יְהַלֵּךְ, "(the righteous individual) *follows* my statutes [literally: *he walks about*
in my statutes]" (Ezek 18:9), וְנוֹעַ יָנוּעוּ בָנָיו וְשִׁאֵלוּ, "May his
children wander about and *beg* [literally: *ask repeatedly*]"
(Ps 109:10), הָרֵס תְּהָרְסֵם וְשַׁבֵּר תְּשַׁבֵּר מַצֵּבֹתֵיהֶם, "you shall
utterly demolish them and *break in pieces* their pillars"
(Exod 23:24).

*(d) Declarative* – involves some kind of proclamation, delocution, or estimative assessment, although the precise
nature of these verbs and their relationship to the facti-
tive is debated: חָפַצְתִּי צַדְּקֶךָ, "I desire *to justify* you [literally:
*to declare* you *righteous*]" (Job 33:32), מִנִּסְתָּרוֹת נַקֵּנִי, "*clear me*
[literally: *declare* me *innocent*] of hidden faults" (Ps 19:13),
טִמֵּא יְטַמְּאֶנּוּ הַכֹּהֵן, "the priest shall *pronounce* him *unclean*"
(Lev 13:44).

As noted, there are simply some uses of the Piel
that cannot be categorized and are, in fact, identical in
meaning to the Qal stem, or have an equivalent simple-
active meaning: בִּקֵּשׁ יְהוָה לוֹ אִישׁ כִּלְבָבוֹ, "YHWH has *sought*
for himself a man after his own heart" (1 Sam 13:14),
וַיַּעַשׂ נֹחַ כְּכֹל אֲשֶׁר צִוָּה אֹתוֹ אֱלֹהִים כֵּן עָשָׂה, "Noah did according to all that God had *commanded* him, so he did"
(Gen 6:22).

[25] Waltke and O'Connor 1990, 414–16; Seow 1995, 174; Lambdin 1971a,
194.

### 3.1.4 *Pual (the Dp stem)*

The Pual is the "causative (with patiency nuance) passive" stem and is the passive counterpart to the Piel. As such, it contains the same four functions of the Piel, though in passive voice (factitive/resultative, denominative, frequentative, and declarative).

#### (a) Factitive/resultative

כְּתֵפֹת עָשׂוּ־לוֹ חֹבְרֹת עַל־שְׁנֵי קִצְווֹתוֹ חֻבָּר

"They made attaching shoulder pieces for it [i.e., the ephod]; *it was attached* at its two ends" (Exod 39:4), וְהַפִּשְׁתָּה וְהַשְּׂעֹרָה נֻכָּתָה, "The flax and the barley were *ruined*" (Exod 9:31).

#### (b) Denominative – וְאָכְלוּ אֹתָם אֲשֶׁר כֻּפַּר בָּהֶם "and they shall eat them [i.e., the food] by which *attonement is made*" (Exod 29:33).

#### (c) Frequentative – וְאֵת שְׂעִיר הַחַטָּאת דָּרֹשׁ דָּרַשׁ מֹשֶׁה וְהִנֵּה שֹׂרָף "Then Moses diligently inquired about the goat of the sin offering, and *it was burned up*" (Lev 10:16).

#### (d) Declarative

אֵלֶּה בִּקְשׁוּ כְתָבָם הַמִּתְיַחְשִׂים וְלֹא נִמְצָאוּ וַיְגֹאֲלוּ מִן־הַכְּהֻנָּה

"These searched their genealogical records, but they could not be found; so they *were considered unclean* for the priesthood" (Ezra 2:62)

One striking feature of the Pual is the high percentage of times it occurs in the participle.[26] The participle comprises no less than 40% of all Pual forms, most of which denote a thing or person for or in which a new condition has been attained: וְהִנֵּה יָדוֹ מְצֹרַעַת כַּשָּׁלֶג, "and behold, his hand *was leprous*, as white as snow" (Exod 4:6), רָשָׁע מַכְתִּיר אֶת־הַצַּדִּיק עַל־כֵּן יֵצֵא מִשְׁפָּט מְעֻקָּל

---

[26] Waltke and O'Connor 1990, 418–19.

"Wickedness surrounds the righteous; therefore, judgment comes forth *perverted*" (Hab 1:4),

וּמֵהֶם מְמֻנִּים עַל־הַכֵּלִים וְעַל כָּל־כְּלֵי הַקֹּדֶשׁ

"And some of them *were appointed* over the vessels and all the vessels of the sanctuary" (1 Chr 9:29).

### 3.1.5 *Hithpael (the HtD stem)*

The Hithpael is the "causative (with patiency nuance) reflexive" and "causative (with active secondary subject) reflexive" stem.

The rudimentary meaning of the Hithpael is the double-status (*reflexive-reciprocal*) counterpart of the Piel and secondarily as a passive form.[27] However, Hithpael verbs are intransitive and often have a reflexive or reciprocal meaning in relation to their active counterparts of the Qal, Piel, or Hiphil type from the same root.[28] The following semantic categories are helpful in classifying verbs in the Hithpael.

*(a) Reflexive* – indicates that the subject of a verb is also its implied object. Stated another way, the direct object, though unspecified, is also the subject of the verb: הִתְחַבְּאוּ, "they *hid themselves*" (1 Sam 14:11), וַיִּתְחַבֵּא הָאָדָם וְאִשְׁתּוֹ מִפְּנֵי יְהוָה, "the man and his wife *hid themselves* from the presence of YHWH" (Gen 3:8), הַכֹּהֲנִים לֹא־הִתְקַדָּשׁוּ, "the priests had not *sanctified themselves*" (2 Chr 30:3).

In some verbal roots, the subject of the *reflexive* Hithpael is not the same as the direct object (which may be expressed), but is rather the same as the indirect object:[29]

---

[27] Joüon and Muraoka 1993, 159–60; Waltke and O'Connor 1990, 424–32; Kautzsch 1910, 149–51; Chisholm 1998, 82; van der Merwe, Naudé, and Kroeze 1999, 82–84; Lambdin 1971a, 248–50.

[28] Lambdin 1971a, 249.

[29] Waltke and O'Connor 1990, 430; Seow 1995, 298.

וַיִּתְפַּשֵּׁט יְהוֹנָתָן אֶת־הַמְּעִיל, "Jonathan *stripped himself* of the robe" (1 Sam 18:4).

***(b) Reciprocal*** – indicates that two or more subjects act in relationship to each other: לְכָה נִתְרָאֶה פָנִים, "Come, let us *look one another* in the face" (2 Kgs 14:8), הִתְקַשְּׁרוּ עָלָיו עֲבָדָיו, "his servants *conspired with one another* against him" (2 Chr 24:25), וָאֶשְׁמַע מִדַּבֵּר אֵלַי, "I heard *someone speaking* with me" (Ezek 43:6).

***(c) Iterative*** – indicates repeated action:

לַהַט הַחֶרֶב הַמִּתְהַפֶּכֶת

"the flame of a *revolving* sword [literally: *turning repeatedly*]" (Gen 3:24), וַיִּתְאַבֵּל עַל־בְּנוֹ יָמִים רַבִּים, "and he [Jacob] *mourned* for his sons many days" (Gen 37:34), אֶת־הָאֱלֹהִים הִתְהַלֶּךְ־נֹחַ, "Noah *walked* with God" (Gen 6:9).[30]

***(d) Denominative*** – indicates a derived verbal idea related to a noun or substantive:

וּבִנְבִיאֵי שֹׁמְרוֹן רָאִיתִי תִפְלָה הִנַּבְּאוּ בַבַּעַל וַיַּתְעוּ אֶת־עַמִּי אֶת־יִשְׂרָאֵל

"Among the *prophets* of Samaria I saw a disgusting thing: *they prophesied* by Baal and led my people astray" (Jer 23:13), וַיִּתְאַנַּף יְהוָה מְאֹד בְּיִשְׂרָאֵל, "YHWH was very *angry* with Israel" (2 Kgs 17:18).

**3.1.6** *Hiphil (the H stem)*

The Hiphil is the "causative (with agency nuance) active" stem. Unlike the Piel causative, where the focus is on the

---

[30] On the special nuances of הלך in the Hithpael and the possibility that it is an "Akkadianism" borrowed into Hebrew, see Waltke and O'Connor 1990, 427–29.

bringing about of a state or condition, the Hiphil causative expresses the cause of an action. The Piel causative tends to focus on the outcome of the action, though with a patiency nuance (i.e, the object is transposed passively into a new state or condition). The subject of a Piel causative changes the object into the state or condition (see Piel *factitive* and *resultative* in section 3.1.3,a). By contrast, the Hiphil causative generally has to do with the causing of an event, this time with an agency nuance. In the Hiphil causation, the object participates in the event denoted by the verbal root.[31]

Generally, the fundamental causative nuance of a Hiphil will be determined by the specific type of verbal root used, and often by the meaning of that root in the Qal and whether it is transitive or intransitive in the Qal. The following semantic categories are helpful in classifying verbs in the Hiphil.

*(a) Causative* – indicates the bringing about of the sense of a verb occurring in the Qal or Niphal. But this causation takes a variety of distinctive connotations, depending on the nature of the root involved.

(a.1) Qal transitives usually become doubly transitive in the Hiphil; that is, they take two objects, a "causing" object and an object of the verbal idea expressed in the root.[32] In this example from Deuteronomy 3:28, the object of causation is represented in the translation by "them," and the object of the verbal idea is "the land": וְהוּא יַנְחִיל אוֹתָם אֶת־הָאָרֶץ, "for he [Joshua] *will cause* them *to inherit* the land."

However, sometimes the second object is omitted, leaving the predicate singly transitive. This is frequently

---

[31] Jenni 1968, 20–52; Waltke and O'Connor 1990, 433–36; Joüon and Muraoka 1993, 162–64.

[32] The terminology "doubly transitive" is that of Lambdin (1972, 211). Waltke and O'Connor refer to "three-place predicates," by which they mean one subject and two objects (Waltke and O'Connor 1990, 441).

the case when the objects of causation are personal,
or where they are abstract nouns or speech acts:[33]
לֹא תָרִיעוּ וְלֹא־תַשְׁמִיעוּ אֶת־קוֹלְכֶם, "Do not shout or *cause*
your voice *to be heard*" (Josh 6:10). Thus, verbs that are transitive in the Qal, but which may appear without an object,
may be either singly or doubly transitive in the Hiphil:
וַאדֹנָי הִשְׁמִיעַ אֶת־מַחֲנֵה אֲרָם קוֹל רֶכֶב קוֹל סוּס קוֹל חַיִל גָּדוֹל,
"And the Lord *had caused* the Aramean army *to hear* the
sound of chariots, and of horses, the sound of a great
army" (2 Kgs 7:6). In this case, שמע takes two objects: the
Aramean army and the sound. But the same root may have
only one object in the Hiphil causative: מִשָּׁמַיִם הִשְׁמַעְתָּ דִּין,
"From the heavens *you uttered* judgment" (Ps 76:9).

(a.2) Qal and Niphal intransitives become singly
transitive in the Hiphil; that is, they take one object.[34] Most common in this category is a large
group of Qal intransitive fientive verbs designating
motion: אֲנִי יְהוָה אֲשֶׁר הוֹצֵאתִיךָ מֵאוּר כַּשְׂדִּים, "I am Yhwh
who *brought you* from Ur of the Chaldeans" (Gen 15:7),
וַיָּשֶׁב יְהוָה עֲלֵהֶם אֶת־מֵי הַיָּם, "and Yhwh *brought back* the
waters of the sea upon them" (Exod 15:19).

Verbal roots that are specifically stative in Qal tend also
to become singly transitive in the Hiphil. Here the term
"factitive" may be used to indicate the transitivizing nature
of the Hiphil, as in the Piel usage:[35] אַל־תַּקְשׁוּ לְבַבְכֶם, "Do
not *harden* your hearts" (Ps 95:8), אֲנִי אַקְשֶׁה אֶת־לֵב פַּרְעֹה,
"I will *harden* Pharaoh's heart" (Exod 7:3),
הוֹבִישׁ יְהוָה אֶת־מֵי יַם־סוּף, "Yhwh *dried up* the waters of the
Sea of Reeds" (Josh 2:10), וַתַּגְדֵּל חַסְדְּךָ, "you have *made
great [or magnified]* your loyal kindness" (Gen 19:19).

[33] Waltke and O'Connor 1990, 442–43.

[34] Waltke and O'Connor 1990, 436–41; Lambdin 1971a, 212.

[35] Seow 1995, 182. On the difficulty of maintaining a distinction between the
Piel factitive and the Hiphil transitivizing causative with Qal stative roots,
see Waltke and O'Connor 1990, 437–38. In general, they conclude that
verbs in the Piel factitive "direct attention to the results of the situation
apart from the event," while the Hiphil "refers to the process."

*(b) Stative* – designates an intransitive causation of verbal roots that are also stative in the Qal, in which the action remains with the subject itself:[36] וּפַרְעֹה הִקְרִיב, "and Pharaoh *drew near*" (Exod 14:10), וַתָּזִדוּ, "and you *became presumptuous*" (Deut 1:43).

At times this Hiphil stative is more specifically *ingressive*, that is, it designates the entry into a state or condition and the continuation in the state or condition: חֲנֹךְ לַנַּעַר עַל־פִּי דַרְכּוֹ גַּם כִּי־יַזְקִין לֹא־יָסוּר מִמֶּנָּה, "Train a youth in the right way to live, and when *he grows old*, he will not depart from it" (Prov 22:6).

At other times, an object simply ellides, leaving an intransitive sense of certain roots in Hiphil:[37] הִקְשִׁיב בְּקוֹל תְּפִלָּתִי, "He [God] *has given heed* [literally: *inclined* (the ear)] to the sound of my prayer" (Ps 66:19). Finally, the absence of an object may also explain certain adverbial Hiphils:[38] הֱטִיבֹתָ, "you *did well*" (1 Kgs 8:18), הִשְׁחִיתוּ, "they *are corrupt*" (Ps 14:1).

*(c) Declarative* – involves proclamation or delocution, or an *estimative* assessment:[39]

וְהִצְדִּיקוּ אֶת־הַצַּדִּיק וְהִרְשִׁיעוּ אֶת־הָרָשָׁע

"and they [judges] will *pardon* [or *declare righteous*] the righteous and *condemn* [or *declare wicked*] the wicked" (Deut 25:1).

*(d) Denominative* – indicates a derived verbal idea related to a noun or substantive. The nominal form is primary

---

[36] Waltke and O'Connor 1990, 439; Joüon and Muraoka 1993, 163; Seow 1995, 183; Lambdin 1971a, 212. Waltke and O'Connor refer to "one-place or inwardly transitive" Hiphils (Waltke and O'Connor 1990, 439).

[37] Joüon and Muraoka 1993, 164.

[38] Joüon and Muraoka 1993, 164.

[39] Waltke and O'Connor 1990, 438–39; Joüon and Muraoka 1993, 163; Seow 1995, 163.

and the verb secondarily derived from it:[40] וְלֹא הֶאֱזִין אֲלֵיכֶם "and he (Yhwh) did not *give ear* to you" (Deut 1:45), וַיִּגַּשׁ הַפְּלִשְׁתִּי הַשְׁכֵּם וְהַעֲרֵב "and the Philistine (Goliath) came forward *morning* and *evening*" (1 Sam 17:16).

*(e) Permissive* – Used rarely, the Hiphil designates an action that is agreeable to the object and allowed by the subject (Lambdin 1972, 212; Waltke and O'Connor 1990, 445): הַרְאָה אֹתִי אֱלֹהִים גַּם אֶת־זַרְעֶךָ "God allowed me to see your children also" (Gen 48:11). Waltke and O'Connor observe a number of other uses of the Hiphil similar to the permissive, in which the relationship between the principal subject and the secondary subject requires a variety of modals in translation: *compulsion, solicitude, toleration, bestowal* (1990, 445–46).

In addition to the difficulty of the overlap between the semantic meaning of certain Piel and Hiphil forms, there are many Hiphil verbs that simply defy classification in any of these categories. Some roots are both transitive and intransitive in different contexts, and we would do well to analyze each derived stem as an independent form without insisting on a discernable connection to the other derived stems.

### 3.1.7 *Hophal (the Hp stem)*

The Hophal is the "causative (with agency nuance) passive" stem and is the passive counterpart to the Hiphil. As such, it contains the same five functions of the Hiphil, though in passive voice (causative, stative, declarative, denominative, permissive). Most frequently in the Hophal, the subject is caused to be in the event signified by the verbal root, whereas the subject of the Pual, by contrast, is made into a state or condition.

---

[40] Waltke and O'Connor 1990, 443–45; Joüon and Muraoka 1993, 163–64; Lambdin 1971a, 213; Seow 1995, 182.

*(a) Causative* – הַנֹּגֵעַ בָּאִישׁ הַזֶּה וּבְאִשְׁתּוֹ מוֹת יוּמָת "anyone, who molests this man or his wife shall certainly *be put to death*" (Gen 26:11), קַח־נָא אֶת־בִּרְכָתִי אֲשֶׁר הֻבָאת לָךְ, "please take my gift which has *been brought* to you (Gen 33:11).

*(b) Stative* – הֲפֹךְ יָדְךָ וְהוֹצִיאֵנִי מִן־הַמַּחֲנֶה כִּי הָחֳלֵיתִי, "turn around (literally: turn your hand), and take me out of the battle, for *I am wounded*" (1 Kgs 22:34).

*(c) Denominative* – וְהָמְלֵחַ לֹא הֻמְלַחַתְּ, "you were not *rubbed with salt*" (Ezek 16:4), חַיַּת הַשָּׂדֶה הָשְׁלְמָה־לָךְ, "the beasts of the field *will be at peace* with you" (Job 5:23).

The change of voice from Hiphil to Hophal means further that in the case of Qal transtives, the primary subject of the Hiphil is no longer designated, and so the double transitivity is dropped. Such roots will designate one object or none at all: וַיֻּגַּד לְרִבְקָה אֶת־דִּבְרֵי עֵשָׂו, "and the words of Esau were told to Rebekah" (Gen 27:42). Similarly with Qal and Niphal intransitives, the Hophal is most often also intransitive so that no object is represented: כְּמַיִם מֻגָּרִים בְּמוֹרָד, "like waters poured down a steep place" (Mic 1:4).[41]

## 3.2 Aspect

As we have seen, the grammatical category *Aspekt* identifies the action as either undefined or progressive ("perfect" or "imperfect").[42] Conjugations indicate aspect in that they denote the relation of an action to the passage of time, especially in reference to its completion, duration, or repetition.[43]

---

[41] For more on the subtle changes from Hiphil to Hophal, see Waltke and O'Connor 1990, 449–51, and Lambdin 1971a, 243–44.

[42] See Waltke and O'Connor 1990, 479–95; Joüon and Muraoka 1993, 359–65; Chisholm 1998, 86.

[43] As regards terminology, we have retained the traditional grammatical designations "perfect" and "imperfect." We recognize that these

### 3.2.1 *Perfect*

The perfect views a situation from the outside, looking upon it as a complete whole.[44] It may refer to an action or state in the past, present, or future, although it tends to view it as a complete situation or action that is temporally undefined (making it similar to the Greek "aorist" tense).[45] Although not required by the morphology, the perfect is frequently used for actions or states reported in the past, often requiring past tense translations. It may also refer to the perfect state, that is, to an event and a state resulting from that event (making the perfect similar to the Greek perfect). The following semantic categories are helpful in further classifying verbs in the perfect.[46]

terms are wholly inadequate, especially for the perfect, as we hope will be clear from our discussion. But a survey of the most widely used beginning grammars reveals a tendency to retain the traditional nomenclature (Hostetter 2000, Seow 1995, Kelley 1992, Lambdin 1971a, Pratico and Van Pelt 2001, etc.). Most of the reference grammars use a combination of terms: hence Joüon's "perfect" and "future," Meyer's interchanging "afformative conjugation"/"perfect" and "preformative conjugation"/"imperfect," and Waltke and O'Connor's "suffix (perfective)" and "prefix (non-perfective)." The reader needs to be aware of the inadequacy of the traditional terms and of the variety of designations for them in the reference grammars (see Rainey 1996, 2:365–66).

[44] Note the careful distinction between viewing a situation "as a complete whole" and viewing a completed action or situation. The perfect does not denote completed action, only that the whole action is in view, which may be placed in the present or future as well as the past. This distinction is clearer when one considers the origins of the BH perfect among second-millennium West Semitic languages as a development from a form related to the Akkadian "stative" or permansive plus personal suffixes, so that it was probably perceived originally as a timeless nominal clause (Moscati 1980, 133; Bergsträsser 1983, 20–23; Rainey 1996, 2:347–66). On the need to abandon "stative" for the Akkadian permansive, see Huehnergard 1987, 229–32.

[45] However, in LBH, the perfect is used only for the past (Sáenz-Badillos 1993, 129).

[46] Kautzsch 1910, 309–13; Waltke and O'Connor 1990, 479–95; Joüon and Muraoka 1993, 359–65; Bergsträsser 1962, 2:25–29; Chisholm 1998,

*(a)* **Complete** – The action or state is viewed as a complete whole, with the beginning and end in view. Usually required is either simple past, present perfect, or pluperfect in translation: וְלַחֹשֶׁךְ קָרָא לָיְלָה, "and the darkness he *called* night" (Gen 1:5), שָׁכַח אֵל, "God *has forgotten*" (Ps 10:11), וְלֹא־יָדַע יַעֲקֹב כִּי רָחֵל גְּנָבָתַם, "Jacob did not know that Rachel *had stolen* them" (Gen 31:32).

*(b)* **Stative** – a state of affairs or a condition usually expressed through a stative verb. Since a stative verb does not denote a "once-and-for-all" completed action, it regularly requires duration, usually present tense in translation: יְדֵיכֶם דָּמִים מָלֵאוּ, "your hands *are full of* blood" (Isa 1:15), דְּבַר־הַתֹּעֵבָה הַזֹּאת אֲשֶׁר שָׂנֵאתִי, "this abominable thing that I *hate*" (Jer 44:4).

*(c)* **Experience** – with a fientive verb denoting a state of mind, usually requiring the present in translation: לֹא יָדַעְתִּי, "I do not *know*" (Gen 4:9). This is common with verbs of perception (ירע) or attitude (אהב): שָׂנֵאתִי מָאַסְתִּי חַגֵּיכֶם, "I *hate*, I *despise* your festivals" (Amos 5:21), אֲנִי יָדַעְתִּי אֶת־זְדֹנְךָ וְאֵת רֹעַ לְבָבֶךָ, "*I know* your impudence and the evil of your heart" (1 Sam 17:28), וְזֶה־אָהַבְתִּי נֶהְפְּכוּ־בִי, "the ones *I love* have turned against me" (Job 19:19).

*(d)* **Rhetorical future** – expresses a vivid future action or situation, which is not yet a reality but considered a certainty from the speaker's rhetorical point of view.[47] As

---

86–89; van der Merwe, Naudé, and Kroeze 1999, 144–46; Williams 1976, 29–30.

[47] Often called the *prophetic perfect*, although this designation may be misleading if we make too much of the distinction between the *rhetorical perfect* and the *future imperfect*. For summaries of the problem, see Waltke and O'Connor 1990, 465 (but see their 490 also), and Joüon and Muraoka 1993, 363; Chisholm 1998, 88; van der Merwe, Naudé, and Kroeze 1999, 146, and especially 364; Williams 1976, 30.

a rhetorical device, the perfect presents future events as if they have already occurred, which often requires the present or future in translation: לָכֵן גָּלָה עַמִּי מִבְּלִי־דָעַת, "therefore my people *will go into exile* for want of knowledge" (Isa 5:13), דָּרַךְ כּוֹכָב מִיַּעֲקֹב, "A star *will come out* of Jacob" (Num 24:17), כִּי עַתָּה תִּתֵּן וְאִם־לֹא לָקַחְתִּי בְחָזְקָה, "But you shall give it now, and if not, *I will take* it by force" (1 Sam 2:16), עָשִׂיתִי אֶת־הַדָּבָר הַזֶּה, "*I will do* this thing" (2 Sam 14:21).

*(e) Proverbial* – denotes actions, events, or facts that are not time conditioned, and considered to be general truths. Also known as the *gnomic perfect,* this usually requires the present tense: וְתֹר וְסִיס וְעָגוּר שָׁמְרוּ אֶת־עֵת בֹּאָנָה, "and the turtledove, swallow, and crane *observe* the time of their coming" (Jer 8:7), יָבֵשׁ חָצִיר נָבֵל צִיץ, "The grass *withers* and the flower *fades*" (Isa 40:7).

*(f) Performative* – describes an action that occurs by means of speaking, usually requiring the present: נָתַתִּי אֹתְךָ עַל כָּל־אֶרֶץ מִצְרָיִם, "*I appoint* you over all the land of Egypt" (Gen 41:41),

בַּיּוֹם הַהוּא כָּרַת יְהוָה אֶת־אַבְרָם בְּרִית לֵאמֹר לְזַרְעֲךָ נָתַתִּי אֶת־הָאָרֶץ הַזֹּאת

"on that day, Yhwh made a covenant with Abraham saying, 'To your descedants, *I give* this land'" (Gen 15:18).

### 3.2.2 *Imperfect*

The imperfect has an even less precise time value than the perfect.[48] In general, the imperfect views actions, events, or states from the inside, meaning that the situation is underway or in process. The speaker or writer views the situation

---

[48] Joüon and Muraoka 1993, 372. Although the term "imperfect" is less than completely satisfying for this aspect of the BH verb, we retain it for the sake of convenience (see Rainey 1986, 7, and 1996, 2:227–28).

as still continuing, in the process of accomplishment, just taking place, or imminent. The imperfect may assume an indicative mood so that the speaker or writer makes an objective statement, which, however, makes no reference to the beginning or end of the situation. As with the perfect aspect, context must determine whether the situation is past, present, or future.[49] At other times, the imperfect may assume a subjunctive or hypothetical mood, describing a dependent situation that is only contingent or possible. Thus, the speaker or writer uses the imperfect when viewing an action as nonspecific, habitual, or probable.

This great variety of uses for the imperfect, together with its close association to the modals (see section 3.3), can be explained partially by developments in the history of the Hebrew language near the end of the second millennium B.C.E. On the basis of comparative Semitic evidence, it appears that the prefixed forms in BH were preceded by four distinct forms: an indicative imperfect (present-future) *yaqtulu*, a subjunctive *yaqtula*, a jussive *yaqtul*, and a preterite *yaqtul*.[50] When Hebrew words lost their final vowels (approximately 1100 B.C.E.), these forms became largely indistinguishable. This may explain why the Bible's uses of the imperfect conjugation include a preterite use and several "contingent" uses (vestiges of the subjunctive in Proto-Hebrew). In addition, the volitive modals (see section 3.3) suggest that *yaqtulu* and the jussive *yaqtul* had merged completely by the time BH was written.[51]

---

[49] However, in LBH, the imperfect is used primarily for the future (Sáenz-Badillos 1993, 129).

[50] The evidence further suggests the presence of an energic form (see Rainey 1986, 10–12, and 1996, 2:221–64; Joüon and Muraoka 1993, 388; Waltke and O'Connor 1990, 496–97). Some scholars also speak of an accent distinguishing Proto-Hebrew jussive and preterite, although this is a moot point (see especially Zevit 1998, 49–65, and compare Joüon and Muraoka 1993, 388).

[51] For more, see Meyer 1992, 18–20, 26–27, 381–84; Waltke and O'Connor 1990, 455–78, 496–502 (esp. 497), 543–47, 566–68; Joüon and Muraoka

The following semantic categories are helpful in further classifying verbs in the imperfect.[52]

*(a) Future* – describes an action anticipated or announced: כִּי־מֶלֶךְ יִמְלֹךְ עָלֵינוּ, "for a king *will reign* over us" (1 Sam 12:12), אַתָּה תָּבוֹא אֶל־אֲבֹתֶיךָ בְּשָׁלוֹם, "you *shall go* to your ancestors in peace" (Gen 15:15). The future imperfect may be used to denote action that is in fact past as far as the speaker or writer is concerned, but prior to some other action: וַיָּבֵא אֶל־הָאָדָם לִרְאוֹת מַה־יִּקְרָא־לוֹ, "and he [YHWH] brought [them] to the man to see what *he would call* them" (Gen 2:19). Likewise, it may denote action in the future that is prior to another anticipated action: וְהַעֲלִיתָ עוֹלָה בַּעֲצֵי הָאֲשֵׁרָה אֲשֶׁר תִּכְרֹת, "and offer it as a burnt offering with the wood of the sacred pole that *you shall cut down*" (Judg 6:26).

*(b) Customary* – denotes an action occurring regularly or customarily. The action may be in the past, in which case the customary imperfect is *iterative*, emphasizing the repeated nature of the action: כָּכָה יַעֲשֶׂה אִיּוֹב כָּל־הַיָּמִים, "This is what Job *would always do*" (Job 1:5). Customary action may also designate the present, in which case it frequently takes on a *proverbial* connotation: בֵּן חָכָם יְשַׂמַּח־אָב, "a wise child *makes* a father *glad*" (Prov 10:1).[53]

*(c) Progressive* – indicates action that is underway or continuing as the writer or speaker describes it. Such

---

1993, 387–89; Sáenz-Badillos 1993, 48–49; Rainey 1986, 4–19; Smith 1991, 12.

[52] Kautzsch 1910, 313–19; Waltke and O'Connor 1990, 496–518; Joüon and Muraoka 1993, 365–73; Lambdin 1971a, 100; Bergsträsser 1962, 2:29–36; Chisholm 1998, 89–94; van der Merwe, Naudé, and Kroeze 1999, 146–49; Williams 1976, 30–32.

[53] For the iterative and proverbial, Waltke and O'Connor speak of "past customary non-perfective," which implies that the situation no longer holds true at the time of the utterance, and "habitual non-perfective" (1990, 502–03 and 506).

actions or events of the present are usually expressed
with participles, but the progressive imperfect emphasizes the present continuous nature of the action, particularly in questions: אָנָה חֵלֵכִי, "where *are you going*?"
(Gen 16:8), לָמָּה תַעֲמֹד בַּחוּץ, "why *are you standing* outside?"
(Gen 24:31).

*(d) Contingent* – expresses action that is dependent upon
other factors in the context. A wide variety of such uses is
possible, often requiring the use of modal helping verbs:
may, can, shall, might, could, should, and so on.

(d.1) *Conditional* – expresses the action of the protasis or introductory clause of a conditional sentence:
כִּי־אֵלֵךְ בְּגֵיא צַלְמָוֶת, "If *I walk* through the darkest valley"
(Ps 23:4), אִם־אֶמְצָא בִסְדֹם חֲמִשִּׁים צַדִּיקִם, "If *I find* in Sodom
fifty righteous people" (Gen 18:26).

(d.2) *Permission* – indicates that the subject is permitted
to take action, usually requiring "may":

מִכֹּל עֵץ־הַגָּן אָכֹל תֹּאכֵל

"You *may freely eat* of every tree in the garden" (Gen 2:16),
יְהוָה מִי־יָגוּר בְּאָהֳלֶךָ מִי־יִשְׁכֹּן בְּהַר קָדְשֶׁךָ, "O YHWH, who
*may abide* in your tent? Who *may dwell* on your holy hill?"
(Ps 15:1).

(d.3) *Obligation* – denotes that some action should
(or should not) be done: מַעֲשִׂים אֲשֶׁר לֹא יֵעָשׂוּ עָשִׂיתָ עִמָּדִי,
"You have done things to me that *ought* not *to be done*"
(Gen 20:9), לֹא־יֵעָשֶׂה כֵן בְּיִשְׂרָאֵל, "such a thing *is not done*
in Israel" (2 Sam 13:12).

(d.4) *Command* – expresses a strong injunction or
prohibition: קִנִּים תַּעֲשֶׂה אֶת־הַתֵּבָה, "*you shall make* rooms
for the ark" (Gen 6:14),

כֹּל אֲשֶׁר־יָלֹק בִּלְשׁוֹנוֹ מִן־הַמַּיִם כַּאֲשֶׁר יָלֹק הַכֶּלֶב תַּצִּיג אוֹתוֹ לְבָד

"all who lap the water with their tongue, just as a dog laps
water, *set* them *apart*" (Judg 7:5).

The use of the imperfect (or the *waw*-consecutive perfect) may connote a command perceived by the speaker as continually valid, or one that need not be performed immediately. Such use of the imperfect may also occur when a superior speaker presents laws or instructions.[54] With the negative particle, such imperfects become prohibitions, which is common in legal literature: לֹא תִגְנֹב, "*you shall not steal*" (Exod 20:15), לֹא תִשְׁמַע אֶל־דִּבְרֵי הַנָּבִיא הַהוּא, "*you shall not listen* to the words of that prophet" (Deut 13:4 [Eng. 13:3]).

*(e) Preterite* – designates specifically past time situations when occurring after אָז, טֶרֶם, and בְּטֶרֶם: אָז יָשִׁיר־מֹשֶׁה וּבְנֵי יִשְׂרָאֵל אֶת־הַשִּׁירָה הַזֹּאת לַיהוָה, "Then Moses and the Israelites *sang* this song to YHWH" (Exod 15:1), וְכֹל שִׂיחַ הַשָּׂדֶה טֶרֶם יִהְיֶה בָאָרֶץ, "and no plant of the field *was* yet in the earth" (Gen 2:5).

Technically, the preterite was a third conjugation that was dying out in BH. Comparison with other Semitic languages reveals that the shortened form of several weak roots – and consistently the Hiphil prefixed forms – could serve in prose as a genuine preterite with אָז, טֶרֶם, and בְּטֶרֶם and in archaic poetry without them.

## 3.3 Modals

In addition to the conjugations expressing statement of fact (perfect and imperfect), Hebrew also has three modals expressing volition: jussive, cohortative, and imperative. These forms evolved independently in the early history of Hebrew, and they therefore constitute a class by function rather than by morphology; that is, they are treated together only because of similar uses, not because they constitute a distinct

[54] Shulman 2001.

conjugation.[55] Together they comprise the variety of ways BH expresses will or volition.[56]

### 3.3.1 *Jussive*

The reader should recall that most roots show no distinction between the jussive and the corresponding imperfect forms. The only exceptions are Hiphil forms, Qal forms of middle weak roots, and all stems of final-*hē* roots.[57]

The jussive expresses the speaker's desire, wish, or command where a second or third person is the subject of the action, although the third person is more common.[58] The following semantic categories are helpful in classifying the jussive.

*(a) Command* – A superior uses the jussive with an inferior as subject: יְהִי אוֹר, "*let there be* light" (Gen 1:3), וְהָעוֹף יִרֶב בָּאָרֶץ, "and *let* birds *multiply* on the earth" (Gen 1:22), שִׁבְעַת יָמִים תּוֹחֵל עַד־בּוֹאִי אֵלֶיךָ, "seven days *you shall wait* until I come to you" (1 Sam 10:8).

At times, this connotes *permission*:

וְיַעַל לִירוּשָׁלַם אֲשֶׁר בִּיהוּדָה וְיִבֶן אֶת־בֵּית יְהוָה אֱלֹהֵי יִשְׂרָאֵל

---

[55] For the hypothesis that the jussive had an independent origin from the imperfect and that they subsequently merged, see discussion under 3.2.2.

[56] Kautzsch 1910, 319–26; Waltke and O'Connor 1990, 564–79; Joüon and Muraoka 1993, 373–79; Bergsträsser 1962, 2:45–53; Chisholm 1998, 103–07; van der Merwe, Naudé, and Kroeze 1999, 150–53; Williams 1976, 34–35.

[57] Kautzsch 1910, 130–31; Hostetter 2000, 70, 97, and 140; Seow 1995, 209, 235–36, and 279–81; Ross 2001, 150, 211, 261, and 277.

[58] In the early stages of Hebrew, the shortened prefix conjugation for expressions of volition could be used in all three persons. But in BH, the jussive occurs only in the third and second persons, although the third is by far the most common (Waltke and O'Connor 1990, 567; Joüon and Muraoka 1993, 138–39 and 376; and Chisholm 1998, 103). Most of the examples included here are third person.

"*let him go up* to Jerusalem which is in Judah, and *let him rebuild* the house of Yнwн, the God of Israel" (Ezra 1:3), וּתְהִי אִשָּׁה לְבֶן־אֲדֹנֶיךָ כַּאֲשֶׁר דִּבֶּר יְהוָה, "and *let her become* the wife of your master's son, as Yнwн has spoken" (Gen 24:51). At other times, the concept of *invitation* is more appropriate: תְּהִי נָא אָלָה בֵּינוֹתֵינוּ, "*let there be* an oath between us" (Gen 26:28).

**(b) Wish** – An inferior uses the jussive with a superior as subject: יְחִי הַמֶּלֶךְ, "*long live* the king" (1 Sam 10:24), וְעַתָּה יֵרֶא פַרְעֹה אִישׁ נָבוֹן וְחָכָם, "and now *let* Pharaoh *select* [literally: *see*] a man who is discerning and wise" (Gen 41:33).

The speaker may use the *jussive of request* by referring to himself or herself indirectly when addressing a superior: וּתְחִי נַפְשִׁי, "and may my life *be saved*" (Gen 19:20). The use of "servant" is a common honorific substitute for a first-person pronoun in such requests: וְעַתָּה יֵשֶׁב־נָא עַבְדְּךָ, "and now please *let* your servant *remain*" (Gen 44:33). Such a request is often followed by the particle נָא: יָשָׁב־נָא עַבְדְּךָ, "*let* your servant *return*" (2 Sam 19:38 [Eng 19:37]). At times, this connotes *advice:* וְיַפְקֵד הַמֶּלֶךְ פְּקִידִים, "and *let* the king *appoint* overseers" (Esth 2:3).

Where the jussive expresses a wish for God to take action, the jussive denotes *prayer:* יֹסֵף יְהוָה לִי בֵּן אַחֵר, "*may* Yнwн *add* to me another son" (Gen 30:24), יָקֵם יְהוָה אֶת־דְּבָרוֹ, "*may* Yнwн *establish* his word" (1 Sam 1:23).

**(c) Benediction** – A superior speaks of God as the subject of the jussive in order to pronounce a blessing for a third party: וִיהִי אֱלֹהִים עִמָּךְ, "and *may* God *be* with you" (Exod 18:19), יְבָרֶכְךָ יְהוָה וְיִשְׁמְרֶךָ, "Yнwн *bless* you and *keep* you" (Num 6:24),[59] וְעַתָּה יַעַשׂ־יְהוָה עִמָּכֶם חֶסֶד וֶאֱמֶת, "and

---

[59] For more on the six jussive verbs (only two in form) in the Aaronic blessing, see Waltke and O'Connor 1990, 566.

now *may* YHWH *show* steadfast love and faithfulness to you" (2 Sam 2:6).

*(d) Prohibition* – with אַל, the command and wish nuances are expressed negatively:[60] וְאַל־תַּעַשׂ לוֹ מְאוּמָה "*do not do* anything to him" (Gen 22:12), אַל־נָא תְהִי מְרִיבָה בֵּינִי וּבֵינֶיךָ "*let there be no* strife between you and me" (Gen 13:8), אַל־נָא יִחַר לַאדֹנָי "O *may* the Lord *not be angry*" (Gen 18:30).

## 3.3.2 *Imperative*

The imperative expresses the speaker's command or instruction directly in the second person. It is interesting to note that the imperative is used only in positive expressions of volition, never in negative commands. Rather, negative commands are expressed with the imperfect preceded by אַל or לֹא, אַל with the imperfect for *immediate prohibition* (section 4.2.3) and לֹא with the imperfect for *permanent prohibition* (section 4.2.11).

The following semantic categories are helpful in classifying the imperative.

*(a) Command* – The speaker urges immediate action: לֶךְ־לְךָ מֵאַרְצְךָ, "*go forth* from your country" (Gen 12:1),[61] שׁוּב אֶל־אֶרֶץ אֲבוֹתֶיךָ, "*return* to the land of your ancestors" (Gen 31:3), בֹּא־אַתָּה וְכָל־בֵּיתְךָ אֶל־הַתֵּבָה, "*go into* the ark, you and all your household" (Gen 7:1), בֹּא דַבֵּר אֶל־פַּרְעֹה מֶלֶךְ מִצְרָיִם, "*go, speak to* Pharaoh king of Egypt" (Exod 6:11). Less immediate action may

---

[60] It is difficult to assign any particular meaning to the few uses of לֹא with the jussive. See Kautzsch 1910, 322.

[61] Note that the use of reflexive לְ with imperatives is common (see 4.1.10). Some have called this the centripetal use of the preposition (Muraoka 1978, 495–98; Waltke and O'Connor 1990, 207–08).

also be commanded by the imperative, although the imperfect is more common: וְכַאֲשֶׁר תִּרְאֶה עֲשֵׂה עִם־עֲבָדֶיךָ, "and *deal (at that time)* with your servants according to what you observe" (Dan 1:13). To this category belong also those imperatives connoting *request* or *wish*: שִׁפְטוּ־נָא בֵּינִי וּבֵין כַּרְמִי, "*judge* between me and my vineyard" (Isa 5:3). In contradistinction to commands expressed by indicative forms (such as imperfects or converted perfects, see sections 3.2.2,d and 3.5.3, respectively), such imperatives are usually perceived by the speaker as urgent and usually valid for one occasion.[62]

*(b) Permission* – The speaker grants permission for the action, which the recipient of the imperative desires to take. This use of the imperative is frequently preceded in the context by an actual request (often a jussive or cohortative of wish): אֶעֱלֶה־נָּא וְאֶקְבְּרָה אֶת־אָבִי . . . עֲלֵה וּקְבֹר אֶת־אָבִיךָ, "let me go up and bury my father . . . *go up* and *bury* your father" (Gen 50:5–6), אֵלֲכָה נָּא . . . לֵךְ לְשָׁלוֹם, "please let me go back . . . *go* in peace" (Exod 4:18).

*(c) Promise* – The speaker assures that the recipient of the imperative will take the action in the future, although the action itself is normally outside the power of the person receiving the order:[63] עֲלֵה רָמֹת גִּלְעָד וְהַצְלַח, "go up to Ramoth-Gilead and *triumph*" (1 Kgs 22:12), וּבַשָּׁנָה הַשְּׁלִישִׁית זִרְעוּ וְקִצְרוּ וְנִטְעוּ כְרָמִים וְאִכְלוּ פִרְיָם, "and in the third year *sow*, *reap*, *plant* vineyards, and *eat* their fruit" (Isa 37:30).

A long form is possible in all derived stems consisting of a suffix ָה, which results in certain other vowel changes

---

[62] For other subtle distinctions between imperatives and commands expressed by indicative forms, see Shulman 2001.

[63] See Waltke and O'Connor's discussion of "heterosis" in which one grammatical form is exchanged for another. So a promise is made more emphatic by the use of an imperative where a present-future imperfect would be expected (1990, 572).

(קָטְלָה or קְטָלָה in the Qal strong verb). This has sometimes been taken as stylistic, emphatic, or polite, but appears to have no discernible difference in nuance from the regular form.[64] Recent studies have suggested it may have been used when the verbal action was directed toward the speaker.[65]

Likewise the particle נָא־, which is frequently added to all three volitive modals (imperatives, jussives, and cohortatives), evinces no discernible difference in meaning. Some authorities continue to suspect that it originally added a nuance of "energy" (so translated "please" or "I pray"),[66] while others have noted its "logical" connotations, implying that the wish of the volitive is a logical consequence of a preceding statement or situation.[67] In any case, the particle could easily be left untranslated.

### 3.3.3 *Cohortative*

The cohortative expresses the speaker's desire, wish, or command, with the first person used as the subject of the action. In general, the cohortative emphasizes the determination behind the action, or one's personal interest in it. The following semantic categories are helpful in classifying the cohortative.

*(a) Resolve* – The speaker expresses self-determination to take an action that is within the speaker's ability: אֵרֲדָה־נָּא וְאֶרְאֶה, "*I must go down* and see" (Gen 18:21), אָגִילָה וְאֶשְׂמְחָה בְּחַסְדֶּךָ, "*I will exult* and *rejoice* in your steadfast love" (Ps 31:8), אָשִׁירָה נָּא לִידִידִי, "*let me sing* now for my beloved" (Isa 5:1), אֲדַבְּרָה בְמַר נַפְשִׁי, "*I will speak* in the

---

[64] Joüon suggests it is purely euphonic (1910, 143 and 378).
[65] Fassberg 1999, 7–13.
[66] Joüon and Muraoka 1993, 350–51.
[67] Lambdin 1971a, 170–71.

bitterness of my soul" (Job 10:1), אָשִׁירָה וַאֲזַמְּרָה לַיהוָה,
"*I will sing* and *I will make melody* to YHWH" (Ps 27:6).[68]

*(b) Wish* – The speaker expresses the desire to take
an action that requires the consent of another:
אֶעְבְּרָה בְאַרְצֶךָ, "*let me pass through* your land" (Deut 2:27),
אֵלְכָה נָּא וְאָשׁוּבָה אֶל־אַחַי אֲשֶׁר־בְּמִצְרַיִם, "*let me go back,
let me return* to my kindred in Egypt" (Exod 4:18),
אֶעְבְּרָה־נָּא וְאָסִירָה אֶת־רֹאשׁוֹ, "*let me go over* and *take off* his
head" (2 Sam 16:9), אֵלְכָה־נָּא הַשָּׂדֶה וַאֲלַקֳטָה בַשִׁבֳּלִים,
"*let me go* to the field and *let me glean* among the ears of
grain" (Ruth 2:2).

At times, the consent seems doubtful, or the speaker
incapable: אָנָּה יְהוָה אַל־נָא נֹאבְדָה בְּנֶפֶשׁ הָאִישׁ הַזֶּה, "please, O
YHWH, *do not let us perish* on account of this man's life"
(Jonah 1:14), עַל־מִי אֲדַבְּרָה וְאָעִידָה, "to whom *shall I speak*
and *give warning*" (Jer 6:10).

*(c) Exhortation* – Plural speakers encourage one another to take action, or to help in the action:
הָבָה נִלְבְּנָה לְבֵנִים, "come, *let us make bricks*" (Gen 11:3),
נְנַתְּקָה אֶת־מוֹסְרוֹתֵימוֹ, "*let us burst* their bonds asunder"
(Ps 2:3), וְנַחְשְׁבָה עַל־יִרְמְיָהוּ מַחֲשָׁבוֹת, "and *let us devise* plans
against Jeremiah" (Jer 18:18).

## 3.4 Nonfinites

The Hebrew nonfinites are not inflected for *Aspekt*; that is,
they make no reference to the action as undefined or progressive (as do the perfect and imperfect conjugations, see
section 3.2). Furthermore, the two Hebrew infinitives are not

---

[68] Here belong third-*hê* verbs that make no distinction between imperfect
and cohortative in form: נַעֲשֶׂה אָדָם בְּצַלְמֵנוּ, "*let us make* humankind in our
image" (Gen 1:26, and compare Gen 2:18 and others). See Kautzsch 1910,
210.

marked by person, gender, or number.[69] The participle is not marked by person, but is so marked for gender and number. The lack of specific inflection leaves these "nonfinites" less restricted in their uses than the conjugations or modals.

The nonfinites are based on verbal roots, but hold a middle position between verbs and nouns. The infinitives are "verbal nouns," displaying some uses similar to those of nouns and others similar to those of verbs. The participle is a "verbal adjective," being formed as a noun with gender and number, and often having functions like an adjective.

### 3.4.1 *Infinitive Construct*

The infinitive construct comes closest to the uses of infinitives in other languages.[70] It is both "atemporal" and "apersonal," meaning that only the context determines the time/aspect features of the action as well as the subject of the action itself.[71] It has a wide and flexible range of uses, most of which occur in relation to another verb. It often functions as a noun in that it may be governed by prepositions and may take pronominal suffixes. Rather than being negated by אַל or לֹא, the infinitive construct takes (לְ)בִלְתִּי.

Technically, the infinitive construct has no semantic function in itself: "The functions of an infinitive refer either to the syntactic function that it fulfills in a clause, or to the semantic relationship between itself and the finite verb."[72] The following semantic categories are helpful in classifying the infinitive construct.[73]

---

[69] Hebrew is not alone among the Northwest Semitic languages in having two infinitives (Harris 1939, 41; Garr 1985, 183–84).

[70] Blau 1976, 47; Bergsträsser 1983, 56; Joüon and Muraoka 1993, 432.

[71] Joüon and Muraoka 1993, 439.

[72] Van der Merwe, Naudé, and Kroeze 1999, 154.

[73] Kautzsch 1910, 347–52; Waltke and O'Connor 1990, 598–611; Joüon and Muraoka 1993, 432–39; Meyer 1992; 399–403; Lambdin 1971a, 128–29; Bergsträsser 1962, 2:53–60; Chisholm 1998, 77–78; van der Merwe, Naudé, and Kroeze 1999, 153–57; Williams 1976, 35–37. On the infinitive construct in epigraphic Hebrew, see Gogel 1998, 270–71.

*(a) Nominal* – when used as a noun or in place of a noun. Thus, the infinitive construct may function in nominative, genitive, or accusative functions.[74]

(a.1) Examples of the infinitive construct as *nominatives*:

עֲנוֹשׁ לַצַּדִּיק לֹא־טוֹב

"*to impose a fine* on the innocent is not good" (Prov 17:26), טוֹב שֶׁבֶת בְּאֶרֶץ־מִדְבָּר מֵאֵשֶׁת מִדְיָנִים וָכָעַס, "It is better *to live* in a desert land than with a contentious and fretful wife" (Prov 21:19), טוֹב תִּתִּי אֹתָהּ לָךְ, "it is good that *I give* her to you" (Gen 29:19).

(a.2) Examples of the infinitive construct as *genitives*: עֵת סְפוֹד וְעֵת רְקוֹד, "a time *of mourning* and a time *of dancing*" (Eccl 3:4), בְּיוֹם אֲכָלְךָ מִמֶּנּוּ מוֹת תָּמוּת, "in the day *when you eat* (literally: *of your eating*) from it, you shall surely die" (Gen 2:17), לֹא־עֵת הֵאָסֵף הַמִּקְנֶה, "it is not time for the cattle *to be gathered together* [literally: time *of being gathered together*]" (Gen 29:7). This category also includes the numerous times the infinitive construct occurs after a preposition (see sections 3.4.1,b–d, f, g).

(a.3) Examples of the infinitive construct as *accusatives*: לֹא אֵדַע צֵאת וָבֹא, "I do not know how *to go out or to come in*" (1 Kgs 3:7), זְכֹר עָמְדִי לְפָנֶיךָ, "remember how *I stood* before you [literally: *my standing* before you]" (Jer 18:20). Just as nouns may be *adverbial accusatives* (see section 2.3), so the infinitive construct may take on *adverbial* force when following a finite verb (often a Hiphil or Piel denominative). In such cases, the infinitive construct takes on the function of the main verb in the English translation: וַתָּרַע לַעֲשׂוֹת, "*you have done* evil" (1 Kgs 14:9), מַדּוּעַ מִהַרְתֶּן בֹּא הַיּוֹם, "why *have you come back* so soon today" (Exod 2:18).

To this category of the infinitive construct as accusatives belong many verbs that require an infinitive to complete their meanings. Thus, the infinitive construct may serve

[74] The *nominal* infinitive construct may occur in any of these functions with the preposition לְ.

as a *verbal complement*: לֹא יוּכַל לִרְאוֹת, "he is not able *to see*"
(Gen 48:10), לֹא־יֹאבֶה יְהוָה סְלֹחַ לוֹ, "Yhwh will not be willing *to pardon* him" (Deut 29:19). The most common verbs
requiring such a complement include ידע (and other verbs
of observation or cognition), חלל (Hiphil, to begin), יסף
(Hiphil, to continue), בקשׁ (Piel, to seek), חדל (to stop),
יכל (to be capable of), מאן (to refuse), נתן (to allow), and
אבה (to be willing).[75]

*(b) Temporal* – locates the action of the finite verb by re-
lating it to the action of the infinitive construct. The uses
of various prepositions on the *temporal* infinitive construct
denote the specific moment in time.[76]

(b.1) The preposition בְּ plus the infinitive (section 4.1.5,b) connotes action that is *simultaneous* with that
of the finite verb, and may be translated "as," "when," or
"while":

בְּשׁוּב דָּוִד מֵהַכּוֹת אֶת־הַפְּלִשְׁתִּי וַתֵּצֶאנָה הַנָּשִׁים מִכָּל־עָרֵי
יִשְׂרָאֵל

"*when* David *returned* from killing the Philistine, the women
came out of all the towns of Israel" (1 Sam 18:6),
בַּיּוֹם הַהוּא בְּשֶׁבֶת עַמִּי יִשְׂרָאֵל לָבֶטַח, "on that day *when* my
people Israel *are dwelling* securely" (Ezek 38:14).

(b.2) The preposition כְּ plus the infinitive (section 4.1.9,c) connotes action that occurs *immediately preceding* that of the finite verb, and may be translated "the
moment when," or "as soon as":

וַיְהִי כְּבוֹא אַבְרָם מִצְרָיְמָה וַיִּרְאוּ הַמִּצְרִים אֶת־הָאִשָּׁה כִּי־יָפָה
הִוא מְאֹד

---

75 Van der Merwe, Naudé, and Kroeze 1999, 154, and Waltke and O'Connor
1990, 602.
76 Such constructions using the infinitive construct are especially frequent
after וַיְהִי (Kautzsch 1910, 347–48). For several other prepositions in addition to the ones discussed here, see Waltke and O'Connor 1990, 604–05.

"*As soon as* Abram *entered* Egypt, the Egyptians saw that the woman was very beautiful" (Gen 12:14), כִּשְׁמֹעַ עֵשָׂו אֶת־דִּבְרֵי אָבִיו וַיִּצְעַק צְעָקָה גְּדֹלָה וּמָרָה עַד־מְאֹד, "*When Esau heard* his father's words, he cried out with an exceedingly great and bitter cry" (Gen 27:34). Similar to בְּ above, כְּ may also point to simultaneous action:

וַיְהִי כִרְאוֹת הַמֶּלֶךְ אֶת־אֶסְתֵּר הַמַּלְכָּה עֹמֶדֶת בֶּחָצֵר נָשְׂאָה
חֵן בְּעֵינָיו

"*The moment* the king *saw* Queen Esther standing in the court, she obtained favor in his sight" (Esth 5:2), וְהִיא כְפֹרַחַת עָלְתָה נִצָּהּ, "*As it was budding,* its blossoms came out" (Gen 40:10).

(b.3) The preposition עַד plus the infinitive (section 4.1.15,b) connotes that the action of the finite verb occurs *during the period extending to* the action of the infinitive, and may be translated "until": לֹא אוּכַל לַעֲשׂוֹת דָּבָר עַד־בֹּאֲךָ שָׁמָּה, "I can do nothing *until* you *arrive* there" (Gen 19:22),

בְּזֵעַת אַפֶּיךָ תֹּאכַל לֶחֶם עַד שׁוּבְךָ אֶל־הָאֲדָמָה

"By the sweat of your face you shall eat bread *until* you *return* to the ground" (Gen 3:19), וַיֵּאָבֵק אִישׁ עִמּוֹ עַד עֲלוֹת הַשָּׁחַר, "and a man wrestled with him *until* daybreak [literally: *until the coming up of* the dawn]" (Gen 32:25).

(b.4) The preposition אַחֲרֵי plus the infinitive (section 4.1.1,b) connotes that the action of the finite verb occurs *subsequent* to the action of the infinitive, and may be translated "after":

וַיִּמָּלֵא שִׁבְעַת יָמִים אַחֲרֵי הַכּוֹת־יְהוָה אֶת־הַיְאֹר

"seven days passed *after* YHWH *had struck* the Nile" (Exod 7:25), וַיְהִי אַחֲרֵי הֵסַבּוּ אֹתוֹ וַתְּהִי יַד־יְהוָה בָּעִיר, "*After* they *brought* it *around* [that is, the ark of the covenant to Gath], the hand of YHWH was against the city" (1 Sam 5:9).

*(c) Purpose* – expresses the reason the action of the finite verb took place (most commonly used with ל, see section 4.1.10,d): וַיָּבֵא אֶל־הָאָדָם לִרְאוֹת מַה־יִּקְרָא־לוֹ, "and he [YHWH] brought [them] to the man *in order to see* what he would call them" (Gen 2:19), אֲנִי יְהוָה אֲשֶׁר הוֹצֵאתִיךָ מֵאוּר כַּשְׂדִּים לָתֶת לְךָ אֶת־הָאָרֶץ הַזֹּאת, "I am YHWH who brought you out from Ur of the Chaldeans *in order to give* to you this land" (Gen 15:7), הוּא יֹצֵא לִקְרָאתֶךָ, "he is coming out *in order to meet* you" (Exod 4:14). Besides ל, the infinitive construct of *purpose* also occurs with לְמַעַן (section 4.1.11,a) and בַּעֲבוּר (Williams 1976, 36).

*(d) Result* – expresses the outcome or consequence of the action of the finite verb. This form of the infinitive normally occurs with ל, and may be translated "and so," "so as," or "so that": וַיִּתְמַכְּרוּ לַעֲשׂוֹת הָרַע בְּעֵינֵי יְהוָה לְהַכְעִיסוֹ, "and they sold themselves to do evil in the sight of YHWH, *so provoking him to anger*" (2 Kgs 17:17), מַדּוּעַ מָצָאתִי חֵן בְּעֵינֶיךָ לְהַכִּירֵנִי, "why have I found favor in your sight *so that you took notice* of me" (Ruth 2:10), וַיְגָרֶשׁ שְׁלֹמֹה אֶת־אֶבְיָתָר מִהְיוֹת כֹּהֵן לַיהוָה לְמַלֵּא אֶת־דְּבַר יְהוָה, "and Solomon banished Abiathar from being priest to YHWH, *so fulfilling* the word of YHWH" (1 Kgs 2:27), בְּךָ בָּחַר יְהוָה אֱלֹהֶיךָ לִהְיוֹת לוֹ לְעַם סְגֻלָּה, "YHWH your God chose you *and so you became* his special people" (Deut 7:6). The distinction between *purpose* and *result* is not always clear, but result generally emphasizes the idea of sequence or progression (Joüon's "consecution" [1991, 436]). Besides ל, the infinitive construct of result also occurs with לְמַעַן.[77]

*(e) Obligation* – expresses the burden of responsibility or necessity when used in verbless clauses:[78]

---

[77] Williams 1976, 36.

[78] Other "modal" uses of the infinitive construct are also possible in verbless clauses. See Waltke and O'Connor 1990, 609–10.

וְעָלַי לָתֶת לְךָ עֲשָׂרָה כֶסֶף וַחֲגֹרָה אֶחָת, "and I *would have had to give* you ten shekels of silver and a belt" (2 Sam 18:11). This use of the infinitive construct often takes a negative particle, and at times the negative obligation becomes *prohibition*: הֲלוֹא לָכֶם לָדַעַת אֶת־הַמִּשְׁפָּט, "is it not for you *to know* justice" (Mic 3:1), אֵין לָבוֹא אֶל־שַׁעַר הַמֶּלֶךְ בִּלְבוּשׁ שָׂק, "no one *was permitted to enter* the king's gate clothed with sackcloth" (Esth 4:2).

**(f) Imminence** – expresses action expected soon or about to take place in constructions with לְ plus infinitive construct in verbless clauses: יְהוָה לְהוֹשִׁיעֵנִי, "YHWH *will soon save me*" (Isa 38:20), וּבְרִיתוֹ לְהוֹדִיעָם, "and he [YHWH] is *about to make known* his covenant to them" (Ps 25:14), וְכַלָּתוֹ אֵשֶׁת־פִּינְחָס הָרָה לָלַת, "and his [Eli's] daughter-in-law, the wife of Phinehas, was pregnant, *about to give birth*" (1 Sam 4:19). For imminent action in past-tense narration, the construction adds a form of הָיָה: וַיְהִי כַּאֲשֶׁר הִקְרִיב לָבוֹא מִצְרָיְמָה, "when he was *about to enter* Egypt" (Gen 12:11), וַיְהִי הַשֶּׁמֶשׁ לָבוֹא, "and as the sun was *at the point of setting*" (Gen 15:12), וַיְהִי הַשַּׁעַר לִסְגּוֹר בַּחֹשֶׁךְ, "and the gate was *about to be shut* at dark" (Josh 2:5).

**(g) Specification** – used with לְ after a verb to clarify or explain further the preceding verbal action, which would otherwise be generally or ambiguously stated. In translation, the *specification* infinitive construct often requires "by ...-ing"):[79] וְאַתֶּם מוֹסִיפִים חָרוֹן עַל־יִשְׂרָאֵל לְחַלֵּל אֶת־הַשַּׁבָּת, "and you are adding to the wrath on Israel *by profaning* the sabbath" (Neh 13:18),

הָלַךְ אַחֲרֵי בְכָל־לְבָבוֹ לַעֲשׂוֹת רַק הַיָּשָׁר בְּעֵינִי

---

[79] Also known as *epexegetical, gerundive,* or *explanatory* infinitive construct (Waltke and O'Connor 1990, 608–09; Joüon and Muraoka 1993, 437–48; Kautzsch 1910, 351; Williams 1976, 36).

"he followed me with all his heart, *by doing* only that which was right in my sight" (1 Kgs 14:8). The specification infinitive construct often has לָלֶכֶת or לַעֲשׂוֹת after שָׁמַר:

וְשָׁמְרוּ בְנֵי־יִשְׂרָאֵל אֶת־הַשַּׁבָּת לַעֲשׂוֹת אֶת־הַשַּׁבָּת לְדֹרֹתָם בְּרִית עוֹלָם

"and the Israelites shall keep the sabbath, *by observing* the sabbath throughout their generations, as a perpetual covenant" (Exod 31:16),

וְשָׁמַרְתָּ אֶת־מִשְׁמֶרֶת יְהֹוָה אֱלֹהֶיךָ לָלֶכֶת בִּדְרָכָיו

"and you must keep the charge of Yhwh your God, *by walking* in his ways" (1 Kgs 2:3).

To this category belongs the nearly ubiquitous לֵאמֹר (Qal infinitive construct of אמר), which is used to frame reported speech, frequently following verbs of speaking or thinking:[80] וַיְדַבֵּר אֱלֹהִים אֶל־נֹחַ לֵאמֹר, "and God spoke to Noah, *by saying*" (Gen 8:15), וַיְבָרֶךְ אֹתָם אֱלֹהִים לֵאמֹר, "and God blessed them, *by saying*" (Gen 1:22). Such usage has taken on a stereotypical formula to mark reported speech.

### 3.4.2 *Infinitive Absolute*

The infinitive absolute is also both "atemporal" and "apersonal," meaning that only the context determines the time/aspect features of the action, as well as the subject of the action itself. This results from the fact that the infinitive absolute, like the infinitive construct, is also uninflected. On the other hand, unlike the infinitive construct, the infinitive absolute does not take prepositions or pronominal suffixes. Even though the two Hebrew infinitives appear similar in form, they apparently had completely different origins and histories.[81]

---

[80] A wide variety of verbs are used with לֵאמֹר. For this term as a "complementizer introducing a highly marked form of direct speech," see Miller 1996, 163–212.

[81] Bergsträsser 1962, 2:61; Waltke and O'Connor 1990, 581–82.

The following semantic categories are helpful in classifying the infinitive absolute.[82]

**(a) Nominal** – when used as a noun or in place of a noun. Thus, the infinitive absolute may serve in nominative, genitive, and accusative functions.

(a.1) Examples of the infinitive absolute functioning as *nominatives*: וְקָרוֹב לִשְׁמֹעַ מִתֵּת הַכְּסִילִים זָבַח, "and *to draw near* to listen is better than the sacrifice offered by fools," (Eccl 4:17 [Eng. 5:1]), וְגַם־הֵיטֵיב אֵין אוֹתָם, "and also *well-doing* is not in them" (Jer 10:5), הַכֵּר־פָּנִים לֹא־טוֹב, "*to show partiality* is not good" (Prov 28:21).

(a.2) Examples of the infinitive absolute functioning as *genitives*:[83] וּבְרוּחַ בָּעֵר, "and by the spirit *of burning*" (Isa 4:4), מִדֶּרֶךְ הַשְׂכֵּל, "from the way *of understanding*" (Prov 21:16). On rare occasions, the infinitive absolute may occur after a preposition.[84]

(a.3) Examples of the infinitive absolute functioning as *accusatives*: חֶמְאָה וּדְבַשׁ יֹאכֵל לְדַעְתּוֹ מָאוֹס בָּרָע וּבָחוֹר בַּטּוֹב, "he shall eat curds and honey by the time he knows *to refuse* the evil and *to choose* the good" (Isa 7:15), לִמְדוּ הֵיטֵב, "learn *to do good*" (Isa 1:17), לֹא יֶאֱהַב־לֵץ הוֹכֵחַ לוֹ, "a scoffer does not love *to be rebuked* [literally: *to reprove himself*]" (Prov 15:12).

**(b) Emphatic** – affirms and intensifies the authenticity or conviction of the verbal action when used with a finite verb of the same verbal root.[85] In one of the most common uses

---

[82] Kautzsch 1910, 339–47; Waltke and O'Connor 1990, 580–97; Joüon and Muraoka 1993, 420–31; Meyer 1992, 403–07; Lambdin 1971a, 158–59; Bergsträsser 1962, 2:61–67; Chisholm 1998, 76–77; van der Merwe, Naudé, and Kroeze 1999, 157–62; Williams 1976, 37–39. On the infinitive absolute in epigraphic Hebrew, see Gogel 1998, 271.

[83] Examples of genitives are rare, and may have different explanations. See Meyer 1992, 404, and Williams 1976, 38.

[84] Williams 1976, 38; Kautzsch 1910, 340.

[85] By using the same root, the *emphatic* infinitive absolute becomes paronomastic; that is, it uses word play to create the emphasis. Earlier grammarians thought of this use as an *internal accusative* or an *accusative*

of the infinitive absolute, the infinitive normally precedes a finite verb of the same root, and is best translated by adverbs such as "certainly," "surely," "indeed," "definitely," and so on:

וְאַבְרָהָם הָיוֹ יִהְיֶה לְגוֹי גָּדוֹל

"and Abraham *will surely become* a great nation" (Gen 18:18), הָעֵד הֵעִד בָּנוּ הָאִישׁ, "the man *solemnly* warned us" (Gen 43:3), הַגִּלְגָּל גָּלֹה יִגְלֶה, "Gilgal *will certainly* go into exile" (Amos 5:5), הִשָּׁמֵד הִשָּׁמְדוּן, "you will be *utterly* destroyed" (Deut 4:26), וְנַקֵּה לֹא יְנַקֶּה יְהוָה, "Yhwh will *by no means* leave the guilty unpunished" (Nah 1:3). Sometimes the particle אַךְ (section 4.2.2) is used for additional emphasis: אַךְ טָרֹף טֹרָף, "he has *surely* been torn to pieces" (Gen 44:28).[86]

At times the *emphatic* infinitive absolute follows the finite verb of the same root: יָצֹא יָצוֹא, "he will *surely* come out" (2 Kgs 5:11). Sometimes this postpositive position seems to connote continuous action or repetition: לַשָּׁוְא צָרַף צָרוֹף, "in vain the refining *goes on*" (Jer 6:29), אֹמְרִים אָמוֹר, "they *keep on* saying" (Jer 23:17), וַיִּשְׁפֹּט שָׁפוֹט, "and he *constantly* acted as a judge" (Gen 19:9). However, while some grammarians continue to accept this durative connotation of the postpositive infinitive absolute, others doubt its validity.[87]

---

*of internal object* (Joüon and Muraoka 1993, 421–22). But comparative evidence from Ugaritic has shown that this use of the infinitive absolute is an extension of its use in the nominative case, and as such is an "appositional" nominative (Meyer 1992, 405) or an absolute complement resulting in what may be called an "intensifying infinitive" (Waltke and O'Connor 1990, 584–88).

[86] The *emphatic* infinitive absolute is also used to strengthen contrasts, indignant questions expecting a negative answer, and conditional clauses. On these, see Kautzsch 1910, 343; Joüon and Muraoka 1993, 422–23; Waltke and O'Connor 1990, 587; or van der Merwe, Naudé, and Kroeze 1999, 159).

[87] Of those who take the first position, see Meyer 1992, 63; Williams 1976, 38; Horsnell 1999, 73; Chisholm 1998, 77; of those who doubt this, see Waltke and O'Connor 1990, 585; Joüon and Muraoka 1993, 425; Seow 1995, 250–51.

Lambdin implies that the postpositive position is more common with intransitive roots.[88]

When the emphatic infinitive absolute follows a finite verb of the same root, it may be coordinated with a second infinitive absolute for simultaneous or durative action: וַיֵּצֵא יָצוֹא וָשׁוֹב, "and it [the raven] *kept flying back and forth*" (Gen 8:7),

וְהַמְאַסֵּף הֹלֵךְ אַחֲרֵי אֲרוֹן יְהוָה הָלוֹךְ וְתָקוֹעַ בַּשּׁוֹפָרוֹת

"the rear guard came after the ark of Yhwh, while they were *blowing the trumpets continually*" (Josh 6:13 *Qere*).[89] The use of the infinitive absolute for הלך in this function appears to have resulted in a formulaic use of the word, which is quite common: וַיֵּלֶךְ אִתָּהּ אִישָׁהּ הָלוֹךְ וּבָכֹה אַחֲרֶיהָ, "and her husband went with her, *weeping as he walked* behind her" (2 Sam 3:16).

*(c) Manner* – describes the way in which an action or situation is performed or the attendant circumstances of the action.[90] This is an infinitive absolute of a different root than the finite verb (and hence not the *emphatic* infinitive absolute). It typically follows the finite verb and modifies it adverbially: רִדְפוּ מַהֵר, "pursue *quickly*" (Josh 2:5), וְנָטָה־לוֹ מִחוּץ לַמַּחֲנֶה הַרְחֵק מִן־הַמַּחֲנֶה, "and he [Moses] pitched it [the tent of meeting] outside the camp, *a good distance* [literally: *far off*] from the camp" (Exod 33:7), וְשָׁחַקְתָּ מִמֶּנָּה הָדֵק, "and you shall beat some of it [incense] *very fine*" (Exod 30:36), וַיַּעַמְדוּ הַכֹּהֲנִים נֹשְׂאֵי הָאָרוֹן בְּרִית־יְהוָה בֶּחָרָבָה בְּתוֹךְ הַיַּרְדֵּן הָכֵן, "and the priests who carried the ark of the covenant of Yhwh stood *firm* on dry ground in the middle of the Jordan" (Josh 3:17).

---

[88] Lambdin 1971a, 158.

[89] Note that the infinitive absolute has been restored in this verse in the *Qere* (הָלוֹךְ), while the *Ketib* has an active participle (הֹלֵךְ).

[90] May be called an *adverbial complement* or an *adverbial infinitive* (Waltke and O'Connor 1990, 588–89).

Certain Hiphil and Piel infinitive absolutes were used for *manner* so naturally and frequently that they came to be treated as adverbs:

אַחְאָב עָבַד אֶת־הַבַּעַל מְעָט יֵהוּא יַעַבְדֶנּוּ הַרְבֵּה

"Ahab served Baal a little; Jehu will serve him *much*" (2 Kgs 10:18), סָרוּ מַהֵר מִן־הַדֶּרֶךְ אֲשֶׁר צִוִּיתִם, "they have *quickly* turned aside from the way I commanded them" (Exod 32:8). The infinitives most often used in this way are הַרְבֵּה (much, many), הֵיטֵב (well, thoroughly), הַשְׁכֵּם (early), הַרְחֵק (far), and מַהֵר (quickly).

*(d) Verbal substitute* – serves the function of a main verb, whether finite verb, modal, or even an infinitive construct:[91] רָגוֹם אֹתוֹ בָאֲבָנִים כָּל־הָעֵדָה, "all the congregation *shall stone* him" (Num 15:35), הִמּוֹל לָכֶם כָּל־זָכָר, "every male among you *shall be circumcised*" (Gen 17:10), וְנָתוֹן אֹתוֹ עַל כָּל־אֶרֶץ מִצְרָיִם, "and *he set* him over all the land of Egypt" (Gen 41:43), זָכוֹר אֶת־יוֹם הַשַּׁבָּת לְקַדְּשׁוֹ, "*remember* the sabbath day, to keep it holy" (Exod 20:8).

### 3.4.3 *Participle*

The participle is formed like a noun (taking gender and number), but has functions like the adjectives (section 2.5), and is thus a "verbal adjective." Like the other nonfinites, the participle is "atemporal," meaning that only the context determines the time/aspect features of the action.[92] Typically, the active participles (Qal active, Piel, and Hiphil)

---

[91] It has been suggested that this use of the infinitive absolute only occurs where one would expect a *waw*-consecutive form, and that this usage is related to the disappearance of the *waw* consecutive in LBH. See Rubenstein 1952, 262–67, and compare the use of the participle as a main verb in pre-exilic narrative, as discussed in Smith 1991, 27–33. For evidence of the same function surviving also in first-millennium Phoenician texts, see Garr 1985, 183–84.

[92] Joüon and Muraoka 1993, 409.

imply continuing or progressing action, whether past,
present, or future. This durative idea is in fact more strongly
expressed by the participle than by the imperfect (Joüon
and Muraoka 1993, 412).[93] The passive participles connote
completed action, often resulting in translation in a relative clause with a perfect or preterite verb (Lambdin 1971a,
18–19 and 158). In certain uses as an adjectival predicate,
the participle has secondarily become a temporal form;
that is, it may become a substitute for the imperfect.[94]
When negated, the participle takes אֵין.

The following semantic categories are helpful in classifying the participle.[95]

*(a) Attributive* – ascribes a quality to a noun. Like the *attributive adjective*, the *attributive participle* forms a phrase with
the noun it modifies, having a single function in the sentence. It stands in apposition to the noun, normally coming
after it and agreeing in gender, number, and definiteness:
לֵב שֹׁמֵעַ, "a *listening* heart" (1 Kgs 3:9), וּבִזְרֹעַ נְטוּיָה, "and by
*an outstretched* arm" (Deut 4:34), אֹזֶן שֹׁמַעַת, "a *hearing* ear"
(Prov 15:31).

Frequently, the participle requires a relative clause in
translation (introduced by "who," "which," or "that"), in
which case the attributive participle is usually definite:

מִבְּכוֹר פַּרְעֹה הַיֹּשֵׁב עַל־כִּסְאוֹ

---

93 The durative or progressive action of the active participles may be represented by a continuous line (i.e., _____ ) while the durative quality of the
imperfect expresses repetition or multiplicity, and may be represented by
a row of dots (i.e., . . . . . . ). See Horsnell 1999, 78.

94 Specifically in LBH, the participle alone functions as a present tense, and
in periphrastic clauses it indicates frequentative action (Sáenz-Badillos
1993, 129).

95 Kautzsch 1910, 355–62; Waltke and O'Connor 1990, 612–31; Joüon and
Muraoka 1993, 409–18; Meyer 1992, 407–12; Lambdin 1971a, 18–19 and
157–58; Bergsträsser 1962, 2:68–74; Horsnell 1999, 78–84; Chisholm
1998, 67–70; van der Merwe, Naudé, and Kroeze 1999, 162–63; Williams
1976, 39–40. On the participles in epigraphic Hebrew, see Gogel 1998,
272–73.

"from the firstborn of Pharaoh *who sits* on his throne" (Exod 11:5), הַיּוֹם הַבָּא, "the day *that is coming*" (Jer 47:4), הַכֶּסֶף הַמּוּשָׁב, "the money *that was returned*" (Gen 43:12), לֻחֹת אֶבֶן כְּתֻבִים בְּאֶצְבַּע אֱלֹהִים, "tablets of stone, *which were written* by the finger of God" (Exod 31:18).[96]

The attributive participle marks neither time nor aspect, both of which must be determined from the context. Thus, הַצָּבָא הַבָּא may mean "the army that came," "the army that is coming," or "the army that will come." In the context of 2 Chronicles 28:9, it can only mean "the army that came," since it is in a narrative context recounting past events.

*(b) Predicate* – expresses an assertion about a noun or pronoun in a nominal clause (i.e., in a clause without a finite verb). Like the *predicate adjective*, the *predicate participle* agrees in gender and number with the noun it modifies, and is always indefinite. The participle may stand before or after the noun or pronoun it modifies: הַשָּׁמַיִם מְסַפְּרִים כְּבוֹד־אֵל, "the heavens *are telling* the glory of God" (Ps 19:2 [Eng Ps 19:1]), בָּרוּךְ אַבְרָם לְאֵל עֶלְיוֹן, "*blessed is* Abram by God Most High" (Gen 14:19).

Because of its verbal character, the predicate participle may have a subject or a direct object, or it may be modified by an adverb or prepositional phrase.[97] As always, the participle does not express tense, but rather the durative or progressive action or condition that may occur in past, present, or future time, depending on the context.

(b.1) *Present* – expresses duration in present time, which is the participle's most natural verbal function due to its durative nature. The *predicate participle* indicating *present* action becomes a substitute for

---

[96] See Waltke and O'Connor's *attributive relative* as a subcategory under *relative participles* (1990, 621–22).

[97] The uses of the *predicate participle* are so similar to finite verbs that some grammars have a separate category of the participle as *verbal substitute,* or "participles as verbs" (see Kelley 1992, 200–01; van der Merwe, Naudé, and Kroeze 1999, 162).

the imperfect: אָנֹכִי בֹּרַחַת, "I *am fleeing*" (Gen 16:8),
לֹא־כֵן אֲנַחְנוּ עֹשִׂים, "we *are not doing* what is right" (2 Kgs
7:9).[98] This may denote general truths just revealed,
or truths valuable for all time: כִּי יָדַע אֱלֹהִים, "for God
*knows*" (Gen 3:5), דּוֹר הֹלֵךְ וְדוֹר בָּא וְהָאָרֶץ לְעוֹלָם עֹמָדֶת, "a
generation *goes* and a generation *comes,* but the earth
*remains* forever" (Eccl 1:4). Occasionally the present predicate participle occurs after הִנֵּה to express immediate
action or conditions requiring observation (hence, the
English, "behold"):[99] הִנֵּה פְלִשְׁתִּים נִלְחָמִים בִּקְעִילָה, "behold
the Philistines *are fighting* against Keilah" (1 Sam 23:1).

(b.2) *Past* – expresses duration in past time:
וְנָהָר יֹצֵא מֵעֵדֶן, "and a river *was flowing out* of Eden"
(Gen 2:10), אֲשֶׁר־הוּא עֹשֶׂה יְהוָה מַצְלִיחַ, "whatever he
[Joseph] *was doing,* YHWH *was prospering* [or whatever he
*did,* YHWH *prospered*]" (Gen 39:23), וַאֲדֹנִיָּה בֶן־חַגִּית מִתְנַשֵּׂא,
"Now Adonijah son of Haggith *was exalting himself* [or,
*exalted himself*]" (1 Kgs 1:5), לוֹט יֹשֵׁב בְּשַׁעַר־סְדֹם, "Lot
*was sitting* in the gateway of Sodom" (Gen 19:1),
סִיחֹן מֶלֶךְ הָאֱמֹרִי אֲשֶׁר יוֹשֵׁב בְּחֶשְׁבּוֹן, "Sihon king of the
Amorites, *who was living* at Heshbon" (Deut 3:2).

The *past predicate participle* frequently occurs after
הִנֵּה to express immediate action which occurred
in the past (see b.1): וְהִנֵּה אֹרְחַת יִשְׁמְעֵאלִים בָּאָה,
"behold, a caravan of Ishmaelites *was coming*" (Gen
37:25), וְהִנֵּה שְׁלֹשָׁה אֲנָשִׁים נִצָּבִים עָלָיו, "behold,
three men *were standing* near him" (Gen 18:2),
וְהִנֵּה אֲנַחְנוּ מְאַלְּמִים אֲלֻמִּים בְּתוֹךְ הַשָּׂדֶה, "behold, we *were*

---

[98] Though specific time reference is still determined by context only. In
Mishnaic Hebrew, the participle actually becomes a finite verb for the
present tense, while it continues to be used for frequentative or iterative
action in both the past and future (Segal 1927, 155–57).

[99] The use of הִנֵּה plus the participle has been identified in recent rhetorical
studies as one of the ways Hebrew narrators change points of view. This
appears to be especially common in circumstantial clauses in which a
narrator shifts the point of view to that of a character in order to narrate
what the character sees as the action unfolds (Berlin 1983, 63). On הִנֵּה
as a focus particle drawing attention to the content of the clause that
follows, see van der Merwe, Naudé, and Kroeze 1999, 328–30.

*binding* sheaves in the field" (Gen 37:7),

וַיְהִי הֵם מְרִיקִים שַׂקֵּיהֶם

"and they *were emptying* their sacks" (Gen 42:35).

The normally atemporal nature of the verbal participle is clarified with the addition of the verb הָיָה to express past time clearly: וּמֹשֶׁה הָיָה רֹעֶה אֶת־צֹאן יִתְרוֹ חֹתְנוֹ, "and Moses *was pasturing* the flock of Jethro his father-in-law" (Exod 3:1), הַבָּקָר הָיוּ חֹרְשׁוֹת, "the oxen *were plowing*" (Job 1:14), מַמְרִים הֱיִיתֶם עִם־יְהוָה, "you *have been rebellious* against YHWH" (Deut 9:24),

וָאֱהִי צָם וּמִתְפַּלֵּל לִפְנֵי אֱלֹהֵי הַשָּׁמָיִם

"and I *was fasting* and *praying* before the God of heaven" (Neh 1:4).

(b.3) *Future* – expresses duration in future time: אָנֹכִי מַמְטִיר עַל־הָאָרֶץ אַרְבָּעִים יוֹם וְאַרְבָּעִים לָיְלָה, "I *will send rain* upon the earth forty days and forty nights" (Gen 7:4), לַמּוֹעֵד הַזֶּה כָּעֵת חַיָּה אַתְּ חֹבֶקֶת בֵּן, "At this season, in due time, you *shall embrace* a son" (2 Kgs 4:16 *Qere*).

Most frequently, the *future predicate participle* is used to announce approaching action, or action that is already in progress:[100] אֲשֶׁר הָאֱלֹהִים עֹשֶׂה הִרְאָה אֶת־פַּרְעֹה, "that which God *is about to do*, he has shown to Pharaoh" (Gen 41:28), כִּי־מַשְׁחִתִים אֲנַחְנוּ אֶת־הַמָּקוֹם הַזֶּה, "for we *are about to destroy* this place" (Gen 19:13). As with the present and past predicate participles, the future predicate participle may indicate especially impending action when introduced with הִנֵּה: וַאֲנִי הִנְנִי מֵבִיא אֶת־הַמַּבּוּל מַיִם עַל־הָאָרֶץ, "and I, even I, *am bringing* a flood of waters upon the earth" (Gen 6:17), הִנְּךָ שֹׁכֵב עִם־אֲבֹתֶיךָ, "you *are about to sleep* with your fathers" (Deut 31:16), הִנְנִי נֹתְנוֹ בְיָדְךָ הַיּוֹם, "look, I *will deliver it* into your hand today" (1 Kgs 20:13). As with the past predicate

---

[100] This announcement of imminent action, which has already in fact begun to take place, is a powerful literary tool in the hands of the Old Testament prophets. Announcements of judgment frequently use this future *predicate participle* for rhetorical effect.

participle, the future may occur with הָיָה to express future
time more clearly: וְכִסֵּא דָוִד יִהְיֶה נָכוֹן לִפְנֵי יְהוָה עַד־עוֹלָם,
"and the throne of David *shall be established* before YHWH
forever" (1 Kgs 2:45).

**(c) Substantive** – functions as a noun, most often occurring with the definite article: בִּימֵי שְׁפֹט הַשֹּׁפְטִים, "In the days
when *the judges* ruled" (Ruth 1:1), קֹנֵה שָׁמַיִם וָאָרֶץ, "*the maker*
of heaven and earth (Gen 14:19), הוֹי בֹּנֶה בֵיתוֹ בְּלֹא־צֶדֶק,
"woe to *the one who builds* his house without righteousness" (Jer 22:13). The definite article may be omitted
in poetry: וְהָלְכוּ גְאוּלִים, "but *redeemed people* shall walk
[there]" (Isa 35:9). As a noun, the *substantive participle*
functions in all the ways nouns are used. Thus, it may
take pronominal suffixes: יְהוָה שֹׁמְרֶךָ, "YHWH is your *keeper*"
(Ps 121:5), may stand in the construct state: שֹׁמְרֵי מִשְׁפָּט,
"*keepers* of justice" (Ps 106:3), or may serve as the object of
a preposition: לְשֹׁמְרֵי בְרִיתוֹ, "to *those who keep* his covenant"
(Ps 103:18). They may also serve in any of the nominative,
genitive, or accusative functions.

The substantive participle serving in the genitive construction may fulfill any of the possible genitive constructions (section 2.2). However, one unique use of the
participle occurs when certain verbs (especially בּוֹא and
יָצָא) serve as constructs bound to another noun, rather
than having an accusative or a prepositional phrase as one
might expect:[101] בָּאֵי שַׁעַר־עִירוֹ, "*those entering* at the gate of
his city" (Gen 23:10), יֹצְאֵי הַתֵּבָה, "*those coming out* of the
ark" (Gen 9:10), יוֹרְדֵי־בוֹר, "*those going down* to the pit"
(Isa 38:18), אֹכְלֵי שֻׁלְחַן אִיזֶבֶל, "*those eating* at Jezebel's table"
(1 Kgs 18:19).

Certain verbal roots were used so widely as substantive participles that they in essence became nouns, most
denoting vocations or other identifying roles: שׁוֹפֵט, "judge
(one who judges)," סוֹפֵר, "scribe (one who recounts),"

---

[101] Joüon and Muraoka 1993, 416.

יֹצֵר, "potter (one who forms)," אוֹיֵב, "enemy (one showing enmity)," and so on.

## 3.5 Verbal Sequences

A specialized form of the conjunction *waw* may be prefixed to finite verbal forms in Hebrew narrative for functions not normally associated with the simple *waw* conjunctive.[102] Grammarians have used a variety of names for this feature of grammar: *waw* consecutive, *waw* inversive, relative *waw*, or *waw* conversive.[103] Each of these labels identifies the same phenomenon with a slightly different emphasis on the function of the *waw* in forming relationships between clauses. Whereas grammarians previously held that the *waw* simply *converted* the meaning of one verbal aspect to another (e.g., an imperfect form converted to a perfect meaning), more recent work demonstrates that the function of the *waw* with a finite verbal form affects not only the aspect of the verb but also the verbal ideas themselves. While the two main forms presented here (imperfects and perfects with *waw* consecutive) have different origins and connotations, in general we may consider *succession in time* or *progression* as the main idea.[104]

The following patterns are important to remember when noting verbal sequences in Hebrew narrative.[105]

[102] The function of *waw* described here is rare in poetry. For the distinctions between narrative (discursive speech) and dialogue (direct speech), see van der Merwe, Naudé, and Kroeze 1999, 164–65; Miller 1996, 1–4 and 14–38. In general, discursive speech (narration) has a relatively limited variety of such functions, whereas dialogue (direct speech) has much more syntactical diversity.

[103] See the beginning grammars for morphological features of the *waw* consecutive. On the terminology "*waw* consecutive," see Rainey (1986, 6).

[104] For our best current understanding of the history and function of the *waw* consecutive, see Smith 1991, esp. 12–15.

[105] Joüon and Muraoka 1993, 379–408; Meyer 1992, 386–89 and 393–94; Waltke and O'Connor 1990, 519–63; Kautzsch 1910, 326–39; Williams 1976, 33–34; Chisholm 1998, 94–112 and 119–33; van der Merwe, Naudé, and Kroeze 1999, 163–72; and for epigraphic Hebrew, see Gogel 1998, 260–68.

### 3.5.1 *Imperfect plus* waw *Consecutive*

In general, the imperfect with *waw* consecutive will connote
the same aspect of the perfect, which will often precede
it in the previous clause.[106] However, the imperfect plus
*waw* consecutive pattern may also succeed a clause with an
imperfect or a participle, or even a nominal clause.[107] In
any case, it generally serves as a substitute for the perfect
aspect, adding only the idea of succession. The following
nuances will be helpful in interpreting the *waw* consecutive
plus imperfect.

*(a) Sequential* – expresses temporal sequence, describing
an action or situation subsequent to a previous action or
situation: וְהָאָדָם יָדַע אֶת־חַוָּה אִשְׁתּוֹ וַתַּהַר וַתֵּלֶד אֶת־קַיִן, "Now
the man knew his wife Eve, _and_ she _conceived_ and _and then
bore_ Cain (Gen 4:1),

וַיַּעֲבֹר דָּוִד הָעֵבֶר וַיַּעֲמֹד עַל־רֹאשׁ־הָהָר

---

[106] So it seems likely that this is really the original preterite tense of pre–
biblical Hebrew (see 3.2.2,e).

[107] Several beginning grammars refer to a "governing verb" that influences
the aspect and meaning of the prefixed *waw* consecutive in fixed relationships, such as perfect plus imperfect, or nonfinite plus imperfect (see
Kelly 1992, 210–16; Seow 1995, 226–27). While these definitions are not
inaccurate, and we recognize that a verb functions in sequence, we have
chosen, for several reasons, not to define verbal sequences solely by the
identification of the governing verb. Firstly, the identification of a governing verb in even simple narrative sequences can be quite complex and
confusing. Secondly, as our examples show, the imperfect *waw* consecutive is often employed without a governing verb. Thirdly, the function of
these verbal sequences is not as clear-cut as the beginning grammars tend
to portray them. For instance, even though many stress the importance
of the perfect plus imperfect sequence in narrative, the reader needs to
be aware that a narrative rarely begins with a perfect verb but, in fact,
more often begins with a *waw* consecutive plus imperfect (Niccacci 1990,
37; for an important exception see his 47). Furthermore, the function
of these verbal sequences seems to differ on the basis of the narratival
or discursive nature of the text at hand (Niccacci 1990, 35–45), a difference that is not given enough coverage by the beginning grammars,
and often not appreciated by beginning and intermediate students.

"Then David crossed over to the other side, *and then he stood* on the top of the mountain" (1 Sam 26:13), וַיָּבֹא מֹשֶׁה וְאַהֲרֹן אֶל־פַּרְעֹה וַיַּעֲשׂוּ כֵן כַּאֲשֶׁר צִוָּה יְהוָה, "So Moses and Aaron came to Pharaoh, *and then they did* just as YHWH commanded" (Exod 7:10).

Within narrative, an action or situation that is not sequential to the main verb, but prior to it (equivalent to the English pluperfect or past perfect), is often presented by avoiding the וַיִּקְטֹל pattern and replacing it with the conjunctive *waw* on a finite form (see section 3.5.4,a). But, occasionally, *waw* consecutive plus imperfect may be used to mark such anterior constructions, which must be discerned from the context (Joüon and Muraoka 1993, 390–91; Zevit 1998):

וַיְדַבֵּר אֲלֵהֶם אֲבִיהֶם אֵי־זֶה הַדֶּרֶךְ הָלָךְ וַיִּרְאוּ בָנָיו אֶת־הַדֶּרֶךְ אֲשֶׁר הָלַךְ אִישׁ הָאֱלֹהִים אֲשֶׁר־בָּא מִיהוּדָה

"Their father spoke to them, 'Which way did he go?' *Now his sons had seen* the way that the man of God who came from Judah *had gone*" (1 Kgs 13:12).

*(b) Consequential* – expresses logical result, describing an action or situation resulting from a previous action or situation: וַיְהִי יְהוָה אֶת־יוֹסֵף וַיְהִי אִישׁ מַצְלִיחַ, "YHWH was with Joseph, *and so* he became a successful man" (Gen 39:2), וַיְכֻלּוּ הַשָּׁמַיִם וְהָאָרֶץ, "*Thus* the heavens and the earth were completed" (Gen 2:1), וַיֶּחֱזַק דָּוִד מִן־הַפְּלִשְׁתִּי בַּקֶּלַע וּבָאֶבֶן, "*So* David prevailed over the Philistine with a sling and a stone" (1 Sam 17:50). This consequential use of the וַיִּקְטֹל pattern may be used to conclude a narrative:

וּתְשֻׁבָתוֹ הָרָמָתָה כִּי־שָׁם בֵּיתוֹ וְשָׁם שָׁפַט אֶת־יִשְׂרָאֵל וַיִּבֶן־שָׁם מִזְבֵּחַ לַיהוָה

"Then he would return to Ramah because his house was there; and there he judged Israel. And *he built* there an altar to Y<small>HWH</small>" (1 Sam 7:17),

וַיְהִי יְהוָה אֶת־יְהוֹשֻׁעַ וַיְהִי שָׁמְעוֹ בְּכָל־הָאָרֶץ

"*So Y<small>HWH</small> was* with Joshua, and his fame _was_ in all the land" (Josh 6:27).

*(c) Narratival* – Due to the frequency of its use, the *waw* consecutive plus imperfect came to be used on its own, independent of a preceding verbal clause, in order to begin a narrative sequence or a new section of narrative: וַיֵּרָא אֵלָיו יְהוָה בְּאֵלֹנֵי מַמְרֵא, "_Now_ Y<small>HWH</small> _appeared_ to him [Abraham] by the oaks of Mamre" (Gen 18:1). This *narratival* use of the וַיִּקְטֹל pattern may even begin a book: וַיִּקְרָא אֶל־מֹשֶׁה וַיְדַבֵּר יְהוָה אֵלָיו מֵאֹהֶל מוֹעֵד, "Y<small>HWH</small> _called_ to Moses and spoke to him from the Tent of Meeting" (Lev 1:1), וַיְדַבֵּר יְהוָה אֶל־מֹשֶׁה בְּמִדְבַּר סִינַי, "*Then* Y<small>HWH</small> *spoke* to Moses in the wilderness of Sinai" (Num 1:1).

The narratival use is especially common with the imperfect of the verb הָיָה to introduce a new narrative or section of a narrative: וַיְהִי אִישׁ אֶחָד מִן־הָרָמָתַיִם צוֹפִים, "*There was* a certain man from Ramathaim Zophim" (1 Sam 1:1), וַיְהִי דְּבַר־יְהוָה אֶל־יוֹנָה, "The word of YHWH _came_ to Jonah" (Jonah 1:1).

*(d) Epexegetical* – clarifies, expands, or paraphrases the clause that precedes it (the simple conjunctive *waw* may be used on nouns to perform a similar function; compare section 4.3.3,d): אֲבָל אִשָּׁה־אַלְמָנָה אָנִי וַיָּמָת אִישִׁי, "Truly, I am a widow; _my husband has died_" (2 Sam 14:5), וַתִּקְרָא שְׁמוֹ מֹשֶׁה וַתֹּאמֶר כִּי מִן־הַמַּיִם מְשִׁיתִהוּ, "She called his name Moses, _saying_, 'Because I drew him out of the water'" (Exod 2:10), מֶה עָשִׂיתָ וַתִּגְנֹב אֶת־לְבָבִי, "What have you done? *You have deceived* me!" (Gen 31:26).

On occasion, the clarification of the verbal action can repeat the main verbal idea:

וְלֹא־זָכַר שַׂר־הַמַּשְׁקִים אֶת־יוֹסֵף וַיִּשְׁכָּחֵהוּ

"The chief cup-bearer did not remember Joseph; *he forgot him*" (Gen 40:23),

הֲלוֹא־הוּא אָבִיךָ קָנֶךָ הוּא עָשְׂךָ וַיְכֹנְנֶךָ

"Is he not your father, who created you, who made you and *established you*?" (Deut 32:6), וְדָוִד נָס וַיִּמָּלֵט בַּלַּיְלָה הוּא,
"David fled; *he escaped* that night" (1 Sam 19:10).

Nearly identical to this use is *specification*, in which *waw* consecutive plus imperfect makes a previous verbal idea more specific:

וַיִּשְׁכְּחוּ אֶת־יְהוָה אֱלֹהֵיהֶם וַיַּעַבְדוּ אֶת־הַבְּעָלִים וְאֶת־הָאֲשֵׁרוֹת

"They forgot YHWH their God, *they served* the Baals and the Ashtoreth" (Judg 3:7), קִנֵּא לֵאלֹהָיו וַיְכַפֵּר עַל־בְּנֵי יִשְׂרָאֵל,
"He was zealous for his God; *thus he made atonement* for the people of Israel" (Num 25:13).

*(e) Dependent* – Following temporal clauses, the וַיִּקְטֹל pattern will present an action or situation that is dependent on the temporal clause: בִּשְׁנַת־מוֹת הַמֶּלֶךְ עֻזִּיָּהוּ וָאֶרְאֶה אֶת־אֲדֹנָי,
"In the year of King Uzziah's death, *I saw* the lord" (Isa 6:1), בִּהְיוֹתָם בַּשָּׂדֶה וַיָּקָם קַיִן אֶל־הֶבֶל אָחִיו, "When they were in the field, Cain *rose up* against Abel, his brother" (Gen 4:8), וַיְהִי כְּשָׁמְעָם אֶת־הַתּוֹרָה וַיַּבְדִּילוּ כָל־עֵרֶב מִיִּשְׂרָאֵל, "When they heard the law, *they separated* all the aliens from Israel" (Neh 13:3).

### 3.5.2 *Perfect plus* waw *Consecutive*

The perfect with *waw* consecutive will connote the same aspect of the imperfect, which will often precede it in the previous clause. However, *waw* consecutive plus perfect may also succeed a clause with an imperative, a perfect, a participle, an infinitive functioning as a finite verb, or a nominal clause. In any case, it generally serves as a substitute for the imperfect aspect, adding only the idea of succession. The following nuances will be helpful in interpreting the *waw* consecutive plus perfect.

*(a) Sequential* – expresses temporal sequence, describing an action or situation subsequent to a previous action or situation:

קָרַע יְהוָה אֶת־מַמְלְכוּת יִשְׂרָאֵל מֵעָלֶיךָ הַיּוֹם וּנְתָנָהּ לְרֵעֶךָ

"Yнwн has torn the kingdom of Israel from you to-day, *and he has given* it to your neighbor" (1 Sam 15:28), אֵצֵא וְהָיִיתִי רוּחַ שֶׁקֶר בְּפִי כָל־נְבִיאָיו, "I will go out, and *I will be* a lying spirit in the mouths of all his prophets" (1 Kgs 22:22), וּבְיוֹם פָּקְדִי וּפָקַדְתִּי עֲלֵיהֶם חַטָּאתָם, "On the day I punish, *I will punish* them for their sin" (Exod 32:34), הָעַלְמָה הָרָה וְיֹלֶדֶת בֵּן וְקָרָאת שְׁמוֹ עִמָּנוּ אֵל, "A virgin will be pregnant and *she will give birth* to a son and *she will call* his name Immanuel" (Isa 7:14).

*(b) Consequential* – expresses logical result, describing an action or situation resulting from a previous action or situation: אֲנִי יְהוָה וְהוֹצֵאתִי אֶתְכֶם, "I am Yнwн, and *I will bring you out*" (Exod 6:6),

וּבְנֵי יִשְׂרָאֵל פָּרוּ וַיִּשְׁרְצוּ וַיִּרְבּוּ וַיַּעַצְמוּ בִּמְאֹד מְאֹד וַתִּמָּלֵא הָאָרֶץ אֹתָם

"The people of Israel were fruitful, and increased greatly, and multiplied and became exceedingly mighty, *so that the land was filled* with them" (Exod 1:7), וְהֵפִיץ יְהוָה אֶתְכֶם בָּעַמִּים וְנִשְׁאַרְתֶּם מְתֵי מִסְפָּר, "Yнwн will scatter you among the peoples, and *you will be left* few in number" (Deut 4:27).

*(c) Volitional* – expresses a command or wish:

וַאֲהַבְתֶּם אֶת־הַגֵּר כִּי־גֵרִים הֱיִיתֶם בְּאֶרֶץ מִצְרָיִם

"*You shall love* the stranger, for you were strangers in the land of Egypt" (Deut 10:19), וּקְשַׁרְתָּם לְאוֹת עַל־יָדֶךָ, "*You shall bind* them as a sign upon your hand" (Deut 6:8). This *volitional* use of the perfect plus *waw* consecutive is often preceded by a clause with a jussive, imperative or cohortative, or an infinitive absolute functioning as an imperative

(see section 3.4.2,d), and functions to express *consecu-tion:*[108] יְבַקְשׁוּ לַאדֹנִי הַמֶּלֶךְ נַעֲרָה בְתוּלָה וְעָמְדָה לִפְנֵי הַמֶּלֶךְ,
"Let them seek a young virgin for my lord the king, *and let her attend* the king" (1 Kgs 1:2),

לֹא־יָמוּשׁ סֵפֶר הַתּוֹרָה הַזֶּה מִפִּיךָ וְהָגִיתָ בּוֹ יוֹמָם וָלַיְלָה

"This book of the law shall not depart from your mouth, but *you shall meditate* on it day and night" (Josh 1:8). The *waw* consecutive plus perfect after a modal, or an equiva-lent infinitive absolute, may emphasize succession, so that the execution of its action or situation is dependent upon the preceding one: עֲשֵׂה כַּאֲשֶׁר דִּבֶּר וּפְגַע־בּוֹ וּקְבַרְתּוֹ, "Do as he has said and strike him down *and then bury* him" (1 Kgs 2:31), וְנִקְרְבָה בְּאַחַד הַמְּקֹמוֹת וְלַנּוּ, "let us approach one of these places, and [then] *spend the night*" (Judg 19:13), בְּנֵה־לְךָ בַיִת בִּירוּשָׁלַםִ וְיָשַׁבְתָּ שָׁם, "Build yourself a house in Jerusalem, *and stay* there" (1 Kgs 2:36).

Frequently, the idea of succession can be nuanced to express purpose or result:[109] עֲלֹה נַעֲלֶה וְיָרַשְׁנוּ אֹתָהּ, "Let us go up at once and *[so] let us possess it*" (Num 13:30), הָלוֹךְ וְרָחַצְתָּ שֶׁבַע־פְּעָמִים בַּיַּרְדֵּן, "Go, *and wash* seven times in the Jordan" (2 Kgs 5:10), וְשׁוּב עִמִּי וְהִשְׁתַּחֲוֵיתִי לַיהוָה אֱלֹהֶיךָ, "Return with me, *so that I may worship* YHWH your God" (1 Sam 15:30), וְזֹאת עֲשׂוּ לָהֶם וְחָיוּ וְלֹא יָמֻתוּ, "Do this to them, *so that they may live* and not die" (Num 4:19).

*(d) Apodictic* – in a conditional sentence, expresses log-ical result, describing an action or situation resulting from (or dependent on) a previous action or situa-tion: אִם־חָפֵץ בָּנוּ יְהוָה וְהֵבִיא אֹתָנוּ אֶל־הָאָרֶץ הַזֹּאת, "If YHWH is pleased with us, *then he will lead* us into this land"

---

[108] Lambdin 1971a, 119; Seow 1995, 243–44.
[109] The perfect plus *waw*-consecutive construction most often follows an im-perative, and is frequently identical to the person, gender, and number of the imperative. As the last two examples in this paragraph illustrate, however, there are some first- and third-person examples of this con-struction that carry a successive idea from an imperative (Joüon and Muraoka 1993, 399–400).

אִם־יִהְיֶה אֱלֹהִים עִמָּדִי...וְהָיָה יְהוָה לִי לֵאלֹהִים (Num 14:8),
"If God will be with me...*then YHWH will be* my God"
(Gen 28:20–21), וְאִם־אֵין מוֹשִׁיעַ אֹתָנוּ וְיָצָאנוּ אֵלֶיךָ, "If there
is no one to deliver us, *then we will surrender* to you"
(1 Sam 11:3).

Quite often, *waw* consecutive plus perfect functions
not to present the apodosis, but to provide an expan-
sion of the idea in either the protasis, or the apod-
osis: אִם־שָׁמוֹעַ תִּשְׁמְעוּ בְּקֹלִי וּשְׁמַרְתֶּם אֶת־בְּרִיתִי, "If you fully
obey my voice *and keep* my covenant" (Exod 19:5),
כִּי תַעַזְבוּ אֶת־יְהוָה וַעֲבַדְתֶּם אֱלֹהֵי נֵכָר, "If you forsake YHWH
and *serve* foreign gods..." (Josh 24:20),

כִּי־יִהְיֶה לָהֶם דָּבָר בָּא אֵלַי וְשָׁפַטְתִּי בֵּין אִישׁ וּבֵין רֵעֵהוּ
וְהוֹדַעְתִּי אֶת־חֻקֵּי הָאֱלֹהִים וְאֶת־תּוֹרֹתָיו

"If they have a dispute, it comes to me, *then I judge* between
a person and that person's neighbor, *and I make known* the
statutes of God and his instructions" (Exod 18:16).

Verbal sequence relationships are not limited to *waw*
consecutive forms, but can also be expressed by verbs
that are prefixed with the simple *waw* conjunctive.
Thus, a *waw* conjunctive on a perfect[110] or imperfect[111]
form can also express succession or consecution. Consi-
der: עָשִׂיתִי לִי גַּנּוֹת וּפַרְדֵּסִים וְנָטַעְתִּי בָהֶם עֵץ כָּל־פֶּרִי, "I made

---

[110] Particularly in LBH, the *waw* conjunctive plus perfect is viewed as a substitute for the *waw* consecutive plus imperfect. This use is based on the
theorized influence of Aramaic, which lacked *waw*-consecutive forms
(Smith 1991, 27–33). However, evidence from the Tel Dan inscription
indicates that there very well could have been a *waw* consecutive plus imperfect construction employed in Aramaic (see Emerton 1994, 255–58;
and 2000, 35). This is in addition to a ninth-century Aramaic inscription
in which this construction is found (*KAI* 202, line 11).

[111] It should be remembered that certain imperfect forms take a shortened
form before the *waw* consecutive and a normal form (so-called longer
form) with *waw* conjunctive. Thus, the imperfect of these verbs makes a
morphological distinction between imperfect with *waw* consecutive and
imperfect with *waw* conjunctive. See beginning grammars for more on
the morphology of the *waw* consecutive.

for myself gardens and parks, *and [then] I planted* in them all kinds of fruit trees" (Eccl 2:5),

וַיִּשְׁתַּחוּ לְכָל־צְבָא הַשָּׁמַיִם וַיַּעֲבֹד אֹתָם וּבָנָה מִזְבְּחוֹת
בְּבֵית יְהוָה

"He worshiped all the hosts of heaven, and he served them, *and he built* altars [for them] in the house of YHWH" (2 Chr 33:3–4), כִּי מִי עָמַד בְּסוֹד יְהוָה וְיֵרֶא וְיִשְׁמַע אֶת־דְּבָרוֹ, "But who has stood in the council of YHWH, *that they should see and hear* his word" (Jer 23:18),

הַאֵין פֹּה נָבִיא לַיהוָה עוֹד וְנִדְרְשָׁה מֵאוֹתוֹ

"Is there not yet a prophet of YHWH here, *so that we may inquire* of him" (1 Kgs 22:7).

Additionally, the *waw* conjunctive on a finite verbal form expresses all the various functions of the *waw* conjunction (see section 4.3.3), in particular, verbal hendiadys (section 4.3.3,g), coordination (section 4.3.3,b), or continuation.[112]

### 3.5.3 *Commands in Verbal Sequences*

As noted, the perfect plus *waw* consecutive may express volition (see section 3.5.2,c). BH may also use the *waw* conjunctive with imperfects and volitives (and at times perfects) to express sequential commands, which may connote succession or purpose.[113]

*(a) Succession* – shows an action that temporally follows the main verb: אַל־נָא יִחַר לַאדֹנִי וַאֲדַבֵּרָה, "May my lord not be angry, *and I shall speak*" (Gen 18:30), שְׁאַל אֶת־נְעָרֶיךָ וְיַגִּידוּ לָךְ, "Ask your young men, *and they will tell* you" (1 Sam 25:8),

וְנִזְעַק אֵלֶיךָ מִצָּרָתֵנוּ וְתִשְׁמַע וְתוֹשִׁיעַ

---

[112] Niccacci 1990, 40, and Waltke and O'Connor 1990, 540–41.
[113] Lambdin 1971a, 119; Seow 1995, 243; Niccacci 1990, 187.

"We will cry out to you in our distress, and *you will hear us*, and *save us*" (2 Chr 20:9), לֵךְ וּבָאתָ־לְּךָ אֶרֶץ יְהוּדָה, "Go, *and [then] enter* into the land of Judah" (1 Sam 22:5).

**(b) Purpose** – expresses the purpose or motivation behind the main verb: וְהָבִיאָה לִּי וְאֹכֵלָה, "Bring it to me, *so that I may eat*" (Gen 27:4),

אָסֻרָה־נָּא וְאֶרְאֶה אֶת־הַמַּרְאֶה הַגָּדֹל הַזֶּה

"Let me turn *in order to see* this great sight" (Exod 3:3), וַהֲרַגְנוּם וְהִשְׁבַּתְנוּ אֶת־הַמְּלָאכָה, "Kill them, *and [so], put a stop* to the work" (Neh 4:5 [Eng. 4:11]), וַאֲשַׁלְּחָה אֶת־הָעָם וְיִזְבְּחוּ לַיהוָה, "I will let the people go, *that they may sacrifice* to YHWH" (Exod 8:4).

### 3.5.4 *Interruptions in Verbal Sequences*

The *waw* conjunctive employed with a verbal idea is also used in narrative texts to present an idea that is strongly disjunctive from the *waw* consecutives in context. This disjunction occurs with both perfect and imperfect verbs, but typically, the *waw* conjunctive is not prefixed onto the verbal form, but an associated noun (that is, either the subject or the object of the noun).[114] The nonsuccessive idea presented by the *waw* conjunctive can express several nuances.

**(a) Distinct subject** – the *waw* conjunctive points to a seemingly successive action performed by a different subject, thereby placing emphasis on an agent who is distinct from the agent of the main verb, and, in effect, presenting an opposition of subjects:

וַיֵּט מֹשֶׁה אֶת־מַטֵּהוּ עַל־הַשָּׁמַיִם וַיהוָה נָתַן קֹלֹת וּבָרָד

---

[114] This "*waw*+subject+finite verb" sequence is variously diagrammed as "w...qatal/w...yiqtol" (Joüon and Muraoka 1993, 390 and 397) or "waw x qatal" (Niccacci 1990, 49–72).

"Moses stretched his staff to the heavens, *and YHWH sent* thunder and hail" (Exod 9:23),

וַיְשַׁלַּח אֶת־הָאֲנָשִׁים וַיֵּלֵכוּ וְהוּא־בָא וַיַּעֲמֹד אֶל־אֲדֹנָיו

"He sent the men away and they left. *But he himself* went and stood before his master" (2 Kgs 5:24–5).

*(b) Simultaneous action* – The *waw* conjunctive expresses an action that is not successive, but simultaneous with the main verb: וַיִּקְרָא אֱלֹהִים לָאוֹר יוֹם וְלַחֹשֶׁךְ קָרָא לָיְלָה, "God called the light day, *and he called* the darkness light" (Gen 1:5), וַיֵּלֶךְ שְׁמוּאֵל הָרָמָתָה וְשָׁאוּל עָלָה אֶל־בֵּיתוֹ גִּבְעַת שָׁאוּל, "Samuel went to Ramah, *and Saul went up* to his house at Gibeah of Saul" (1 Sam 15:34), וְהָרְגוּ אֹתִי וְאֹתָךְ יְחַיּוּ, "They will kill me, but *they will let you live*" (Gen 12:12).

*(c) Anterior action* – The *waw* conjunctive signals an action or situation that is out of chronological order in the narratival flow, and is equivalent to the English pluperfect or present perfect in narratives of past time. On occasion, parenthetical remarks within a narrative will be presented in this manner:[115]

וַיָּבֹא לָבָן בְּאֹהֶל יַעֲקֹב וּבְאֹהֶל לֵאָה וּבְאֹהֶל שְׁתֵּי הָאֲמָהֹת
וְלֹא מָצָא וַיֵּצֵא מֵאֹהֶל לֵאָה וַיָּבֹא בְּאֹהֶל רָחֵל וְרָחֵל
לָקְחָה אֶת־הַתְּרָפִים

---

[115] Some assert that this pluperfect use is expressed not only by the *waw* conjunctive but also by the perfect plus *waw* conjunctive (Waltke and O'Connor 1990, 541–42, and Johnson 1979, 41; and cf. וַיַּרְא עֵשָׂו כִּי־בֵרַךְ יִצְחָק אֶת־יַעֲקֹב וְשִׁלַּח אֹתוֹ פַּדֶּנָה אֲרָם, "Esau saw that Isaac blessed Jacob, and *had sent him* to Padan-Aram" [Gen 28:6]). Niccacci further states that the perfect plus *waw* conjunctive expresses background or parenthetical comments in narrative (1990, 35). Recently, Zevit has argued that authors of BH narrative could mark pluperfect or present-perfect time unambiguously by following a narratival past-time clause with the following sequence: *waw* conjunctive plus subject (noun or pronoun) plus perfect finite verb (Zevit 1998, 15–37).

"Laban went into Jacob's tent, and into Leah's tent, and into the tent of the two maid-servants, but he did not find [them]. He came out from Leah's tent, and went into Rachel's tent, but *Rachel had taken* the household idols..."(Gen 31:33–34),

וּשְׁמוּאֵל מֵת וַיִּסְפְּדוּ־לוֹ כָּל־יִשְׂרָאֵל וַיִּקְבְּרֻהוּ בָרָמָה וּבְעִירוֹ וְשָׁאוּל הֵסִיר הָאֹבוֹת וְאֶת־הַיִּדְּעֹנִים מֵהָאָרֶץ

"Samuel was dead, and all Israel mourned for him, and they buried him in Ramah, his city. And Saul *had expelled* the mediums and the spiritists from the land" (1 Sam 28:3),

וַיִּתְחַפֵּשׂ מֶלֶךְ יִשְׂרָאֵל וַיָּבוֹא בַּמִּלְחָמָה וּמֶלֶךְ אֲרָם צִוָּה אֶת־שָׂרֵי הָרֶכֶב אֲשֶׁר־לוֹ שְׁלֹשִׁים וּשְׁנַיִם

"The king of Israel disguised himself and went into battle. Now, the king of Aram *had commanded* the thirty-two officers of his chariots" (1 Kgs 22:30–31).

# 4 *Particles*

I n addition to nouns and verbs, Hebrew syntax employs another category of words, often referred to as *particles*. This is an inclusive term often used for a wide-ranging number of parts of speech. Here we will use it to refer to prepositions, adverbs, conjunctions, the particles of existence and nonexistence, and the particles הִנֵּה and וְהִנֵּה.[1]

## 4.1 Prepositions

In general, prepositions in BH are difficult to categorize because their function in the syntax may be viewed from a variety of perspectives. As relational terms standing before nouns (or noun equivalents), prepositions may be viewed primarily as "nominal" in orientation and function.[2] On the other hand, most of the Hebrew prepositions have no obvious morphological connection to nouns, and their nature as "particles" is frequently evident in their function as adverbs or conjunctions. However, a third perspective, the "semantic" perspective of prepositions, has become increasingly more prominent in modern grammars, and is important to consider here. In

---

[1] Because Hebrew grammars traditionally include so many parts of speech under the rubric, some have chosen to use "other word classes," or something of the like (van der Merwe, Naudé, and Kroeze 1999, 271).

[2] On these three perspectives of Hebrew prepositions, see Waltke and O'Connor 1990, 187–90.

essence, this perspective means that some prepositions in particular uses have connotations determined by the verb with which they are used. In other words, the meaning of certain prepositions is not so much determined by morphological origins or by use with specific nouns as it is by the particular pattern of *verb plus preposition plus object*. Because of the use of these patterns, it is insufficient to study only the use of prepositions in isolation, as we will present them here. It will also be necessary to consider the way individual prepositions are used with particular verbs, which is ultimately a lexical matter. Since the meaning of some prepositions is determined by the verbs that govern them, it is necessary for the exegete to learn particular prepositions used with certain verbs, or to use the lexica for specific verbs to determine their meaning when used with a given preposition.

The following are the most common prepositions (in alphabetical order) and their uses.[3]

### 4.1.1 אַחַר / אַחֲרֵי

*(a) Spatial* – indicates localization, especially "behind" a place: אַחֲרֵי הַמִּשְׁכָּן, "*behind* the tabernacle" (Num 3:23), עוֹמֵד אַחַר כָּתְלֵנוּ, "he is standing *behind* our wall" (Song 2:9).[4] Related to this spatial use is the *directional* use of אַחַר. In BH, the four directional compass points are often expressed from an eastward-facing position, so that left and right represent north and south respectively, while front and back represent east and west. Hence, "behind" (אַחַר) represents "west": הִנֵּה אַחֲרֵי קִרְיַת יְעָרִים, "it is *west* of Kiriath-jearim" (Judg 18:12).

---

[3] Waltke and O'Connor 1990, 190–225; van der Merwe, Naudé, and Kroeze 1999, 277–94; Williams 1976, 44–63; Kautzsch 1910, 377–84; Bauer and Leander 1991, 634–47; Joüon and Muraoka 1993, 482–92. In addition to these, the lexica are also frequently important for the study of these prepositions, especially *DCH* and *HALOT*.

[4] The particle in its plural construct (אַחֲרֵי) also serves as a substantive, referring to "back parts, rear" (*DCH* 1:199–200; BDB 30).

*(b) Temporal* – points to an event that comes chronologically "after" another event. The preposition normally precedes the noun or verb denoting the first event: וַיְהִי אַחַר הַדְּבָרִים הָאֵלֶּה, "It happened *after* these things" (1 Kgs 21:1), אַחֲרֵי בֹאוֹ מֵחֶבְרוֹן, "*after* coming from Hebron" (2 Sam 5:13), אַחֲרֵי הוֹלִידוֹ אֶת־שֵׁת, "*after* he became the father of Seth" (Gen 5:4).

At times, אַחַר serves as an adverb of time expressing *manner,* and is best translated by the English adverb "afterward": אַחַר תֵּלֵךְ, "*afterward* she may go" (Gen 24:55), וְאַחַר יָלְדָה בַּת, "and *afterward* she bore a daughter" (Gen 30:21), וְאַחַר בָּאוּ מֹשֶׁה וְאַהֲרֹן וַיֹּאמְרוּ אֶל־פַּרְעֹה, "and *afterward* Moses and Aaron went and said to Pharaoh" (Exod 5:1).[5]

*(c) Metaphorical* – denoting a behavior patterned after or according to that of another, or in support of another: וַיֵּלֶךְ אַחַר חַטֹּאת יָרָבְעָם, "and he *followed* [literally: *went after*] the sins of Jeroboam" (2 Kgs 13:2), אַחַר עֵינַי הָלַךְ לִבִּי, "my heart has *followed* [literally: *gone after*] my eyes" (Job 31:7), וִהְיִתֶם גַּם־אַתֶּם וְגַם־הַמֶּלֶךְ אֲשֶׁר מָלַךְ עֲלֵיכֶם אַחַר יְהוָה אֱלֹהֵיכֶם, "and both you and the king who reigns over you will *follow* [literally: *be after*] YHWH your God" (1 Sam 12:14).

### 4.1.2 אֶל / אֶל־

*(a) Terminative* – marks movement "to" or "into" something, especially when the goal of the movement is reached: כִּי־תָבֹא אֶל־הָאָרֶץ, "when you come *into* the land" (Deut 17:14), לֹא־יָרַד אוּרִיָּה אֶל־בֵּיתוֹ, "Uriah did not go down *to* his house" (2 Sam 11:10), וַיֵּצֵא אֶל־אֶחָיו, "and he [Moses] went out *to* his brothers" (Exod 2:11), גּוֹי לֹא־יְדָעוּךָ אֵלֶיךָ יָרוּצוּ, "nations that do not know you shall run *to* you" (Isa 55:5). This may become "on(to)"

---

[5] When occurring in the plural construct form, the adverbial takes the compound אַחֲרֵי־כֵן (see *HALOT* 1:36; *DCH* 1:197; BDB 30).

or "upon" when the motion is vertical:[6] וַיִּפֹּל יְהוֹשֻׁעַ אֶל־פָּנָיו,
"and Joshua fell _on_ his face" (Josh 5:14), יָאֵר יְהוָה פָּנָיו אֵלֶיךָ,
"may YHWH make his face shine _on_ you" (Num 6:25),
וַתִּכְבַּד יַד־יְהוָה אֶל־הָאַשְׁדּוֹדִים, "and the hand of YHWH was
heavy _upon_ the people of Ashdod" (1 Sam 5:6).

The motion or movement takes on a *directional* connotation when the goal is not reached, sometimes resulting in a translation "toward(s)" or "in the direction
of": אֶשְׁתַּחֲוֶה אֶל־הֵיכַל־קָדְשְׁךָ, "I will bow down _toward_
your holy temple" (Ps 5:8), וַיִּפְנוּ אֶל־הַמִּדְבָּר, "they [the
Israelites] turned _toward_ the wilderness" (Exod 16:10),
וָאֶרְאֶה וְהִנֵּה־יָד שְׁלוּחָה אֵלָי, "and I looked and a hand was
extended _to_ me" (Ezek 2:9).

Often in the *terminative* use of אֶל/אֶל־, as with
some of the other uses that follow (see especially the
*declarative* and *perceptual*), the preposition also serves
to mark a simple *indirect object*:[7] וְנָתַן אֵלֶיךָ אוֹת, "and he
gives [_to_] you a sign" (Deut 13:2), קָחֶם־נָא אֵלַי וַאֲבָרֲכֵם,
"bring them _to_ me that I may bless them" (Gen 48:9),
וַיִּשְׁלַח יַעֲקֹב מַלְאָכִים לְפָנָיו אֶל־עֵשָׂו, "and Jacob sent messen-
gers before him _to_ Esau" (Gen 32:4).

*(b) Estimative* – expresses interest/advantage or indiffer-
ence/disadvantage in something, and often requires "for"
or "against" in translation: כִּי הִנְנִי אֲלֵיכֶם, "see now, I am
_for_ you" (Ezek 36:9), וְאֶקְבְּצָה אֶל־אֲדֹנִי הַמֶּלֶךְ אֶת־כָּל־יִשְׂרָאֵל,
"and let me gather all Israel _for_ my lord the king"
(2 Sam 3:21), וְנַבְקִעֶנָּה אֵלֵינוּ, "and let us conquer it
_for_ ourselves," (Isa 7:6), חֲרוֹן אַף־יְהוָה אֶל־יִשְׂרָאֵל, "YHWH's
fierce anger _against_ Israel" (Num 32:14). An extreme
variant of the *estimative* אֶל/אֶל־ is its use with mil-
itaristic verbs, the most obvious being לחם in the
Niphal (וְנִלְחֲמוּ אֵלֶיךָ, "and they will fight _against_ you,"

---

[6] See *DCH* 1:260–64 for the distinction between horizontal and vertical
motion.

[7] Or the so-called datival use (see Waltke and O'Connor 1990, 193).

[Jer 1:19]), but occurring with many other verbs as well: וַיִּפְשְׁטוּ אֶל־הַגִּבְעָה, "and they marauded *against* Gibeah" (Judg 20:37), מַה־לִּי וָלָךְ כִּי־בָאתָ אֵלַי לְהִלָּחֵם בְּאַרְצִי, "what is there between us that you have come *against* me to fight against my land" (Judg 11:12).[8]

*(c) Declarative* – involves proclamation or locution (marking the object/recipient of a verb of speech), and at times with an *estimative* connotation as well. An extension of the *terminative* use of אֶל/־אֶל, the *declarative* marks the recipient of verbs of speech (דבר, קרא, אמר, ספר, etc.): וַיֹּאמֶר אֶל־הָאִשָּׁה, "and he [the serpent] said *to* the woman" (Gen 3:1), דַּבְּרוּ עַל־לֵב יְרוּשָׁלַם וְקִרְאוּ אֵלֶיהָ, "speak tenderly to Jerusalem, and cry *to* her" (Isa 40:2), וּקְרָא אֵלֶיהָ אֶת־הַקְּרִיאָה אֲשֶׁר אָנֹכִי דֹּבֵר אֵלֶיךָ, "and proclaim *to* it [Nineveh] the message that I tell [*to*] you" (Jonah 3:2), וַיְסַפֵּר אֶל־אָבִיו וְאֶל־אֶחָיו, "and he related it *to* his father and *to* his brothers" (Gen 37:10).

*(d) Perceptual* – marks one's disposition or predilection toward another person or place. As another extension of the *terminative*, the *perceptual* marks the recipient of verbs of perception (ראה, שמע, etc.), aptitude (זכר, ידע, בין, שמר), or emotion (רנן, עגב, etc.): שָׁמַע יְהוָה אֶל־עָנְיֵךְ, "YHWH has given heed *to* your affliction" (Gen 16:11), וַיֵּרָא יְהוָה אֶל־אַבְרָם, "and YHWH appeared *to* Abram" (Gen 12:7), לָמָּה לֹא שְׁמַרְתָּ אֶל־אֲדֹנֶיךָ הַמֶּלֶךְ, "Why have you not kept watch *over* your lord the king" (1 Sam 26:15), לֹא יָבִינוּ אֶל־פְּעֻלֹּת יְהוָה, "they do not regard [literally: understand *about*] the works of YHWH" (Ps 28:5), נוֹדַעְתִּי אֲלֵיהֶם, "I [YHWH] made myself known *to* them" (Ezek 20:9), יִזָּכֵר עֲוֹן אֲבֹתָיו אֶל־יְהוָה, "let the iniquity of his fathers be remembered *before* YHWH" (Ps 109:14), לִבִּי וּבְשָׂרִי יְרַנְּנוּ אֶל אֵל־חָי, "my heart and my flesh sing for

---

[8] For many other examples, see *DCH* 1:267–68, section 6.

וַתַּעְגֹּב עַל־מְאַהֲבֶיהָ אֶל־אַשּׁוּר ,(Ps 84:3) joy *to* the living God" "and she [Oholah] lusted after her lovers, *after* the Assyrians" (Ezek 23:5).

With verbs of writing, giving, or commanding, the *perceptual* use of אֶל/אַל, may connote "addressed to" or "intended for": וַיִּכְתֹּב דָּוִד סֵפֶר אֶל־יוֹאָב, "and David wrote a letter *intended for* Joab" (2 Sam 11:14), וְאִגֶּרֶת אֶל־אָסָף, "and [let] a letter [be] *addressed to* Asaph" (Neh 2:8).

*(e) Addition* – denotes circumstances over and above certain others, requiring such translations as "in addition to," or "as well as": אִשָּׁה אֶל־אֲחֹתָהּ לֹא תִקָּח, "You shall not marry a woman *in addition to* her sister" (Lev 18:18), הוֹסַפְתָּ חָכְמָה וָטוֹב אֶל־הַשְּׁמוּעָה אֲשֶׁר שָׁמָעְתִּי, "You have added wisdom and prosperity *together with* the report which I heard" (1 Kgs 10:7).

*(f) Spatial* – indicates localization, especially "at," "in," "by," "in the vicinity of," or "alongside":

קָבַר אַבְרָהָם אֶת־שָׂרָה אִשְׁתּוֹ אֶל־מְעָרַת שְׂדֵה הַמַּכְפֵּלָה

"Abraham buried Sarah his wife *in* the cave of the field at Machpelah" (Gen 23:19),

כִּי אִם־אֶל־הַמָּקוֹם אֲשֶׁר־יִבְחַר יְהוָה אֱלֹהֶיךָ לְשַׁכֵּן שְׁמוֹ שָׁם

"but *at* the place where YHWH your God chooses to establish his name" (Deut 16:6), הוּא־בָא וַיַּעֲמֹד אֶל־אֲדֹנָיו, "he went in and stood *in the presence of* his master" (2 Kgs 5:25).

*(g) Specification* – clarifies or explains further what immediately precedes, which would otherwise be generally or ambiguously stated. This use of the preposition often requires "about" or "concerning": וַתִּשְׁמַע אֶת־הַשְּׁמֻעָה אֶל־הִלָּקַח אֲרוֹן הָאֱלֹהִים וּמֵת חָמִיהָ וְאִישָׁהּ, "and she heard the news *concerning* the capture of the ark of God and the death of her father-in-law and husband"

(1 Sam 4:19), לָכֵן כֹּה־אָמַר יְהוָה אֶל־מֶלֶךְ אַשּׁוּר, "therefore, thus says YHWH *concerning* the king of Assyria" (Isa 37:33), כִּי תוֹרֵם אֶל־הַדֶּרֶךְ הַטּוֹבָה אֲשֶׁר יֵלְכוּ־בָהּ, "indeed, teach them *about* the good way in which they should walk" (2 Chr 6:27).

At times, the use of אֶל/אֶל־, for specification takes on a *causal* connotation: הִתְאַבֵּל שְׁמוּאֵל אֶל־שָׁאוּל, "Samuel grieved *concerning* [*because of*] Saul" (1 Sam 15:35), אֶל־הַכַּעַס אֲשֶׁר הִכְעַסְתָּ, "*because* of the provocation with which you have provoked" (1 Kgs 21:22).

## 4.1.3 אֵצֶל

**Spatial** – Expresses concepts of nearness or close proximity, usually requiring "beside," "with," or "near": וַיַּצִּיגוּ אֹתוֹ אֵצֶל דָּגוֹן, "and he set it *beside* Dagon" (1 Sam 5:2), וַתַּעֲמֹדְנָה אֵצֶל הַפָּרוֹת עַל־שְׂפַת הַיְאֹר, "and they stood *near* the other cows on the bank of the Nile" (Gen 41:3).

## 4.1.4 אֵת / אֶת־

**(a) Accompaniment** – This preposition[9] shows attendant circumstances: אַתָּה וּבָנֶיךָ אִתָּךְ, "you and your children *with* you" (Num 18:2), וַיִּתְהַלֵּךְ חֲנוֹךְ אֶת־הָאֱלֹהִים, "And Enoch walked *with* God" (Gen 5:22), וַיְהִי אֱלֹהִים אֶת־הַנַּעַר, "God was *with* the young boy" (Gen 21:20). A finer nuance of the usage is the *personal accompaniment*, which expresses accompaniment for the purpose of providing help: קָנִיתִי אִישׁ אֶת־יְהוָה, "I have gotten a man *with the help of* YHWH" (Gen 4:1), וַיֵּדְעוּ כִּי מֵאֵת אֱלֹהֵינוּ נֶעֶשְׂתָה הַמְּלָאכָה הַזֹּאת, "They knew that this work was accomplished *with the help of* our God" (Neh 6:16).

---

[9] This preposition is presumably based on the root אתת since suffixed forms double the -*t*- (אִתִּי, and note the Akkadian preposition *itti*). Thus, it should not be confused with the definite direct object marker, which may be based on the root אות in light of its forms with suffixes (אוֹתִי).

*(b) Possession* – expressing ownership:

הִנֵּה־הַכֶּסֶף אִתִּי אֲנִי לְקַחְתִּיו

"behold, the silver is _with_ me, I took it" (Judg 17:2), מַה־אִתָּנוּ, "What do we have [lit: What (is) _with us_]" (1 Sam 9:7), הַנָּבִיא אֲשֶׁר־אִתּוֹ חֲלוֹם יְסַפֵּר חֲלוֹם, "The prophet who _has a dream_ (literally: the prophet, to whom, _a dream is with him_), may tell the dream" (Jer 23:28).

*(c) Complement* – with verbs of speaking, dealing, or making: וַיְדַבֵּר אִתָּם קָשׁוֹת, "and he spoke harshly _with_ them" (Gen 42:7), וִידַעְתֶּם כִּי־אֲנִי יְהוָה בַּעֲשׂוֹתִי אִתְּכֶם, "Then you will know that I am Yнwн, when I have dealt _with you_" (Ezek 20:44).

*(d) Spatial* – denotes a sense of nearness or proximity: בְּצַעֲנַנִּים אֲשֶׁר אֶת־קֶדֶשׁ, "in Zaanannim, which is _near_ Kedesh" (Judg 4:11 *Qere*), וַיֹּאמֶר יְהוָה הִנֵּה מָקוֹם אִתִּי, "Yнwн said, 'See, there is a place _beside_ me" (Exod 33:21), אֶל־הַמֶּרְכָּבָה בְּמַעֲלֵה־גוּר אֲשֶׁר אֶת־יִבְלְעָם, "[so they shot him] in the chariot, at the ascent of Gur, which is _by Ibleam_" (2 Kgs 9:27).

## 4.15 בְּ

*(a) Spatial* – This preposition[10] indicates localization, especially "in," "at" or "on" a place:

לַעֲשׂוֹת זְבָחִים בְּבֵית־יְהוָה בִּירוּשָׁלַ͏ִם

"to offer sacrifices _in_ the house of Yнwн _at_ Jerusalem" (1 Kgs 12:27), וַיִּזְבַּח יַעֲקֹב זֶבַח בָּהָר, "Then Jacob offered a sacrifice _on_ the mountain" (Gen 31:54), הַכְּנַעֲנִי אָז בָּאָרֶץ, "the Canaanites were then _in_ the land" (Gen 12:6).

---

[10] Approximately 58% of the uses of בְּ in the Bible are *spatial,* while only about 16% are temporal (Jenni 1992, 69). For a complete list of uses and numerous examples, see *HALOT* 1:104–05; *DCH* 2:82–86.

With certain verbs of motion or movement, בְּ denotes
the route "through": וַיַּעֲבֹר אַבְרָם בָּאָרֶץ, "and Abram passed
*through* the land" (Gen 12:6), קוּם הִתְהַלֵּךְ בָּאָרֶץ, "rise up,
walk *through* the land" (Gen 13:17). At other times, בְּ
refers to the movement "into" or rest "in" a place ("terminative"): הַבָּאִים אַחֲרֵיהֶם בַּיָּם, "those who went after them
*into* the sea" (Exod 14:28), וְשִׁלַּח אֶת־הַשָּׂעִיר בַּמִּדְבָּר, "and he
shall send forth the goat *into* the wilderness" (Lev 16:22),
בְּנֵי אָדָם בְּצֵל כְּנָפֶיךָ יֶחֱסָיוּן, "all people may take refuge *in* the
shadow of your wings" (Ps 36:8). Included in this cate-
gory of localization are those times when בְּ connotes "in
the domain of," that is, inclusion "among" or "within"
a group: וְהֵפִיץ יְהוָה אֶתְכֶם בָּעַמִּים וְנִשְׁאַרְתֶּם מְתֵי מִסְפָּר בַּגּוֹיִם,
"Yhwh will scatter you *among* the peoples and you shall
be left few in number *among* the nations" (Deut 4:27),
אוֹדְךָ בָעַמִּים אֲדֹנָי, "I will give thanks to you, O Lord,
*among* the peoples" (Ps 57:10). At times, בְּ appears to
connote movement or action away "from" a place, es-
pecially in poetry: אֲדֹנָי מָעוֹן אַתָּה הָיִיתָ לָּנוּ בְּדֹר וָדֹר, "Lord,
you have been our dwelling place *from* all generations"
(Ps 90:1), אֵין יְשׁוּעָתָה לּוֹ בֵאלֹהִים, "he has no salvation
*from* God" (Ps 3:3), דַּיַּן אַלְמָנוֹת אֱלֹהִים בִּמְעוֹן קָדְשׁוֹ, "a pro-
tector of widows is God *from* his sanctuary" (Ps 68:6),
הֲלִיכוֹת אֵלִי מַלְכִּי בַקֹּדֶשׁ, "the processions of my God, my
King, *from* the sanctuary" (Ps 68:25).[11]

### (b) Temporal – expresses a moment or point of time when
an action takes place: בְּיוֹם עֲשׂוֹת יְהוָה אֱלֹהִים אֶרֶץ וְשָׁמָיִם, "*in*
the day when Yhwh God made earth and the heavens"
(Gen 2:4), בְּיוֹם בְּרֹא אֱלֹהִים אָדָם, "*in* the day when God created humankind" (Gen 5:1), בִּימֵי קְצִיר־חִטִּים, "*in* the days
of wheat harvest" (Gen 30:14), וַיָּבֹא יַעֲקֹב מִן־הַשָּׂדֶה בָּעֶרֶב,

---

[11] The so-called double meaning of בְּ ("in" and "from") has been heavily
debated in light of Ugaritic evidence, which seems to support "from"
in these poetic contexts, especially in the Psalms. For bibliography, see
*DCH* 2:602. See also on לְ in 4.1.10.

"and Jacob came from the field _in_ the evening"
(Gen 30:16), בְּכָל־עֵת אֹהֵב הָרֵעַ, "a friend loves _at_ all
times" (Prov 17:17). When used with the infinitive
construct, בְּ frequently connotes "when," or "when-
ever": בְּהִבָּרְאָם, "_when_ they [the heavens and the earth]
were created" (Gen 2:4), בְּצֵאתָם מִמִּצְרָיִם, "_when_ they [the
Israelites] came out of Egypt" (Josh 5:4); and see the
famous examples in the verses following the Shema:
וְדִבַּרְתָּ בָּם בְּשִׁבְתְּךָ בְּבֵיתֶךָ וּבְלֶכְתְּךָ בַדֶּרֶךְ וּבְשָׁכְבְּךָ וּבְקוּמֶךָ, "and
you shall speak of them [God's words] _when_ you sit at home
and _when_ you are on the road, _when_ you lie down and _when_
you rise" (Deut 6:7).

*(c) Instrumental* – refers to an inanimate object used to perform a certain action: בַּשֵּׁבֶט יַכּוּ, "_with_ a rod they will smite
[him]" (Mic 4:14), וְהָרַגְתִּי אֶתְכֶם בֶּחָרֶב, "and I will kill you
_with_ the sword" (Exod 22:23). Similar to this use is the בְּ
of *material,* which indicates the material with which something is made or formed: וְצֹרֵף בַּזָּהָב יְרַקְּעֶנּוּ, "and a gold-
smith overspreads it _with_ gold" (Isa 40:19).

*(d) Adversative* – indicates a relationship of disadvantage:
יָדוֹ בַכֹּל וְיַד כֹּל בּוֹ, "his hand shall be _against_ everyone and
everyone's hand _against_ him" (Gen 16:12). In some contexts, the *adversative* בְּ connotes "in spite of" in translation:
לֹא־יַאֲמִינוּ בִי בְּכֹל הָאֹתוֹת אֲשֶׁר עָשִׂיתִי בְּקִרְבּוֹ, "they do not believe in me _in spite of_ all the signs that I have done among
them" (Num 14:11).

*(e) Specification* – clarifies or explains further an immediately preceding verbal action, which would otherwise be
generally or ambiguously stated:

וְשָׂמַחְתָּ בְכָל־הַטּוֹב אֲשֶׁר נָתַן־לְךָ יְהוָה

"and you shall rejoice _in_ all the good which YHWH has
given to you" (Deut 26:11). The בְּ of *specification* may also
particularize the parts of which the general whole consists:
וַיִּגְוַע כָּל־בָּשָׂר הָרֹמֵשׂ עַל־הָאָרֶץ בָּעוֹף וּבַבְּהֵמָה וּבַחַיָּה וּבְכָל־הַשֶּׁרֶץ,

"and all flesh died that moved on the earth – birds, cattle, wild animals, all swarming creatures" (Gen 7:21),

וַיְמָרְרוּ אֶת־חַיֵּיהֶם בַּעֲבֹדָה קָשָׁה בְּחֹמֶר וּבִלְבֵנִים וּבְכָל־עֲבֹדָה בַּשָּׂדֶה

"and they made their lives bitter with hard service – *in* mortar and *in* brick and *in* all field service" (Exod 1:14).

*(f) Causal* – identifies a cause or reason: אִישׁ בְּחֶטְאוֹ יוּמָתוּ, "each person shall be put to death *because of* his own sin" (Deut 24:16),

הֵן הֵנָּה הָיוּ לִבְנֵי יִשְׂרָאֵל בִּדְבַר בִּלְעָם לִמְסָר־מַעַל בַּיהוָה

"behold, these women caused the Israelites, *because* of the word of Balaam, to act treacherously against YHWH" (Num 31:16),

וּרְאִיתֶם אֶת־כְּבוֹד יְהוָה בְּשָׁמְעוֹ אֶת־תְּלֻנֹּתֵיכֶם עַל־יְהוָה

"and you shall see the glory of YHWH, *because* he has heard your complaining against YHWH" (Exod 16:7), בְּעָזְבְכֶם אֶת־מִצְוֹת יְהוָה, *because* you have forsaken the commands of YHWH" (1 Kgs 18:18). The preposition may be combined with אֲשֶׁר to form a causal conjunction: בַּאֲשֶׁר אַתְּ־אִשְׁתּוֹ, "*because* you are his wife" (Gen 39:9), בַּאֲשֶׁר יְהוָה אִתּוֹ, "*because* YHWH was with him" (Gen 39:23).[12]

*(g) Accompaniment* – denotes circumstances occurring "together with": יֵצְאוּ בִּרְכֻשׁ גָּדוֹל, "they shall come out *with* great possessions" (Gen 15:14), נְטֵה אֶת־יָדְךָ בְּמַטֶּךָ, "stretch out your hand *with* your staff" (Exod 8:1), בְּעֶצֶב תֵּלְדִי בָנִים, "*with* pain you shall bring forth children" (Gen 3:16), וַיֵּצֵא אֱדוֹם לִקְרָאתוֹ בְּעַם כָּבֵד, "and Edom came out against them *with* a large force" (Num 20:20).

---

[12] *HALOT* 1:99 at §B,c; *DCH* 1:433 at §4c(5).

*(h) Essence*[13] – marks identity of a noun in the context, occasionally with a predicate, and connoting "(having the same nature) as" or "(consisting) of": נַעֲשֶׂה אָדָם בְּצַלְמֵנוּ, "let us make humankind [*in the same nature*] *as* our image" (Gen 1:26), בִּדְמוּת אֱלֹהִים עָשָׂה אֹתוֹ, "*as* the likeness of God he made him" (Gen 5:1), וָאֵרָא אֶל־אַבְרָהָם אֶל־יִצְחָק וְאֶל־יַעֲקֹב בְּאֵל שַׁדָּי, "and I appeared to Abraham, Isaac, and Jacob *as* God Almighty" (Exod 6:3), הִנֵּה אֲדֹנָי יְהוָה בְּחָזָק יָבוֹא, "behold, Lord YHWH comes *as* a mighty one" (Isa 40:10), וַיָּגָר שָׁם בִּמְתֵי מְעָט, "and he [Jacob] sojourned there [*consisting*] *of* men few in number" (Deut 26:5).

*(i) Manner* – describes the way in which an action or situation is performed or the attendant circumstances of the action. In such cases, בְּ has an adverbial force: בֹּכִים בְּקוֹל גָּדוֹל, "weeping *aloud* [literally: *with* a great voice]" (Ezra 3:12), וְעַתָּה שׁוּב וְלֵךְ בְּשָׁלוֹם, "go back now, and go *peaceably* [literally: *in* peace]" (1 Sam 29:7).

*(j) Price* – indicating the cost or price of something, and at times connoting "at the risk of" or "in exchange for": בְּכֶסֶף מָלֵא יִתְּנֶנָּה לִי, "let him give it to me *at the cost of* full silver [i.e., full price]" (Gen 23:9), אֶעֱבָדְךָ שֶׁבַע שָׁנִים בְּרָחֵל בִּתְּךָ הַקְּטַנָּה, "I will serve you seven years *as the price of* your younger daughter Rachel" (Gen 29:18), וַיָּמִירוּ אֶת־כְּבוֹדָם בְּתַבְנִית שׁוֹר אֹכֵל עֵשֶׂב, "and they changed their glory *in exchange for* the image of an ox that eats grass" (Ps 106:20).

## 4.1.6 בֵּין

Denotes the interval "between" two points, usually *spatial* and occasionally *temporal*. In 80 percent of its

---

[13] Known by older grammarians as *beth essentiae* (Kautzsch 1910, 379). See Joüon and Muraoka 1993, 486–87, and *DCH* 2:84–85.

occurrences, בֵּין is paired with itself ("...וּבֵין...בֵּין")
in order to denote the interval between two points or
two parties, in which case the second בֵּין is not repeated
in translation:[14] בֵּין בֵּית־אֵל וּבֵין הָעָי, "*between* Bethel
and Ai" (Gen 13:3), וַיְהִי שָׁלוֹם בֵּין יִשְׂרָאֵל וּבֵין הָאֱמֹרִי,
"and there was peace *between* Israel and the
Amorites" (1 Sam 7:14), בְּרִית בֵּינִי וּבֵינֶךָ, "[let there
be] a treaty *between* me and you" (1 Kgs 15:19),
הַתּוֹרֹת אֲשֶׁר נָתַן יְהוָה בֵּינוֹ וּבֵין בְּנֵי יִשְׂרָאֵל בְּהַר סִינַי, "the laws,
which Yнwн established *between* himself and the Israelites
on Mount Sinai" (Lev 26:46). The second בֵּין of the idiom
may be repeated, in which case the idea appears to be "between A (on the one hand) and B and C (on the other)":
וַיִּכְרֹת יְהוֹיָדָע אֶת־הַבְּרִית בֵּין יְהוָה וּבֵין הַמֶּלֶךְ וּבֵין הָעָם, "Then
Jehoiada made a covenant *between* Yнwн on the one hand,
and the king and people on the other" (2 Kgs 11:17).[15]

In other occurrences, בֵּין is used only once, and stands
before the plural or dual of a noun or with plural suffixes to refer to a group, in which case the preposition
may denote "among": אֱלֹהֵי אַבְרָהָם וֵאלֹהֵי נָחוֹר יִשְׁפְּטוּ בֵינֵינוּ,
"the God of Abraham and the God of Nahor judge *between*
us" (Gen 31:53), רִיב בֵּין אֲנָשִׁים, "a dispute *between* men"
(Deut 25:1), מְשַׁלֵּחַ מְדָנִים בֵּין אַחִים, "and one who sows dis-
cord *among* brothers" (Prov 6:19).[16]

## 4.1.7 בַּעַד / בְּעַד־

*(a) Spatial* – indicates localization, especially "behind"
something: הָאָרֶץ בְּרִחֶיהָ בַעֲדִי לְעוֹלָם, "[I went down to] the
earth whose bars [are closed] *behind* me forever" (Jonah 2:7
[Eng. 2:6]). With the verb "close, shut" (סגר), the concept
is to close off or shut up inside: וַיִּסְגֹּר יְהוָה בַּעֲדוֹ, "and Yнwн

---

[14] For the statistics, see Waltke and O'Connor 1990 (199–201) and *DCH*
2:146–49.

[15] For more on this, and other variations of the idiom, see *DCH* 2:146.

[16] On such uses as "inclusive," and on the distinction between *inclusive* and
*exclusive* uses of בֵּין, see Waltke and O'Connor 1990 (199–201).

וּבָאתָ וְסָגַרְתָּ הַדֶּלֶת בַּעֲדֵךְ, closed it _behind_ him" (Gen 7:16), "and go in and shut the door _behind_ you" (2 Kgs 4:4), סָגַר יְהוָה בְּעַד רַחְמָהּ, "Yhwh _closed_ her womb" (1 Sam 1:6).

With verbs of motion (בוא, ירד [Hi]), נפל, etc.), the preposition often denotes a sense of movement "through" an object: בְּעַד הַחַלּוֹנִים יָבֹאוּ כַּגַּנָּב, "_through_ the windows they enter like a thief" (Joel 2:9), וַתּוֹרִדֵם בַּחֶבֶל בְּעַד הַחַלּוֹן, "then she let them down by a rope _through_ the window" (Josh 2:15).

Used metaphorically, the spatial sense of "around" or "round about" can take on an _advantage_ idea related to the next usage:

הֲלֹא־אַתָּה שַׂכְתָּ בַעֲדוֹ וּבְעַד־בֵּיתוֹ וּבְעַד כָּל־אֲשֶׁר־לוֹ מִסָּבִיב

"Have you not put a fence _around_ him, his house, and all that he has, on every side?" (Job 1:10 *Qere*), אַתָּה יְהוָה מָגֵן בַּעֲדִי, "You, O Yhwh, are a shield _around_ me" (Ps 3:4).

**(b) Advantage** – indicates a relationship of interest or advantage, often requiring "for" or "on behalf of": יִתְפַּלֵּל בַּעַדְךָ וֶחְיֵה "he will pray _for_ you and you will live" (Gen 20:7), אוּלַי אֲכַפְּרָה בְּעַד חַטַּאתְכֶם, "perhaps I can make atonement _for_ your sin" (Exod 32:30), וְכַפֵּר בַּעַדְךָ וּבְעַד הָעָם, "and make atonement _for_ yourself and _for_ the people" (Lev 9:7),

לְכוּ דִרְשׁוּ אֶת־יְהוָה בַּעֲדִי וּבְעַד־הָעָם וּבְעַד כָּל־יְהוּדָה

"Go, inquire of Yhwh _on my behalf,_ and _on behalf of_ the people and all Judah" (2 Kgs 22:13).

### 4.1.8 יַעַן

**Causal** – More often used as a conjunction, יַעַן denotes a causal sense: יַעַן כָּל־תּוֹעֲבֹתָיִךְ, "_because_ of all your abominations" (Ezek 5:9), יַעַן מָאַסְתָּ אֶת־דְּבַר יְהוָה וַיִּמְאָסְךָ מִמֶּלֶךְ,

"*Because* you rejected the word of Yhwh, he has rejected you as king" (1 Sam 15:23). For more specific constructions in which the particle appears, refer to "Causal Clauses" (section 5.2.5).

## 4.1.9 כְּ

כְּ, unlike other prepositions, has no spatial use, and has a temporal use only with the infinitive construct. Instead, it shows comparison or correspondence relationships.

*(a) Agreement* – The preposition often denotes a sense of *agreement in quantity or measure*: יֹסֵף עֲלֵיכֶם כָּכֶם אֶלֶף פְּעָמִים, "[may Yhwh] make you a thousand times *as* many as you are" (Deut 1:11). This type of quantitative agreement can be *approximate* as well: וַיֵּשְׁבוּ שָׁם כְּעֶשֶׂר שָׁנִים, "they lived there *about* ten years" (Ruth 1:4), כְּאַרְבָּעִים אֶלֶף חֲלוּצֵי הַצָּבָא, "*about* forty thousand armed for war" (Josh 4:13).

Along with quantitative agreement, כְּ also expresses agreement in *kind* or *quality* as well: וִהְיִיתֶם כֵּאלֹהִים, "you will be *like* God" (Gen 3:5),

הֲלוֹא יְדַעְתֶּם כִּי־נַחֵשׁ יְנַחֵשׁ אִישׁ אֲשֶׁר כָּמֹנִי

"Do you not know that a man *like me* practices divination?" (Gen 44:15), וּבָעֶרֶב יִהְיֶה עַל־הַמִּשְׁכָּן כְּמַרְאֵה־אֵשׁ עַד־בֹּקֶר, "In the evening, [the cloud] was over the tabernacle, *like the appearance of fire*, until morning" (Num 9:15).

*(b) Correspondence* – a comparison that establishes an equivalence between the things that are compared, and often clarifying the identity of what is compared: הוּא כְּאִישׁ אֱמֶת, "he *is truly* a man of truth" (Neh 7:2). This is especially common with the כְּ...כְּ construction: וְהָיָה כָעָם כַּכֹּהֵן כַּעֶבֶד כַּאדֹנָיו, "And it shall be, *as with* the people, *so with* the priest; *as with* the slave, *so with* his master" (Isa 24:2).

*(c)* **Temporal** – with the infinitive construct, expresses "when" or "as soon as": וְהָיָה כִּרְאוֹתוֹ כִּי־אֵין הַנַּעַר וָמֵת, "*As soon as he sees* that the boy is not with us, he will die" (Gen 44:31),

וַיְצַו אַבְשָׁלוֹם אֶת־נְעָרָיו לֵאמֹר רְאוּ נָא כְּטוֹב לֵב־אַמְנוֹן בַּיַּיִן וְאָמַרְתִּי אֲלֵיכֶם הַכּוּ אֶת־אַמְנוֹן וַהֲמִתֶּם אֹתוֹ

"Absalom commanded his servants, saying 'Watch; *when Amnon's heart is merry* with wine, and I say to you "Strike Amnon," then put him to death'" (2 Sam 13:28).

### 4.1.10 לְ

*(a)* **Spatial** – most often, indicates *direction* "to" or "toward" the object of the preposition:

הֲבוֹא נָבוֹא אֲנִי וְאִמְּךָ וְאַחֶיךָ לְהִשְׁתַּחֲוֹת לְךָ אָרְצָה

"Will we indeed come, I and your mother and your brothers, to bow down *to you*, to the ground?" (Gen 37:10), הָרִיעוּ לֵאלֹהִים בְּקוֹל רִנָּה, "Shout *to* God, with a voice of joy" (Ps 47:2 [Eng. 47:1]),

With verbs of motion, spatial לְ can take on a *terminative* sense, expressing movement wherein the goal is reached: הַיּוֹם בָּא לָעִיר, "he came *to* the city today" (1 Sam 9:12), וַיִּשְׁלַח הָאֱלֹהִים מַלְאָךְ לִירוּשָׁלַ͏ִם, "and God sent a messenger *to* Jerusalem" (1 Chr 21:15). Occasionally, the *spatial* לְ has an ablative function, indicating movement "away from" the object: לֹא יִמְנַע־טוֹב לַהֹלְכִים בְּתָמִים, "He does not withhold goodness *from* those who walk in uprightness" (Ps 84:12), וְלֵיהוִה אֲדֹנָי לַמָּוֶת תּוֹצָאוֹת, "Escape *from* death belongs to Yʜwʜ, the lord" (Ps 68:21 [Eng. 68:20]).

*(b)* **Locative** – locates the object of the preposition "in" or "at" a certain point: וַתֵּשֶׁב לִימִינוֹ, "she sat *at* his right" (1 Kgs 2:19), לַפֶּתַח חַטָּאת רֹבֵץ, "Sin is crouching *at* the door" (Gen 4:7), וַיַּעֲלוּ וַיָּתֻרוּ אֶת־הָאָרֶץ מִמִּדְבַּר־צִן עַד־רְחֹב לְבֹא חֲמָת,

"They went up and spied out the land from the wilderness of Zin to Reho, _at_ Lebo Hamath" (Num 13:21).

*(c) Temporal* – similar to the *locative* use, *temporal* לְ locates the object of the preposition "in," "at," or "during" a certain period of time: וַתָּבֹא אֵלָיו הַיּוֹנָה לְעֵת עֶרֶב, "the dove came to him _at_ the time of evening" (Gen 8:11), וְהָבִיאוּ לַבֹּקֶר זִבְחֵיכֶם, "Bring your sacrifices _in_ the morning" (Amos 4:4). Temporal לְ also functions to indicate movement toward a moment in time, or the duration of an action/situation "until" a moment in time: כָּל־יָמֶיךָ לְעוֹלָם, "all your days _to eternity_" (Deut 23:7 [Eng 23:6]), וְלֹא־יָלִין מִן־הַבָּשָׂר אֲשֶׁר תִּזְבַּח בָּעֶרֶב בַּיּוֹם הָרִאשׁוֹן לַבֹּקֶר, "None of the flesh which you slaugher in the evening of the first day shall remain overnight _until_ the morning" (Deut 16:4).

*(d) Purpose* – frequently with the infinitive construct, in order to show the aim or goal of another verb: הַמָּאוֹר הַגָּדֹל לְמֶמְשֶׁלֶת הַיּוֹם, "the greater light _to rule_ the day" (Gen 1:16), וַיּוֹצֵא מֹשֶׁה אֶת־הָעָם לִקְרַאת הָאֱלֹהִים מִן־הַמַּחֲנֶה, "then Moses brought the people out from the camp _to meet_ God" (Exod 19:17),

אַתָּה יָדַעְתָּ אֶת־דָּוִד אָבִי כִּי לֹא יָכֹל לִבְנוֹת בַּיִת לְשֵׁם יְהוָה אֱלֹהָיו

"You know that David my father was unable _to build_ a house for the name of YHWH his god" (1 Kgs 5:17 [Eng 5:3]).

Related to this use is the *causal*, where לְ shows the motive behind an action: אִישׁ הָרַגְתִּי לְפִצְעִי, "I have killed a man _for wounding me_" (Gen 4:23),

לֹא תִתְגֹּדְדוּ וְלֹא־תָשִׂימוּ קָרְחָה בֵּין עֵינֵיכֶם לָמֵת

"You shall not cut yourselves or shave your foreheads _because_ of the dead" (Deut 14:1).

*(e) Quasi datival* – לְ has several datival uses. One of the more common indicates the indirect object of verbs of

giving, speaking, listening, or sending: תִּתֶּן־לוֹ, "you will give *to him*" (Deut 15:14),

אֶלֶף לַמַּטֶּה אֶלֶף לַמַּטֶּה לְכֹל מַטּוֹת יִשְׂרָאֵל תִּשְׁלְחוּ לַצָּבָא

"A thousand from each tribe of all the tribes of Israel you shall send *to the war*" (Num 31:4),

חֲלֹא הוּא אָמַר־לִי אֲחֹתִי הוּא

"Did he himself not say *to me*, 'She is my sister'?" (Gen 20:5).

(e.1) *Interest/advantage* – Sometimes called the *ethical dative*, לְ marks the person or object for whom an action is directed or intended: אַל־תִּבְכּוּ לְמֵת, "Do not weep *for* the dead" (Jer 22:10), הַטוֹב לְךָ כִּי־תַעֲשֹׁק, "Is it right *for you* to oppress?" (Job 10:3),

שִׂימָה בְּפִיהֶם לְמַעַן תִּהְיֶה־לִּי הַשִּׁירָה הַזֹּאת לְעֵד בִּבְנֵי יִשְׂרָאֵל

"Put it in their mouths, so that this song will be a witness *for me* against the people of Israel" (Deut 31:19).

לְ sometimes expresses the exact opposite, indicating that an action or situation is directed "against" someone or something: גַּם־אָנֹכִי אוֹתְךָ מֵחֲטוֹ־לִי, "I also kept you from sinning *against* me" (Gen 20:6).

(e.2) *Product* – with verbs of making, indicates a thing that is made, or a person who is altered, either in status or in form: וְאֶעֶשְׂךָ לְגוֹי גָּדוֹל, "I will make you [*into*] a great nation" (Gen 12:2), וַיִּבֶן יְהוָה אֱלֹהִים אֶת־הַצֵּלָע אֲשֶׁר־לָקַח מִן־הָאָדָם לְאִשָּׁה, "And YHWH God made the rib which he took from Adam *into a woman*" (Gen 2:22), יָצָא מִמְּקֹמוֹ לָשׂוּם אַרְצֵךְ לְשַׁמָּה, "He has gone out from his place to make your land *into a desolation*" (Jer 4:7).

*(f) Possession* – shows that the object of the preposition is in possession of something: כַּסְפְּךָ וּזְהָבְךָ לִי־הוּא, "your silver and your gold are *mine* [literally: *to/for me*]" (1 Kgs 20:3), הַמֵּת לְיָרָבְעָם בָּעִיר יֹאכְלוּ הַכְּלָבִים, "Anyone *belonging to Jeroboam* who dies in the city, the dogs will eat" (1 Kgs 14:11).

The *possessive* use of לְ is quite frequent with the particle of existence, to show possession, or with the particle of nonexistence, to show lack of possession. See sections 4.4.1 and 4.4.2.

**(g) Genitival** – nouns in a genitival relationship formed by the construct chain necessarily agree in definiteness. BH forms genitive relationships between nouns that do not agree in definiteness by הִנֵּה רָאִיתִי בֵּן לְיִשַׁי בֵּית הַלַּחְמִי, "Behold, I have seen *a son of Jesse*, the Bethlehemite" (1 Sam 16:18), וְאִתְּכֶם יִהְיוּ אִישׁ אִישׁ לַמַּטֶּה, "*A man of each tribe* will be with you" (Num 1:4).

**(h) Specification** – calls attention to the object of the preposition: וּלְיִשְׁמָעֵאל שְׁמַעְתִּיךָ, "With *regard* to Ishmael, I have heard you ..." (Gen 17:20),

שְׁלֹף חַרְבְּךָ וּמוֹתְתֵנִי פֶּן־יֹאמְרוּ לִי אִשָּׁה הֲרָגָתְהוּ

"Draw your sword and kill me, so that it will not be said *of me*, 'A woman killed him'" (Judg 9:54), לֹא־יַסִּפוּ לְאֵלֶּה לֹא יִסַּג כְּלִמּוֹת, "If they do not speak out *concerning these things*, reproaches will not be turned back" (Mic 2:6).

**(i) Normative** – often translated "according to," classifies the object of the preposition, sometimes dividing a larger whole into parts: הִתְיַצְּבוּ לִפְנֵי יְהוָה לְשִׁבְטֵיכֶם וּלְאַלְפֵיכֶם, "present yourselves before YHWH *according* to your tribes and *according* to your thousands" (1 Sam 10:19), עֵץ פְּרִי עֹשֶׂה פְּרִי לְמִינוֹ, "fruit trees bearing fruit of its kind" (Gen 1:11), בְּנֵי מְרָרִי לְמִשְׁפְּחֹתָם לְבֵית־אֲבֹתָם תִּפְקֹד אֹתָם, "As for the Merarites, you shall number them *by their families* and *by their fathers's households*" (Num 4:29).

**(j) Manner** – expresses action that is in accordance with a certain standard or principles, which is denoted by the preposition:

יַצֵּב גְּבֻלֹת עַמִּים לְמִסְפַּר בְּנֵי יִשְׂרָאֵל

"He fixed the boundaries of the people *according to* the number of the people of Israel" (Deut 32:8), לֹא־לְמַרְאֵה עֵינָיו יִשְׁפּוֹט וְלֹא־לְמִשְׁמַע אָזְנָיו יוֹכִיחַ, "He will not judge *by* what his eyes will see, and he will not make a decision *by* what his ears hear" (Isa 11:3).

**(k) Estimative** – expresses the opinion or perception held by the object of the preposition: (cf. *DCH* 4:484a): וָאֶהְיֶה תָמִים לוֹ, "I was blameless *to him*" (2 Sam 22:24), כִּי מָרְדֳּכַי הַיְּהוּדִי מִשְׁנֶה לַמֶּלֶךְ אֲחַשְׁוֵרוֹשׁ וְגָדוֹל לַיְּהוּדִים, "For Mordecai the Jew was second to the King Ahasuerus and *great among the Jews*" (Esth 10:3). Where a divine name is the object of an *estimative* לְ, the *superlative* is intended, וְנִינְוֵה הָיְתָה עִיר־גְּדוֹלָה לֵאלֹהִים, "Nineveh was an *exceedingly* great city" or "Nineveh was a great city *in the eyes of* God" (Jonah 3:3).

**(l) Agent** – With passive verbs, לְ often indicates the one who performs the action: בָּרוּךְ אַבְרָם לְאֵל עֶלְיוֹן קֹנֵה שָׁמַיִם וָאָרֶץ, "Blessed be Abram, *by God* most high, maker of heaven and earth" (Gen 14:19), וְנִבְחַר מָוֶת מֵחַיִּים לְכֹל הַשְּׁאֵרִית, "Death will be chosen, rather than life, *by all the remnant*" (Jer 8:3).

**(m) Reflexive** – The לְ preposition also functions *reflexively*, where the object of the preposition is always the same as the subject of the verb. This use is especially common with verbs of motion or with imperatives. לֶךְ־לְךָ, "*Go*!" (Gen 12:1), קוּם בְּרַח־לְךָ אֶל־לָבָן אָחִי חָרָנָה, "*Arise, and flee* to Laban, my brother; to Haran" (Gen 27:43), וַיֹּאמֶר יְהוָה אֶל־מֹשֶׁה כְּתָב־לְךָ אֶת־הַדְּבָרִים הָאֵלֶּה, "YHWH said to Moses, '*Write* these words'" (Exod 34:27).

## 4.1.11 לְמַעַן

*(a) Purpose* – Paired with an infinitive form, the preposition functions to show *purpose:*

וְיֵהוּא עָשָׂה בְעָקְבָּה לְמַעַן הַאֲבִיד אֶת־עֹבְדֵי הַבָּעַל

"But Jehu did it in cunning, *in order to destroy* the servants of Baal" (2 Kgs 10:19),

אִמְרִי־נָא אֲחֹתִי אָתְּ לְמַעַן יִיטַב־לִי בַעֲבוּרֵךְ

"Please say that you are my sister, *so that* it will go well for me because of you" (Gen 12:13).

*(b) Causal* – denotes the cause of an action or situation: וַיִּתְעַבֵּר יְהוָה בִּי לְמַעַנְכֶם, "and YHWH was angry with me *because* of you" (Deut 3:26),

הַשֵּׁבֶט הָאֶחָד יִהְיֶה־לּוֹ לְמַעַן עַבְדִּי דָוִד וּלְמַעַן יְרוּשָׁלַם

"He will have one tribe, *because* of my servant David and because of Jerusalem" (1 Kgs 11:32).

## 4.1.12 לִפְנֵי

This preposition is a compound of the simple preposition לְ prefixed to the substantive פָּנִים in the construct state.

*(a) Locative* – The basic *locative* sense of the preposition points to what is "before," or "in front of": וְאַבְרָהָם עוֹדֶנּוּ עֹמֵד לִפְנֵי יְהוָה, "and Abraham was still standing *before* YHWH" (Gen 18:22),

וְהִנַּחְתָּם בְּאֹהֶל מוֹעֵד לִפְנֵי הָעֵדוּת אֲשֶׁר אִוָּעֵד לָכֶם שָׁמָּה

"Deposit them in the tent of meeting *in front of* the testimony, where I meet with you" (Num 17:19 [Eng 17:4]).

Though translated "before," the particle can place emphasis not on the location of its object but on the fact that the object has been placed at one's disposal, or possession: הִנֵּה־רִבְקָה לְפָנֶיךָ קַח וָלֵךְ, "Here is Rebe-kah *before* you; take her and go" (Gen 24:51), אִתָּנוּ תֵּשֵׁבוּ וְהָאָרֶץ תִּהְיֶה לִפְנֵיכֶם, "You shall dwell with us, and the land shall be open *before* you" (Gen 34:10).

*(b) Temporal* – points to an action that occurred in the past relative to the concurrent situation in the context, that is "before": שְׁנָתַיִם לִפְנֵי הָרַעַשׁ, "two years *before* the earthquake" (Amos 1:1), לִפְנֵי קָצִיר, "*before* the harvest" (Isa 18:5).

*(c) Perceptual* – expresses someone's personal view, or in-troduces events or situations that comes to one's atten-tion: מֶה־חַטָּאתִי לִפְנֵי אָבִיךָ כִּי מְבַקֵּשׁ אֶת־נַפְשִׁי, "What is my sin *against* your father that he seeks my life?" (1 Sam 20:1), וַתִּשָּׁחֵת הָאָרֶץ לִפְנֵי הָאֱלֹהִים, "The earth was corrupt *in the sight* of God" (Gen 6:11),

מִכֹּל חַטֹּאתֵיכֶם לִפְנֵי יְהוָה תִּטְהָרוּ

"You will be clean from all your sins *before* YHWH" (Lev 16:30).

**4.1.13 מִן**

*(a) Source* – One of the most common uses of מִן designates where something or someone originated: אִבְצָן מִבֵּית לָחֶם, "Ibzan *from* Bethelehem" (Judg 12:8),

וְעַתָּה קְחוּ לָכֶם שְׁנֵי עָשָׂר אִישׁ מִשִּׁבְטֵי יִשְׂרָאֵל

"Now, take for yourselves twelve men *from* the tribes of Israel" (Josh 3:12).

מִן can place emphasis not just on the point of origin but also movement *away from* that point of ori-gin, making it *ablative*: לְהוֹצִיאָם מֵאֶרֶץ מִצְרַיִם, "to bring them out *from* the land of Egypt" (Exod 12:42), וְיָצָאתִי אַחֲרָיו וְהִכִּתִיו וְהִצַּלְתִּי מִפִּיו, "I went after him and I struck him and I rescued [the lamb] *from his mouth*" (1 Sam 17:35).

*(b) Temporal* – similar to *source,* marks the beginning point of a given temporal period:

אֲנִי הִתְהַלַּכְתִּי לִפְנֵיכֶם מִנְּעֻרַי עַד־הַיּוֹם הַזֶּה

"I have walked before you *from my youth* until this day" (1 Sam 12:2), וּמָלַךְ יְהוָה עֲלֵיהֶם בְּהַר צִיּוֹן מֵעַתָּה וְעַד־עוֹלָם, "Yhwh will reign over them in Mount Zion *from now,* until eternity" (Mic 4:7),

מִן־הַיּוֹם אֲשֶׁר הוֹצֵאתִי אֶת־עַמִּי אֶת־יִשְׂרָאֵל מִמִּצְרַיִם

"*Since the day* when I brought my people Israel out of Egypt..." (1 Kgs 8:16).

*(c) Material* – identifies the material with which an action is performed, most often with verbs of formation: וַיִּיצֶר יְהוָה אֱלֹהִים אֶת־הָאָדָם עָפָר מִן־הָאֲדָמָה, "And Yhwh God formed man *from* the dust of the ground" (Gen 2:7), מַסֵּכָה מִכַּסְפָּם, "Idols made *from their silver*" (Hos 13:2).

*(d) Causal* – shows the reason or rationale behind an action: הָרִים רָעֲשׁוּ מִמֶּנּוּ, "The mountains quake *because* of him" (Nah 1:5), חָלִילָה לִּי מֵיהוָה אִם־אֶעֱשֶׂה אֶת־הַדָּבָר הַזֶּה לַאדֹנִי, "Far be it from me, *because* of Yhwh, to do this thing against my lord" (1 Sam 24:7 [Eng 24:6]), וַיַּנַּח שְׁלֹמֹה אֶת־כָּל־הַכֵּלִים מֵרֹב מְאֹד מְאֹד, "Solomon left all the vessels unweighed, *because* they were very numerous" (1 Kgs 7:47).

In showing cause, מִן can at times designate the agent of a passive verb: לֹא־יִכָּרֵת כָּל־בָּשָׂר עוֹד מִמֵּי הַמַּבּוּל, "All flesh shall never again be cut off *by the water* of a flood" (Gen 9:11).

*(e) Estimative* – expresses the opinion of one who is making an evaluation or judgment:

כִּי־כָבֵד מִמְּךָ הַדָּבָר לֹא־תוּכַל עֲשֹׂהוּ לְבַדֶּךָ

"For the task is too hard *for you*; you are not able to do it alone" (Exod 18:18),

קָטֹנְתִּי מִכֹּל הַחֲסָדִים וּמִכָּל־הָאֱמֶת אֲשֶׁר עָשִׂיתָ אֶת־עַבְדֶּךָ

"I am *unworthy of* the steadfast love and faithfulness you have shown to your servant" (Gen 32:11 [Eng 32:10]).

*(f) Partitive* – designates a part of a larger whole: יָצְאוּ מִן־הָעָם, "*Some* of the people went out..." (Exod 16:27), וַיָּמוּתוּ מֵעַבְדֵי הַמֶּלֶךְ וְגַם עַבְדְּךָ אוּרִיָּה הַחִתִּי מֵת, "*Some of the servants* of the king are dead, as well as your servant, Uriah the Hittite" (2 Sam 11:24), טוֹב־עַיִן הוּא יְבֹרָךְ כִּי־נָתַן מִלַּחְמוֹ לַדָּל, "The generous man is blessed, because he gives *some of his food* to the poor" (Prov 22:9).

*(g) Privative* – marks something missing or lacking from the object of the preposition: בָּתֵּיהֶם שָׁלוֹם מִפָּחַד, "their houses stand *without* fear" (Job 21:9), כִּי־אָז תִּשָּׂא פָנֶיךָ מִמּוּם, "Then, indeed, you could lift up your face *without* blemish" (Job 11:15), כָּל־קְצִינַיִךְ נָדְדוּ־יַחַד מִקֶּשֶׁת אֻסָּרוּ, "All your rulers have fled together, they have been captured *without* the bow" (Isa 22:3).

*(h) Comparative* – BH does not have a comparative morpheme (-*er* in English), but rather, uses מִן in comparative relationships (see section 2.5.4). Typically, the preposition is prefixed to the noun that is to be surpassed, and preceded by the adjective, although the word order is not always static, particularly in poetry: מַה־מָּתוֹק מִדְּבַשׁ, "What is *sweeter than* honey?" (Judg 14:18), עַם גָּדוֹל וָרָם מִמֶּנּוּ, "The people are *bigger* and *taller* than we are" (Deut 1:28), וַיֶּחְכַּם מִכָּל־הָאָדָם, "He was *wiser* than all people" (1 Kgs 5:11 [Eng 4:31]), אָרוּר אַתָּה מִכָּל־הַבְּהֵמָה וּמִכֹּל חַיַּת הַשָּׂדֶה, "Cursed are you *more than* all cattle, and *more than* all the beasts of the field" (Gen 3:14), טוֹבִים הַשְּׁנַיִם מִן־הָאֶחָד, "Two are *better than* one" (Eccl 4:9).

*(i) Compound* – מִן is commonly used to form compound particles with other prepositions, sometimes carrying the force of only one of the particles, but at other times carrying the combined meaning of both particles. Compare: לֹא־יָסוּר שֵׁבֶט מִיהוּדָה וּמְחֹקֵק מִבֵּין רַגְלָיו, "The scepter shall not depart from Judah, nor the ruler's staff *from between* his feet" (Gen 49:10); מִבֵּין עֳפָאיִם יִתְּנוּ־קוֹל, "They lift up voices *among* the branches" (Ps 104:12), אֵין־כָּמוֹךָ אֱלֹהִים בַּשָּׁמַיִם מִמַּעַל וְעַל־הָאָרֶץ מִתָּחַת, "There is no god like you in heaven *above*, or on the earth *below*" (1 Kgs 8:23); וְהוֹצֵאתִי אֶתְכֶם מִתַּחַת סִבְלֹת מִצְרַיִם, "I will bring you out *from under* the burdens of the Egyptians" (Exod 6:6).

## 4.1.14 מִפְּנֵי

This preposition is a compound construction, consisting of the simple preposition מִן prefixed to the substantive פָּנִים in the construct form.

*(a) Ablative* – with verbs of motion, indicates motion *away from* a position "before" or "in front of" the object of the preposition: וַתֹּאמֶר מִפְּנֵי שָׂרַי גְּבִרְתִּי אָנֹכִי בֹּרַחַת, "and she said 'I am fleeing *from* my mistress Sarah'" (Gen 16:8), וַיִּסַּע עַמּוּד הֶעָנָן מִפְּנֵיהֶם וַיַּעֲמֹד מֵאַחֲרֵיהֶם, "and the pillar of cloud moved *from in front* of them and stood behind them" (Exod 14:19), אָנֹכִי אוֹרִישֵׁם מִפְּנֵי בְּנֵי יִשְׂרָאֵל, "I will drive them out *from before* the people of Israel" (Josh 13:6).

*(b) Spatial* – marks a location "before" or "in front of" the object of the preposition: הַס מִפְּנֵי אֲדֹנָי יְהוִה, "Be silent *before* the lord, Yʜᴡʜ" (Zeph 1:7), אַל־תֵּחַת מִפְּנֵיהֶם, "Do not be dismayed *before* them" (Jer 1:17).

*(c) Causal* – denotes the cause of an action or situation: וַיָּבֹא נֹחַ וּבָנָיו וְאִשְׁתּוֹ וּנְשֵׁי־בָנָיו אִתּוֹ אֶל־הַתֵּבָה מִפְּנֵי מֵי הַמַּבּוּל, "Then Noah and his wife and the wives of his sons with him went into the ark *because* of the waters of the

flood" (Gen 7:7), וַיָּגָר מוֹאָב מִפְּנֵי הָעָם מְאֹד, "Moab was in great fear, *because* of the people" (Num 22:3), וַיָּנָס יוֹתָם וַיִּבְרַח וַיֵּלֶךְ בְּאֵרָה וַיֵּשֶׁב שָׁם מִפְּנֵי אֲבִימֶלֶךְ אָחִיו, "Then Jotham escaped and fled, and went to Beer, and remained there *because* of Abimelech, his brother" (Judg 9:21).

### 4.1.15 עַד

*(a) Locative* – marks the the extent, limit, or goal of movement ("as far as," "up to," "to"): עַד־צַוָּאר יַגִּיעַ, "it will reach *up to* the neck" (Isa 8:8), וַיָּבֹאוּ עַד־חָרָן וַיֵּשְׁבוּ שָׁם, "They went *as far as* Haran, and settled there" (Gen 11:31), וְלֹא־שַׁבְתֶּם עָדַי, "You have not returned *to me*" (Amos 4:6).

*(b) Temporal* – indicates the duration of an action: יֵצֵא אָדָם לְפָעֳלוֹ וְלַעֲבֹדָתוֹ עֲדֵי־עָרֶב, "People go out to their work and their labor *until* evening" (Ps 104:23), לֹא־בָאתֶם עַד־עָתָּה אֶל־הַמְּנוּחָה, "You have *not yet* (literally: *until now*) come upon the inheritance (Deut 12:9), עַד־מָתַי מֵאַנְתָּ לֵעָנֹת מִפָּנָי, "*How long* (literally: *until when*) will you refuse to humble yourself before me?" (Exod 10:3).

*(c) Degree* – Quite frequently, עַד is conjoined to the מְאֹד to express a large quantity of a substantive, or an extreme quality of an action or attribute: וְהַנַּעֲרָה יָפָה עַד־מְאֹד, "The girl was *very* beautiful" (1 Kgs 1:4), וַתְּהִי הַמִּלְחָמָה קָשָׁה עַד־מְאֹד בַּיּוֹם הַהוּא, "The battle was *very* fierce on that day" (2 Sam 2:17), אַל־תִּקְצֹף יְהוָה עַד־מְאֹד, "Do not be *exceedingly* angry, O YHWH" (Isa 64:8 [Eng 64:9]).

### 4.1.16 עַל

*(a) Spatial/locative* – עַל shows a variety of spatial/locative uses:

(a.1) *Vertical relationship* – indicates a location "over" or "upon" an object: רוּחַ אֱלֹהִים מְרַחֶפֶת עַל־פְּנֵי הַמָּיִם, "the spirit of God was hovering *over* the surface of the water" (Gen 1:2), הַשֶּׁמֶשׁ יָצָא עַל־הָאָרֶץ וְלוֹט בָּא צֹעֲרָה, "The sun had risen *over* the earth, when Lot came to Zoar" (Gen 19:23), וַיֵּט אַהֲרֹן אֶת־יָדוֹ עַל מֵימֵי מִצְרַיִם, "Aaron held out his arms *over* the waters of Egypt" (Exod 8:2), כַּאֲשֶׁר הָיִיתִי בִּימֵי חָרְפִּי בְּסוֹד אֱלוֹהַּ עֲלֵי אָהֳלִי, "When I was in the prime of my days, my God was *over* my tent" (Job 29:4).

With some verbs of motion, עַל can take on a *terminative* sense, expressing the end goal of vertical motion: וַיֵּרֶד הָעַיִט עַל־הַפְּגָרִים, "the bird of prey came down *upon* the carcasses" (Gen 15:11),

וַיִּשָּׂא בִלְעָם אֶת־עֵינָיו וַיַּרְא אֶת־יִשְׂרָאֵל שֹׁכֵן לִשְׁבָטָיו וַתְּהִי עָלָיו רוּחַ אֱלֹהִים

"Baalam lifted his eyes and he saw Israel camping tribe by tribe. And the spirit of God came *upon him*" (Num 24:2).

(a.2) *Horizontal relationship* – indicates a location "at" or "beside": וַיִּבֶן עַל־קִיר הַבַּיִת, "He built *against* the walls of the house..." (1 Kgs 6:5),

וַיֹּאמֶר יְהוָה אֶל־מֹשֶׁה וְאֶל־אַהֲרֹן בְּהֹר הָהָר עַל־גְּבוּל אֶרֶץ־אֱדוֹם

"Then Yʜwʜ spoke to Moses and to Aaron at Mount Hor, *at the border* of the land of Edom" (Num 20:23), חוֹמָה הָיוּ עָלֵינוּ, "They were a wall *around* us" (1 Sam 25:16).

**(b) Duty** – The preposition can mark a burden or duty that impinges on a person: עָלַי לָתֶת לְךָ עֲשָׂרָה כָסֶף, "I would *have had [literally: it would have been upon me]* to give you ten [pieces] of silver" (2 Sam 18:11), שָׁלוֹם לָךְ רַק כָּל־מַחְסוֹרְךָ עָלָי, "Peace to you; only, let me take care of your needs [literally: all your needs are *upon me*]" (Judg 19:20), זִבְחֵי שְׁלָמִים עָלָי, "*I had to make* sacrifices of well-being" (Prov 7:14).

*(c) Rank* – indicates a person's rank, or responsibility over another: יוֹאָב בֶּן־צְרוּיָה עַל־הַצָּבָא, "Joab, son of Zeruiah, was *over* the army" (2 Sam 8:16),

הַגֵּר אֲשֶׁר בְּקִרְבְּךָ יַעֲלֶה עָלֶיךָ מַעְלָה מָּעְלָה

"The alien in your midst shall rise *above you*, higher and higher" (Deut 28:43), אֲדֹנָי אָתָּה טוֹבָתִי בַּל־עָלֶיךָ, "You are my lord; I have no good greater than you" (Ps 16:2).

*(d) Causal* – expresses the *cause* of an action or situation: הִנְּךָ מֵת עַל־הָאִשָּׁה, "You will certainly die *because* of this woman" (Gen 20:3),

וַיִּקְרָא שֵׁם הַמָּקוֹם מַסָּה וּמְרִיבָה עַל־רִיב בְּנֵי יִשְׂרָאֵל

"He called the name of the place Massah and Meribah *because* of the quarrel of the people of Israel" (Exod 17:7), כִּי־עָלֶיךָ הֹרַגְנוּ כָל־הַיּוֹם, "*Because of you*, we are being killed all day long" (Ps 44:23 [Eng 44:22]), כִּי־בְזַעַף עִמּוֹ עַל־זֹאת, "... for he was angry with him *because* of this" (2 Chr 16:10).

The *causal* use of עַל is frequent when conjoined with the particle כֵּן:

הֵילִילוּ כִּי קָרוֹב יוֹם יְהוָה כְּשֹׁד מִשַּׁדַּי יָבוֹא עַל־כֵּן כָּל־יָדַיִם תִּרְפֶּינָה

"Wail, for the day of Yʜwʜ is near. It will come as destruction from the Almighty. *Therefore*, all hands will fall limp" (Isa 13:6–7 [Eng 13:6]), עַל־כֵּן יַעֲזָב־אִישׁ אֶת־אָבִיו וְאֶת־אִמּוֹ, "*For this reason*, a man will leave his father and his mother" (Gen 2:24).

*(e) Manner* – behavior or action *according to* a standard: נִשְׁבַּע יְהוָה וְלֹא יִנָּחֵם אַתָּה־כֹהֵן לְעוֹלָם עַל־דִּבְרָתִי מַלְכִּי־צֶדֶק, "Yʜwʜ has sworn, and he will not change his mind. 'You are a priest forever, *according* to the order of Melchizedek'" (Ps 110:4), הוֹצִיאוּ אֶת־בְּנֵי יִשְׂרָאֵל מֵאֶרֶץ מִצְרַיִם עַל־צִבְאֹתָם, "Bring out the people of Israel from the land of Egypt

*according* to their hosts" (Exod 6:26),

עַל־כֵּן קָרְאוּ לַיָּמִים הָאֵלֶּה פוּרִים עַל־שֵׁם הַפּוּר

"Therefore, they called these days Purim, *according* to the name of Pur" (Esth 9:26).

*(f) Adversative* – shows action directed *against* another: וְאִם־לֹא תַשְׁלִים עִמָּךְ וְעָשְׂתָה עִמְּךָ מִלְחָמָה וְצַרְתָּ עָלֶיהָ, "But if it does not make peace with you, and makes war against you, then you shall make siege *against* it" (Deut 20:12), וַיִּקְשֹׁר עָלָיו בַּעְשָׁא בֶן־אֲחִיָּה לְבֵית יִשָּׂשכָר, "Then Baasha, the son of Ahijah of the house of Issachar, conspired *against* him" (1 Kgs 15:27),

וַיֵּלֶךְ אֶת־יְהוֹרָם בֶּן־אַחְאָב מֶלֶךְ יִשְׂרָאֵל לַמִּלְחָמָה עַל־חֲזָאֵל מֶלֶךְ־אֲרָם

"He went with Jehoram, son of Ahab, king of Israel, to fight *against* Hazael, king of Aram" (2 Chr 22:5).

Adversative עַל also shows that an action can occur, despite circumstances that make it seem unlikely to the speakers: וְעַתָּה יֵשׁ־מִקְוֶה לְיִשְׂרָאֵל עַל־זֹאת, "Yet now, there is hope for Israel, *in spite* of this" (Ezra 10:2), כִּי עַל־כָּל־אֵלֶּה וַתֹּאמְרִי כִּי נִקֵּיתִי, "Yet *in spite* of all these things, you said 'I am innocent.'" (Jer 2:34–35).

*(g) Accompaniment* – denotes circumstances that occur with another: לֹא שָׁתָם עַל־צֹאן לָבָן, "he did not set them *with* the flock of Laban" (Gen 30:40), לֹא־תִשְׁחַט עַל־חָמֵץ דַּם־זִבְחִי, "You shall not offer the blood of my sacrifice *with* leavened bread" (Exod 34:25), וְאֶת־מַלְכֵי מִדְיָן הָרְגוּ עַל־חַלְלֵיהֶם, "They killed the kings of Midian, *along with* the rest of their slain" (Num 31:8).

Similarly, עַל can express a sense of *addition*: שֶׁבֶר עַל־שֶׁבֶר נִקְרָא, "Disaster *upon* disaster is proclaimed" (Jer 4:20).

**(h) Interest** – עַל with verbs of thinking, feeling, or emotions marks the object of interest: יָגִיל עָלַיִךְ בְּרִנָּה, "he will rejoice *over* you with shouts of joy!" (Zeph 3:17), וָאַגִּיד לָהֶם אֶת־יַד אֱלֹהַי אֲשֶׁר־הִיא טוֹבָה עָלַי, "I told them of how the hand of my God had been gracious *upon me*" (Neh 2:18).

**(i) Emotive** – functions to highlight or emphasize the subject of the emotion, as well as the expression of emotion: בְּהִתְעַטֵּף עָלַי נַפְשִׁי אֶת־יְהוָה זָכָרְתִּי, "When my life was *ebbing away* (literally: in feebleness *upon me*), I remembered YHWH" (Jonah 2:8 [Eng 2:7]), נֶהְפַּךְ עָלַי לִבִּי, "My heart is turned *over* within me" (Hos 11:8).

## 4.1.17 עִם

**(a) Accompaniment** – This preposition expresses additional participants in the discourse through a sense of *accompaniment*:[17] וַיֹּאכְלוּ וַיִּשְׁתּוּ הוּא וְהָאֲנָשִׁים אֲשֶׁר־עִמּוֹ, "Then he and the men who were *with* him ate and drank" (Gen 24:54), עַתָּה שְׁמַע בְּקֹלִי אִיעָצְךָ וִיהִי אֱלֹהִים עִמָּךְ, "Now, listen to my voice, I will give you counsel, and may God be *with* you" (Exod 18:19).

Similarly, עִם expresses a sense of *addition*:

עִם־עָרֵיהֶם הֶחֱרִימָם יְהוֹשֻׁעַ

"Joshua exterminated them *along with* their cities" (Josh 11:21), הַאַף תִּסְפֶּה צַדִּיק עִם־רָשָׁע, "Will you indeed sweep away the righteous *along with* the wicked?" (Gen 18:23).

**(b) Personal complement** – resembles a datival function, to mark the recipient of an action: וַעֲשֵׂה־חֶסֶד עִם אֲדֹנִי אַבְרָהָם,

---

[17] BDB notes that the comitative/accompaniment sense of אֵת is much more intimate and expresses closer association than the comitative sense of עִם (37).

"And show kindness _to_ my master Abraham" (Gen 24:12),
וְלֹא אִם־עוֹדֶנִּי חָי וְלֹא־תַעֲשֶׂה עִמָּדִי חֶסֶד יְהוָה וְלֹא אָמוּת, "If I
am still alive, will you show _to me_ the faithfulness of Yhwh,
that I may not die?" (1 Sam 20:14),

הִנֵּה אָנֹכִי בָּא אֵלֶיךָ בְּעַב הֶעָנָן בַּעֲבוּר יִשְׁמַע הָעָם בְּדַבְּרִי עִמָּךְ

"Behold, I will come to you in a pillar of cloud, so that the
people will hear when I speak _with_ you" (Exod 19:9).

Similarly, this preposition may indicate dealings
or relationships with another: תָּמִים תִּהְיֶה עִם יְהוָה אֱלֹהֶיךָ,
"Be blameless _before_ Yhwh, your god" (Deut 18:13),
וְהָיָה לְבַבְכֶם שָׁלֵם עִם יְהוָה אֱלֹהֵינוּ, "Let your hearts be wholly
devoted _to_ Yhwh, our god" (1 Kgs 8:61).

**_(c) Locative_** – marks a locality or position:

וַיֵּשֶׁב יִצְחָק עִם־בְּאֵר לַחַי רֹאִי

"and Isaac lived _near_ Beer-lahai-roi" (Gen 25:11),
וַיִּשְׁלַח יְהוֹשֻׁעַ אֲנָשִׁים מִירִיחוֹ הָעַי אֲשֶׁר עִם־בֵּית אָוֶן, "Joshua sent
out men from Jericho to Ai, which is _near_ Beth-Aven"
(Josh 7:2), הֵמָּה עִם־בֵּית מִיכָה, "[When] they were _near_ the
house of Micah" (Judg 18:3).

**_(d) Restrictive_** – presents an exception to a circumstance
or action: רְאוּ עַתָּה כִּי אֲנִי אֲנִי הוּא וְאֵין אֱלֹהִים עִמָּדִי, "See now
that I, I am he, and there is no god _besides_ me" (Deut 32:39),
מִי־לִי בַשָּׁמָיִם וְעִמְּךָ לֹא־חָפַצְתִּי בָאָרֶץ, "Whom do I have in
heaven _but you_, and I desire nothing else on earth"
(Ps 73:25), יְהוָה אֵין־עִמְּךָ לַעְזוֹר, "O Yhwh, there is no one
besides you to help" (2 Chr 14:10 [Eng 14:11]).

## 4.1.18 תַּחַת

**_(a) Vertical relationship_** – This preposition locates an object
"under" another: יִהְיוּ אֵפֶר תַּחַת כַּפּוֹת רַגְלֵיכֶם, "they will be

ashes _under_ the soles of your feet" (Mal 3:21 [Eng 4:3]),
יֻקַּח־נָא מְעַט־מַיִם וְרַחֲצוּ רַגְלֵיכֶם וְהִשָּׁעֲנוּ תַּחַת הָעֵץ, "Let a little
water be brought and wash your feet, and rest yourselves
_under_ the tree" (Gen 18:4), וְהִיא יוֹשֶׁבֶת תַּחַת־תֹּמֶר דְּבוֹרָה,
"She used to sit _under_ the oak of Deborah" (Judg 4:5),
זֶה רָע בְּכֹל אֲשֶׁר־נַעֲשָׂה תַּחַת הַשָּׁמֶשׁ, "This is an evil in all that
is done _under_ the sun" (Eccl 9:3).

*(b) Static position* – The locative תַּחַת can also express
a *static position* of "on the spot," or "in that place":
וְעָמַדְנוּ תַחְתֵּינוּ וְלֹא נַעֲלֶה אֲלֵיהֶם, "We will stand _in our place,_
and we will not go up to them" (1 Sam 14:9), שְׁבוּ אִישׁ תַּחְתָּיו,
"Remain, every person, _in their place_" (Exod 16:29),
לֹא־רָאוּ אִישׁ אֶת־אָחִיו וְלֹא־קָמוּ אִישׁ מִתַּחְתָּיו שְׁלֹשֶׁת יָמִים, "They
could not see one another, and they did not rise _from their
place_ for three days" (Exod 10:23).

*(c) Metaphorical* – expresses *subordination* or *obedience* to the
influence of another: וַתִּכָּנַע מוֹאָב בַּיּוֹם הַהוּא תַּחַת יַד יִשְׂרָאֵל,
"On that day, Moab was subdued _under_ the hand
of Israel" (Judg 3:30), תַּחַת אָוֶן רָאִיתִי אָהֳלֵי כוּשָׁן, "I
saw the tents of Cushan _under_ distress" (Hab 3:7),
אִם־לֹא שָׁכַב אִישׁ אֹתָךְ וְאִם־לֹא שָׂטִית טֻמְאָה תַּחַת אִישֵׁךְ, "If no
man has lain with you, and if you have turned to unclean-
ness _under the authority_ [literally: _under_] your husband..."
(Num 5:19).

*(d) Substitution* – A common secondary use of תַּחַת is to
show *substitution,* that is, "instead of" or "in the place
of": שָׁת־לִי אֱלֹהִים זֶרַע אַחֵר תַּחַת הֶבֶל, "God has appointed
to me another offspring _in place of_ Abel" (Gen 4:25),
וַיַּמְלֵךְ פַּרְעֹה נְכֹה אֶת־אֶלְיָקִים בֶּן־יֹאשִׁיָּהוּ תַּחַת יֹאשִׁיָּהוּ אָבִיו,
"Pharaoh Neco made Eliakim, son of Josiah,
king _in place of_ Josiah, his father" (2 Kgs 23:34),
וַיֵּשֶׁב שְׁלֹמֹה עַל־כִּסֵּא יְהוָה לְמֶלֶךְ תַּחַת־דָּוִיד אָבִיו, "Then
Solomon sat on the throne of YHWH, as king, _in place of_
David his father" (1 Chr 29:23).

## 4.2 Adverbs

The adverb in any language is typically the most complicated and least understood of the traditional parts of speech. It is elusive due to its wide range of functions, modifying a single word or an entire clause, as well as because an adverb can be classified as other parts of speech. In BH, both levels of complexity are present in the adverbs. Many, if not most, of the adverbs in BH can function as conjunctions or prepositions. To complicate matters, adverbial function is not limited to the adverbs in BH; it can be performed by accusatives (section 2.3.2), by infinitives absolute (section 3.4.2,b and c), and by certain verb plus verb constructions (see section 4.3.3,g on hendiadys).[18] BH adverbs have two major divisions: Those that modify clauses or words in a way that is related to the discourse are the *clausal/item* adverbs.[19] Those that specify the time, place, or manner of the predicated situation are called the *constituent* adverbs. There are some adverbs that are classified in both groups; thus, the distinction seems to lie in syntax, not morphology.

The following are the most common adverbs and their uses.[20]

### 4.2.1 אָז / אָזַי

(a) *Temporal* – Typically rendered "then," this adverb[21] functions to indicate a subsequent action within the

---

[18] Waltke and O'Connor 1990, 656. The authors note that the verbs שׁוּב and יָסַף are paired with other verbs to indicate a repetition or continuation of action.

[19] Item adverbs, which modify single words, are quite rare in BH. Because they serve a function similar to the clausal adverbs, they should be considered together. See Waltke and O'Connor 1990, 656; van der Merwe, Naudé, and Kroeze 1999, 58 and 305–20.

[20] Kautzsch 1910, 483–84; Waltke and O'Connor 1990, 655–73; van der Merwe, Naudé, and Kroeze 1999, 305–20; Williams 1976, 63–66; Bauer and Leander 1991, 630–34; Joüon and Muraoka 1993, 329–36. See also BDB, *HALOT,* and *DCH.*

[21] אָזַי is the poetic form of the adverb.

וַיַּאֲמִינוּ בַּיהוָה וּבְמֹשֶׁה עַבְדּוֹ אָז יָשִׁיר־מֹשֶׁה וּבְנֵי יִשְׂרָאֵל, discourse:
"Then they believed in Yʜwʜ and in Moses, his servant. *Then* Moses and the people of Israel sang" (Exod 14:31–15:1),

וּלְשֵׁת גַּם־הוּא יֻלַּד־בֵּן וַיִּקְרָא אֶת־שְׁמוֹ אֱנוֹשׁ אָז הוּחַל לִקְרֹא בְּשֵׁם יְהוָה

"To Seth, to him also, was born a son, and he called his name Enosh. *Then* people began to call on the name of Yʜwʜ" (Gen 4:26),

אָבִיךָ חֲלוֹא אָכַל וְשָׁתָה וְעָשָׂה מִשְׁפָּט וּצְדָקָה אָז טוֹב לוֹ

"Did your father not eat and drink, and do justice and righteousness? *Then* it was well with him" (Jer 22:15).

**(b) Logical** – often marks a logical turn in the flow of the discourse: יָשַׁנְתִּי אָז יָנוּחַ לִי, "I would have slept, *and* [*as a result*] I would have been at rest" (Job 3:13),

לֹא־יָמוּשׁ סֵפֶר הַתּוֹרָה הַזֶּה מִפִּיךָ וְהָגִיתָ בּוֹ יוֹמָם וָלַיְלָה לְמַעַן תִּשְׁמֹר לַעֲשׂוֹת כְּכָל־הַכָּתוּב בּוֹ כִּי־אָז תַּצְלִיחַ אֶת־דְּרָכֶךָ וְאָז תַּשְׂכִּיל

"This book of the law shall not depart from your mouth, but you shall meditate upon it day and night, so that you may be careful to do all that is written in it. *For then* you shall make your way prosperous, and *then* you shall succeed" (Josh 1:8),

וְלֹא־יָסַף עוֹד מַלְאַךְ יְהוָה לְהֵרָאֹה אֶל־מָנוֹחַ וְאֶל־אִשְׁתּוֹ אָז יָדַע מָנוֹחַ כִּי־מַלְאַךְ יְהוָה הוּא

"The messenger of Yʜwʜ did not appear again to Manoah and his wife; *then* Manoah knew that it was the messenger of Yʜwʜ" (Judg 13:21).

**(c) Condition** – can also introduce the apodosis of a conditional statement, and often implies the fulfillment of that condition:

אִם־תְּבַקְשֶׁנָּה כַכָּסֶף וְכַמַּטְמוֹנִים תַּחְפְּשֶׂנָּה אָז תָּבִין יִרְאַת יְהוָה
וְדַעַת אֱלֹהִים תִּמְצָא

"If you seek her as silver, and search for her as hidden treasure, *then* you will understand the fear of YHWH and you will find the knowledge of God" (Prov 2:4–5), אַחֲלֵי אֲדֹנִי לִפְנֵי הַנָּבִיא אֲשֶׁר בְּשֹׁמְרוֹן אָז יֶאֱסֹף אֹתוֹ מִצָּרַעְתּוֹ, "Ah that my lord were before the prophet that is in Samaria, *then* he would cure him of his leprosy" (2 Kgs 5:3), לוּלֵי תוֹרָתְךָ שַׁעֲשֻׁעָי אָז אָבַדְתִּי בְעָנְיִי, "If your law had not been my delight, *then* I would have perished in my affliction" (Ps 119:92).

## 4.2.2 אַךְ

*(a) Restrictive* – often functions to establish a clarification of or mild contrast with ideas preceding in the discourse. It is a restriction or limitation, however, and not a strong disjunction because there is not a complete reversal of what has preceded. Rather, there is a limitation placed on the previous clause(s):

כָּל־פֶּטֶר רֶחֶם לְכָל־בָּשָׂר אֲשֶׁר־יַקְרִיבוּ לַיהוָה בָּאָדָם וּבַבְּהֵמָה
יִהְיֶה־לָּךְ אַךְ פָּדֹה תִפְדֶּה אֵת בְּכוֹר הָאָדָם

"Every first issue of the womb of all flesh, which they offer to YHWH, whether man or animal, shall be yours. *Nevertheless* the firstborn of man you shall redeem." (Num 18:15), וַיִּשָּׁאֶר אַךְ־נֹחַ וַאֲשֶׁר אִתּוֹ בַּתֵּבָה, "*Only* Noah, and those who were with him in the ark, [were] left" (Gen 7:23),

אַל־תִּירָאוּ אַתֶּם עֲשִׂיתֶם אֵת כָּל־הָרָעָה הַזֹּאת אַךְ אַל־תָּסוּרוּ
מֵאַחֲרֵי יְהוָה

"Do not fear. You have committed all this evil; *yet* do not turn from serving YHWH" (1 Sam 12:20).

*(b) Asseverative* – Often rendered "surely," אַךְ introduces a statement or expression of truth, or highlights an

unexpected truth, quite often in speech or colloquial language, by expressing a conviction as to its correctness:[22] אַךְ נֶגֶד יְהוָה מְשִׁיחוֹ, "*Surely* before YHWH is his anointed" (1 Sam 16:6), אַךְ מֶלֶךְ־יִשְׂרָאֵל הוּא, "*Surely* it is the king of Israel" (1 Kgs 22:32), אַךְ עַצְמִי וּבְשָׂרִי אָתָּה, "*Surely* you are my bone and my flesh" (Gen 29:14).

### 4.2.3  אַל

While translated much like לֹא ("not"), אַל may be found in specific constructions.

*(a) Prohibition* – typically negates imperatival forms to denote a *specific* or *immediate prohibition*: אַל־תִּשְׂמַח יִשְׂרָאֵל, "*Do not rejoice*, O Israel" (Hos 9:1), נָקִי וְצַדִּיק אַל־תַּהֲרֹג, "*Do not kill* the innocent and the righteous" (Exod 23:7), הֲלוֹא צִוִּיתִיךָ חֲזַק וֶאֱמָץ אַל־תַּעֲרֹץ וְאַל־תֵּחָת, "Have I not commanded you? Be strong and courageous! *Do not tremble*, and *do not be dismayed*" (Josh 1:9).

*(b) Negative volition* – As the negation of the modals jussive and cohortative, אַל expresses their same nuances negatively, usually in the form of a negative wish or negative prayer: אַל־יִמְשְׁלוּ־בִי, "*Do not let them* rule over me" (Ps 19:14), אַל־נָא תְהִי מְרִיבָה בֵּינִי וּבֵינֶיךָ, "*Let there be no strife* between me and you" (Gen 13:8), אַל־יֵצֵא אִישׁ מִמְּקֹמוֹ בַּיּוֹם הַשְּׁבִיעִי, "*Let no one go out* from their place on the seventh day" (Exod 16:29).

### 4.2.4  אַף

The first of two major coordinating adverbs (גַּם being the second), אַף[23] is closer to the simple וְ conjunction, and

---

[22] Waltke and O'Connor 1990, 670.
[23] Generally more common in poetry and later prose, while גַּם is more common to prose.

may at times be translated simply "and." In general, it also associates its clause (i.e., one that follows it) with a preceding clause (Waltke and O'Connor 1991, 663).

*(a) Addition* – indicates that an entity is added to another: אַף־אֲנִי בַּחֲלוֹמִי, "I *also* had a dream [literally: *also* I in my dream]" (Gen 40:16),

וְזָכַרְתִּי אֶת־בְּרִיתִי יַעֲקוֹב וְאַף אֶת־בְּרִיתִי יִצְחָק וְאַף אֶת־בְּרִיתִי
אַבְרָהָם אֶזְכֹּר

"Then I will remember my covenant with Jacob; I will remember *also* my covenant with Isaac and *also* my covenant with Abraham" (Lev 26:42), לְךָ יוֹם אַף־לְךָ לָיְלָה, "Yours is the day, yours *also* the night (Ps 74:16).

When the entity added is unexpected, אַף may be translated "even" and is sometimes said to be an *emphatic* use of the particle, although the concept of emphasis is too broad to be of much use:[24] וְיִסַּרְתִּי אֶתְכֶם אַף־אָנִי, "I, *even* I, will punish you myself" (Lev 26:28). Such a use may occur in questions: הַאַף אָמְנָם אֵלֵד וַאֲנִי זָקַנְתִּי, "Shall I indeed *even* bear a child, now that I am old?" (Gen 18:13).

*(b) Asseverative*[25] – Especially in poetry, אַף introduces a statement or expression of truth and expresses a conviction as to its correctness: אַף־נַחֲלָת שָׁפְרָה עָלָי, "*Surely* my heritage is beautiful to me" (Ps 16:6), אַף מִן־קָמַי תְּרוֹמְמֵנִי, "*Indeed* you exalted me above my adversaries" (Ps 18:49 [Eng 18:48]).

*(c) Rhetorical* – A variation of the *asseverative*, this particle is often combined with כִּי to express a comparative assertion in which two clauses are related, the second one bearing persuasive force: זֶבַח רְשָׁעִים תּוֹעֵבָה אַף כִּי־בְזִמָּה יְבִיאֶנּוּ, "the

---

[24] Joüon and Muraoka 1993, 618.

[25] The asseverative/emphatic use of אַף, as well as גַּם (4.2.5), may not be original to either particle, but a nuance of their primary use as particles denoting addition (Muraoka 1985, 142–43).

sacrifice of the wicked is an abomination; *how much more* when he brings it with evil intent" (Prov 21:27). This may also be expressed negatively (i.e., with a negated first clause):

הִנֵּה הַשָּׁמַיִם וּשְׁמֵי הַשָּׁמַיִם לֹא יְכַלְכְּלוּךָ אַף כִּי־הַבַּיִת הַזֶּה אֲשֶׁר בָּנִיתִי

"Even heaven and the highest heavens cannot contain you; *how much less* this house that I have built!" (1 Kgs 8:27).

This *rhetorical* use of אַף כִּי may actually introduce a *rhetorical question,* in which the assertion of the clause is confirmed in light of the preceding clause:

הִנֵּה אֲנַחְנוּ פֹה בִיהוּדָה יְרֵאִים וְאַף כִּי־נֵלֵךְ קְעִלָה אֶל־מַעַרְכוֹת פְּלִשְׁתִּים

"Look, we are afraid here in Judah; *how much more* then if we go to Keilah against the armies of the Philistines?" (1 Sam 23:3), אַף כִּי־נִתְעָב וְנֶאֱלָח אִישׁ־שֹׁתֶה כַמַּיִם עַוְלָה, "*What then* of one loathsome and foul, a person who drinks wrongdoing like water?" (Job 15:16).

### 4.2.5 גַּם

The second of two major coordinating adverbs (אַף being the first), גַּם has quite similar uses, although it is much more common in prose, while אַף is more common in poetry. In general, גַּם may modify either a word or clause, in which case it also associates its clause (i.e., one that follows it) with a preceding clause.

*(a) Addition* – often used to point out an additional participant or party within the discourse: וַתִּתֵּן גַּם־לְאִישָׁהּ עִמָּהּ, "and she gave *also* to her husband with her" (Gen 3:6). When the additional event or statement is unexpected or illogical, "even" may be the best translation: וַיִּפֶן פַּרְעֹה וַיָּבֹא אֶל־בֵּיתוֹ וְלֹא־שָׁת לִבּוֹ גַּם־לָזֹאת, "Then Pharaoh turned and went into his house, and he did not take *even* this to heart" (Exod 7:23),

אֵין עֹשֵׂה־טוֹב אֵין גַּם־אֶחָד, "there is no one who does good, not _even_ one" (Ps 14:3).

This usage is not uncommon with an independent personal pronoun following immediately after the particle: גַּם־אַתָּה לֹא־תָבֹא שָׁם, "_even_ you shall not enter there" (Deut 1:37), גַּם־אַתָּה חֻלֵּיתָ כָמוֹנוּ, "you _also_ have become as weak as we" (Isa 14:10). This use of גַּם is a means of focusing on the pronoun's antecedent within the specific clause marked by the particle (van der Merwe, Naudé, and Kroeze 1999, 314, and 311–18 on גַּם and אַף as "focus particles").

The use of גַּם as a "double conjunction" is a variation on the _addition_ use, and typically denotes the inclusion of _both_ entities preceded by the particle:[26] וַיַּעַל עִמּוֹ גַּם־רֶכֶב גַּם־פָּרָשִׁים, "_both_ chariots _as well as_ charioteers went up with him" (Gen 50:9), גַּם־תֶּבֶן גַּם־מִסְפּוֹא רַב עִמָּנוּ, "we have plenty of _both_ straw _and_ fodder" (Gen 24:25).

_(b) Asseverative_ – adds emphasis or certainty to an idea: וְהָיָה אִם־לֹא יַאֲמִינוּ גַּם לִשְׁנֵי הָאֹתוֹת הָאֵלֶּה, "But, if they will not believe _even_ these two signs" (Exod 4:9), גַּם בֵּין הָעֳמָרִים תְּלַקֵּט וְלֹא תַכְלִימוּהָ, "Let her glean _even_ among the sheaves and do not insult her" (Ruth 2:15).

When found at the end of a speech or exposition, or at the end of lists, גַּם may be _climactic_: גַּם־בְּרוֹשִׁים שָׂמְחוּ לְךָ, "_even_ the cypress trees exult over you" (Isa 14:8), לְכוּ עִבְדוּ אֶת־יְהוָה רַק צֹאנְכֶם וּבְקַרְכֶם יֻצָּג גַּם־טַפְּכֶם יֵלֵךְ עִמָּכֶם, "Go, serve YHWH, only let your flocks and herds be detained; _even_ your little ones may go with you" (Exod 10:24).

_(c) Concessive_ – indicates that an action that is or was expected to lead to another action will not, or leads to an unexpected action: בְּחָנוּנִי גַּם־רָאוּ פָעֳלִי, "they tested me, _even though_ they saw my works" (Ps 95:9), הֹבִישׁוּ כִּי תוֹעֵבָה עָשׂוּ גַּם־בּוֹשׁ לֹא־יֵבֹשׁוּ, "They acted

---

[26] See van der Merwe, Naudé, and Kroeze 1999, 239 and 314–15, and especially point 5.2(ii) on page 316.

shamefully. They committed abomination. *Yet* they were
not at all shamed" (Jer 8:12).

### 4.2.6 הַרְבֵּה

***Degree*** – As an adverb, הַרְבֵּה[27] expresses a great, abundant,
or extreme degree of action, and is often used with מְאֹד[28]
הִנֵּה הִסְכַּלְתִּי וָאֶשְׁגֶּה הַרְבֵּה מְאֹד, "Yes, I have been foolish, and
have erred *very greatly*" (1 Sam 26:21), וָאִירָא הַרְבֵּה מְאֹד,
"Then I was *very much* afraid" (Neh 2:2).

The particle also functions *adjectivally*, to indicate a
large amount of a substantive: וְגַם־הַרְבֵּה נָפַל מִן־הָעָם וַיָּמֻתוּ,
"Also, *many* of the people fell and they died" (2 Sam 1:4),
אַל־תִּירָא אַבְרָם אָנֹכִי מָגֵן לָךְ שְׂכָרְךָ הַרְבֵּה מְאֹד, "Do not fear,
Abram, I am a shield to you. Your reward shall be *very great*"
(Gen 15:1).

### 4.2.7 יוֹמָם

***Temporal locative*** – This adverb[29] functions to designate a
general point in time, "by day" or "daytime," when an action
takes place: וַעֲנַן יְהוָה עֲלֵיהֶם יוֹמָם, "the cloud of YHWH was
over them *by day*" (Num 10:34),

וַיְהִי כַּאֲשֶׁר יָרֵא אֶת־בֵּית אָבִיו וְאֶת־אַנְשֵׁי הָעִיר מֵעֲשׂוֹת יוֹמָם וַיַּעַשׂ
לָיְלָה

"Because he was too afraid of his father's house and of the
men of the city to do it *by day*, he did it at night" (Judg 6:27),

---

[27] This adverb illustrates the complexity of Hebrew adverbs generally, since
it is in form a Hiphil infinitive absolute. Along with the adverbial function,
the infinitive also functions as an adjective, as well as a substantive.

[28] *HALOT* 1:255.

[29] The frequentative or repetitive use of the יוֹמָם is noted in BDB (401) and
Seow (44). BDB notes that the repetitive use of this adverb is most often
found in poetry, and within a merism, where it is paired with לָיְלָה. It may
be, however, that the repetitive force comes not from the adverb alone,
but is expressed by the merism instead. For more on merisms in BH, see
Krašovec (1977 and 1983).

וְהוֹצֵאתָ כֵלֶיךָ כִּכְלֵי גוֹלָה יוֹמָם לְעֵינֵיהֶם, "Bring your baggage out *during the day* in their sight, like baggage for exile" (Ezek 12:4).

### 4.2.8 כֹּה

*(a) Manner* – indicates that an action takes place or took place in a certain manner, and often takes "thus" in translation. With verbs of speech, this use often introduces the content of speech: כֹּה תֹאמַר לִבְנֵי יִשְׂרָאֵל, "*thus* you shall say to the children of Israel" (Exod 3:14), לָמָּה תַעֲשֶׂה כֹה לַעֲבָדֶיךָ, "Why do you deal *this way* [*thusly*] with your servants" (Exod 5:15),

וַיָּסֹבּוּ אֶת־הָעִיר בַּיּוֹם הַשֵּׁנִי פַּעַם אַחַת וַיָּשֻׁבוּ הַמַּחֲנֶה כֹּה עָשׂוּ שֵׁשֶׁת יָמִים

"On the second day, they surrounded the city once and returned to camp. They did *thusly* for six days" (Josh 6:14).

*(b) Demonstrative/locative* – points demonstratively to the place of action or discourse: שִׂים כֹּה נֶגֶד אַחָי, "Set it *here* before my brothers" (Gen 31:37), הִתְיַצֵּב כֹּה עַל־עֹלָתֶךָ, "Stand *here*, by your burnt offering" (Num 23:15), וַיֹּאמֶר הַמֶּלֶךְ סֹב הִתְיַצֵּב כֹּה וַיִּסֹּב וַיַּעֲמֹד, "The king said 'Turn around and stand *here*.' So he turned around and stood still" (2 Sam 18:30).

Rarely, this locative sense refers to a temporal period: וְהִנֵּה לֹא־שָׁמַעְתָּ עַד־כֹּה, "Indeed, you have not listened until *now*" (Exod 7:16).

### 4.2.9 כִּי

The particle כִּי has a tremendous variety of uses, several of which have adverbial force, which are detailed under "Conjunctions" (see section 4.3.4).[30]

---

[30] *DCH* 4:383–91

**4.2.10** כֵּן

*(a) Comparative* – typically used in the apodosis of a comparison: כְּעֵינֵי שְׁפָחָה אֶל־יַד גְּבִרְתָּהּ כֵּן עֵינֵינוּ אֶל־יְהוָה, "As the eyes of a maid to the hand of her mistress, *so* our eyes look to Yʜwʜ" (Ps 123:2), וַיְהִי כַּאֲשֶׁר פָּתַר־לָנוּ כֵּן הָיָה, "As he interpreted to us, *so* it turned out" (Gen 41:13).

In variation of this use, כֵּן appears in a clause that is not a comparative apodosis, but nevertheless has a comparative force (hence, *manner*): כֵּן יֹאבְדוּ כָל־אוֹיְבֶיךָ יְהוָה "*Thus* perish all your enemies, O Yʜwʜ" (Judg 5:31), וְהָיוּ לִמְאוֹרֹת בִּרְקִיעַ הַשָּׁמַיִם לְהָאִיר עַל־הָאָרֶץ וַיְהִי־כֵן, "'and let them be for lights in the expanse of heaven to give light onto the earth.' And it was *so*" (Gen 1:15).

*(b) Compound forms of* כֵּן – The compound form לָכֵן typically indicates a response to a statement of conditions ("the foregoing being the case, therefore...")[31] וְאֵת פֹּעַל יְהוָה לֹא יַבִּיטוּ וּמַעֲשֵׂה יָדָיו לֹא רָאוּ לָכֵן גָּלָה עַמִּי, "But they do not consider the deeds of Yʜwʜ nor do they consider the work of his hands; *therefore*, my people go into exile" (Isa 5:12–13),

אֹתֶם עֲזַבְתֶּם אוֹתִי וַתַּעַבְדוּ אֱלֹהִים אֲחֵרִים לָכֵן לֹא־אוֹסִיף
לְהוֹשִׁיעַ אֶתְכֶם

"You have forsaken me and served other gods; *therefore*, I will no longer deliver you" (Judg 10:13),

יַעַן אֲשֶׁר־הִכְרַתִּי מִמֵּךְ צַדִּיק וְרָשָׁע לָכֵן תֵּצֵא חַרְבִּי מִתַּעְרָהּ
אֶל־כָּל־בָּשָׂר מִנֶּגֶב צָפוֹן

"Because I will cut off from you the righteous and the wicked; *therefore*, my sword will go out from its sheath against all flesh from south to north" (Ezek 21:9 [Eng 21:4]).

---

[31] Waltke and O'Connor 1990, 666.

The compound form עַל־כֵּן often introduces a statement of effect, linking two clauses with a causal link:

כִּי אֶת־מַעְשַׂר בְּנֵי־יִשְׂרָאֵל אֲשֶׁר יָרִימוּ לַיהוָה תְּרוּמָה נָתַתִּי
לַלְוִיִּם לְנַחֲלָה עַל־כֵּן אָמַרְתִּי לָהֶם בְּתוֹךְ בְּנֵי יִשְׂרָאֵל לֹא
יִנְחֲלוּ נַחֲלָה

"Because of the tithe of the sons of Israel, which they offer as an offering to YHWH, I have given to the Levites for an inheritance; *therefore,* I have said concerning them, 'They shall have no inheritance among the children of Israel' " (Num 18:24), עַל־כֵּן קָרָא שְׁמָהּ בָּבֶל כִּי־שָׁם בָּלַל יְהוָה שְׂפַת כָּל־הָאָרֶץ, "*Therefore,* its name is called Babel, because there, YHWH confused the languages of the whole earth" (Gen 11:9).

### 4.2.11 לֹא

*Negation* – The primary use of this adverb is to negate verbal clauses.[32] The particle functions to negate a verbal idea in an independent verbal clause: רָעָה לֹא רָאִינוּ, "we did *not* see evil" (Jer 44:17), אָנֹכִי לֹא אֶהְיֶה כְּאַחַת שִׁפְחֹתֶיךָ, "I am *not* like one of your maidservants" (Ruth 2:13), נֶגַע־וְקָלוֹן יִמְצָא וְחֶרְפָּתוֹ לֹא תִמָּחֶה, "He will find wounds and disgrace, and his reproach will *not* be blotted out" (Prov 6:33).

The negative force of לֹא can also be used with commands to denote a *general* or *permanent prohibition:* לֹא תֹאכַל מִמֶּנּוּ, "you *shall not* eat from it" (Gen 2:17), וְכֹל אֲשֶׁר אֵין־לוֹ סְנַפִּיר וְקַשְׂקֶשֶׂת לֹא תֹאכֵלוּ, "but anything that does not have fins and scales, *you shall not eat*" (Deut 14:10), וּבַיּוֹם הַשְּׁבִיעִי מִקְרָא־קֹדֶשׁ יִהְיֶה לָכֶם כָּל־מְלֶאכֶת עֲבֹדָה לֹא תַעֲשׂוּ, "And on the seventh day you shall have have a holy convocation; *you shall not do* any laborious work" (Num 28:25).

---

[32] Occasionally, and in contrast with the negative particle אַל, לֹא will be used to negate only one word, typically a nominal form: לֹא־טוֹב הֱיוֹת הָאָדָם לְבַדּוֹ, "it is not good for the man to be alone" (Gen 2:18).

At times, לֹא negates verbless clauses or prepositional phrases: לֹא בִי־הִיא, "it is *not* in me" (Job 28:14),
לֹא־טוֹב הַדָּבָר אֲשֶׁר אַתָּה עֹשֶׂה, "The thing you are doing is
*not good*" (Exod 18:17),

וַתַּעֲשֶׂה אָדָם כִּדְגֵי הַיָּם כְּרֶמֶשׂ לֹא־מֹשֵׁל בּוֹ

"You have made humanity like fish in the sea, like crawling
things with *no ruler* over them" (Hab 1:14).

### 4.2.12 מְאֹד

***Intensive*** – The intensive adverbial use of מְאֹד points
to a high degree or magnitude in the force of the
verb: וְאַבְרָם כָּבֵד מְאֹד, "Abram was *very* rich" (Gen 13:2),
וְיִרְאוּ מִכֶּם וְנִשְׁמַרְתֶּם מְאֹד, "They will be afraid of you; so
be *very* careful" (Deut 2:4), וַיִּרְאוּ מְאֹד מְאֹד, "They *were
overcome with fear*" (2 Kgs 10:4),

וַיִּקְצֹף הַמֶּלֶךְ מְאֹד וַחֲמָתוֹ בָּעֲרָה בוֹ

"Then the king became *very angry*, and his anger burned
within him" (Esth 1:12).

The particle also intensifies an adjective:

הָאָרֶץ אֲשֶׁר עָבַרְנוּ בָהּ לָתוּר אֹתָהּ טוֹבָה הָאָרֶץ מְאֹד מְאֹד

"The land which we went through to spy out is a *very good*
land" (Num 14:7),

וַיְהִי כְּכַלּוֹת יְהוֹשֻׁעַ וּבְנֵי יִשְׂרָאֵל לְהַכּוֹתָם מַכָּה גְדוֹלָה־מְאֹד

"When Joshua and the people of Israel had finished
slaying them with a *great slaughter* … " (Josh 10:20),
כִּי־גָדוֹל יוֹם־יְהוָה וְנוֹרָא מְאֹד וּמִי יְכִילֶנּוּ, "For the day of Yhwh
is great and *very terrible*; who can endure it?" (Joel 2:11).

In addition to the adverbial use, מְאֹד can also
function adjectivally to denote a "large amount,"
frequently when paired with either הרבה or רב:
וּמִבֶּטַח וּמִבֵּרֹתַי עָרֵי הֲדַדְעֶזֶר לָקַח הַמֶּלֶךְ דָּוִד נְחֹשֶׁת הַרְבֵּה מְאֹד,
"From Betah and Berothai, cities of Hadadezer, King

David took a *large amount* of copper" (2 Sam 8:8), וַתִּתֵּן לַמֶּלֶךְ מֵאָה וְעֶשְׂרִים כִּכַּר זָהָב וּבְשָׂמִים הַרְבֵּה מְאֹד, "She gave to the king 120 talents of gold and a *large amount* of spices" (1 Kgs 10:10).

### 4.2.13 עוֹד

***Manner*** – expresses a *continual* or *persistent* nature of the verbal clause: וְאַבְרָהָם עוֹדֶנּוּ עֹמֵד לִפְנֵי יְהוָה, "and Abraham was *still* standing before YHWH" (Gen 18:22), עוֹדֶנִּי הַיּוֹם חָזָק כַּאֲשֶׁר בְּיוֹם שְׁלֹחַ אוֹתִי מֹשֶׁה, "I am *still as strong* as the day when Moses sent me" (Josh 14:11), וּמַלְתֶּם אֵת עָרְלַת לְבַבְכֶם וְעָרְפְּכֶם לֹא תַקְשׁוּ עוֹד, "So, circumcise the foreskins of your hearts, and stiffen your neck *no longer*" (Deut 10:16),

עוֹדֶנּוּ הָאָרֶץ לְפָנֵינוּ כִּי דָרַשְׁנוּ אֶת־יְהוָה אֱלֹהֵינוּ

"The land is *still* ours, because we have sought YHWH, our God" (2 Chr 14:6).

This particle also indicates a *repeated* nature of a verbal clause: וַיֵּדַע אָדָם עוֹד אֶת־אִשְׁתּוֹ, "Adam had relations with his wife *again*" (Gen 4:25),

בִּי אֲדוֹנִי אִישׁ הָאֱלֹהִים אֲשֶׁר שָׁלַחְתָּ יָבוֹא־נָא עוֹד אֵלֵינוּ

"O lord, please let the man of God, whom you sent, come to us *again*" (Judg 13:8), וַתַּהַר עוֹד וַתֵּלֶד בַּת, "She conceived *again* and gave birth to a daughter" (Hos 1:6).

### 4.2.14 עַתָּה

***(a) Temporal*** – places focus on time that is concurrent with the perspective of the discourse, and is most often rendered "now": עַתָּה יָדַעְתִּי כִּי הוֹשִׁיעַ יְהוָה מְשִׁיחוֹ, "*now* I know that YHWH saves his anointed" (Ps 20:7), וַתָּבוֹא וַתַּעֲמוֹד מֵאָז הַבֹּקֶר וְעַד־עַתָּה זֶה, "So she came and she stayed from this morning until *now*" (Ruth 2:7), אַתָּה עַתָּה תַּעֲשֶׂה מְלוּכָה עַל־יִשְׂרָאֵל,

"Do you _now_ reign over Israel" (1 Kgs 21:7),
וְגַם־עַתָּה נְאֻם־יְהֹוָה שֻׁבוּ עָדַי בְּכָל־לְבַבְכֶם וּבְצוֹם וּבְבְכִי וּבְמִסְפֵּד
"'Yet even _now_,' declares YHWH, 'Return to me with all
your hearts, and in fasting, weeping, and mourning'"
(Joel 2:12).

**(b) Logical** – typically occurs through the compound form
וְעַתָּה and usually indicates a shift in the argument or flow of
the discourse without a break in the theme. Frequently, this
is also accompanied by a temporal shift as well, when one
reflects on past events and commits to present or future
action:

אַתֶּם חֲטָאתֶם חֲטָאָה גְדֹלָה וְעַתָּה אֶעֱלֶה אֶל־יְהֹוָה אוּלַי אֲכַפְּרָה בְּעַד
חַטַּאתְכֶם

"You yourselves have committed a great sin; and _now_ I will
go up to YHWH, perhaps I can make atonement for your
sin" (Exod 32:30),

הֵן הָאָדָם הָיָה כְּאַחַד מִמֶּנּוּ לָדַעַת טוֹב וָרָע וְעַתָּה פֶּן־יִשְׁלַח יָדוֹ
וְלָקַח גַּם מֵעֵץ הַחַיִּים

"Indeed, humanity has become like one of us, knowing
good and evil; _and now_, they might stretch out their hand
and take also from the tree of life" (Gen 3:22),

מַדּוּעַ אֵינְכֶם מְחַזְּקִים אֶת־בֶּדֶק הַבָּיִת וְעַתָּה אַל־תִּקְחוּ־כֶסֶף
מֵאֵת מַכָּרֵיכֶם

"Why do you not repair the damages to the house?
_Now, therefore_, do not take any money from your acquain-
tances" (2 Kgs 12:8 [Eng 12:7]).

### 4.2.15 רַק

**(a) Restrictive** – functions to place a limit on an idea:
רַק אֶתְכֶם יָדַעְתִּי מִכֹּל מִשְׁפְּחוֹת הָאֲדָמָה, "You, _only_, have I
known among all the nations of the earth" (Amos 3:2),
וַיַּעַשׂ הָרַע בְּעֵינֵי יְהֹוָה רַק לֹא כְּמַלְכֵי יִשְׂרָאֵל אֲשֶׁר הָיוּ לְפָנָיו, "He
did evil in the eyes of YHWH, _though_ not like the

kings of Israel who were before him" (2 Kgs 17:2), רַק הַבָּמוֹת לֹא־סָרוּ עוֹד הָעָם מְזַבְּחִים וּמְקַטְּרִים בַּבָּמוֹת, "*Only* the high places were not removed. The people still sacrificed and burned incense on the high places" (2 Kgs 14:4).

Occasionally, this restrictive idea can be expanded into a complete contrast between two ideas: וַיַּעַשׂ הַיָּשָׁר בְּעֵינֵי יְהוָה רַק לֹא כְּדָוִד אָבִיו, "He did right in the eyes of YHWH, *but* not like his father David" (2 Kgs 14:3).

With discourse involving instruction, the restrictive force of רַק can also indication a *clarification*: הִנֵּה כָל־אֲשֶׁר־לוֹ בְּיָדֶךָ רַק אֵלָיו אַל־תִּשְׁלַח יָדֶךָ, "See, all that he has is in your hands; *only*, do not send forth your hand upon him" (Job 1:12),

אָנֹכִי אֲשַׁלַּח אֶתְכֶם . . . רַק הַרְחֵק לֹא־תַרְחִיקוּ לָלֶכֶת

"I will let you go ... *only*, do not go very far away" (Exod 8:24),

וְאִם־לֹא תֹאבֶה הָאִשָּׁה לָלֶכֶת אַחֲרֶיךָ וְנִקִּיתָ מִשְּׁבֻעָתִי זֹאת רַק אֶת־בְּנִי לֹא תָשֵׁב שָׁמָּה

"If the woman is not willing to go with you, you will be free from this my oath. *Only*, you must not take my son back there" (Gen 24:8).

**(b) Asseverative** – expresses a conviction as to the correctness of an observation:

אָמַרְתִּי רַק אֵין־יִרְאַת אֱלֹהִים בַּמָּקוֹם הַזֶּה

"I thought, there is *certainly* [literally: I *only* thought there is] no fear of God at all in this place" (Gen 20:11), רַק עַם־חָכָם וְנָבוֹן הַגּוֹי הַגָּדוֹל הַזֶּה, "*Surely*, this great nation is a wise and discerning people" (Deut 4:6).

## 4.2.16 שָׁם

**(a) Locative** – points demonstratively to a place, "there," which is the realm of action: וּבָאתָ עַד־בָּבֶל שָׁם תִּנָּצֵלִי, "Go to Babylon, *there* you will be rescued" (Mic 4:10),

וַיָּשֶׂם שָׁם אֶת־הָאָדָם אֲשֶׁר יָצָר

"*There* he placed the man whom he had formed" (Gen
2:8), שָׁם תֹּאכְלֵךְ אֵשׁ תַּכְרִיתֵךְ חֶרֶב, "*There* the fire will
consume you, the sword will cut you down" (Nah 3:15),
וַיַּעַשׂ לוֹ שָׁם סֻכָּה וַיֵּשֶׁב תַּחְתֶּיהָ בַּצֵּל עַד אֲשֶׁר יִרְאֶה מַה־יִּהְיֶה בָּעִיר,
"He made for himself *there* a booth, and he sat under
it until he could see what would happen to the city"
(Jonah 4:5).

With the relative pronoun אֲשֶׁר, שָׁם functions to introduce a relative clause that points to location:

הָעֲרָפֶל אֲשֶׁר־שָׁם הָאֱלֹהִים

"the thick cloud *where* God was" (Exod 20:21),
וַיֵּלֶךְ לְמַסָּעָיו מִנֶּגֶב וְעַד־בֵּית־אֵל עַד־הַמָּקוֹם אֲשֶׁר־הָיָה שָׁם אָהֳלוֹ,
"He went on his journeys, from the Negeb to Bethel, to
the place *where* his tent had been" (Gen 13:3 *Qere*).

*(b) Terminative* – Typically with verbs of motion, and suffixed with the *he locale*, שָׁם has a *terminative* sense, placing
emphasis on the end goal of movement, rather than a static
location: אִמָּלְטָה נָּא שָׁמָּה, "Please let me escape *to there*" (Gen
19:20), יְהוֹשֻׁעַ בֶּן־נוּן הָעֹמֵד לְפָנֶיךָ הוּא יָבֹא שָׁמָּה, "Joshua, son
of Nun, who stands before you; he will enter *there*" (Deut
1:38), וַיָּנֻסוּ שָׁמָּה כָּל־הָאֲנָשִׁים וְהַנָּשִׁים וְכֹל בַּעֲלֵי הָעִיר, "All the
men and women, and all the leaders of the city fled to
*there*" (Judg 9:51).

### 4.2.17 תָּמִיד

*(a) Manner* – most often expresses a *continual* or
*persistent* manner of the action: שִׁוִּיתִי יְהוָה לְנֶגְדִּי תָמִיד,
"I have set Yʜᴡʜ *continually* before me" (Ps 16:8),
עֵינַי תָּמִיד אֶל־יְהוָה, "my eyes are *ever* toward Yʜᴡʜ" (Ps
25:15), עַל־מִי לֹא־עָבְרָה רָעָתְךָ תָּמִיד, "on whom has your evil
not passed *continually*" (Nah 3:19).

## 4.3 Conjunctions

Conjunctions join words, phrases, or clauses and express relations between them. They may be of two types: coordinate conjunctions and subordinate conjunctions. The first of these conjoin grammatically equivalent nouns or clauses; in BH, these are וְ and אוֹ.[33] The second type, subordinate conjunctions, conjoin a subordinate clause to the main clause, and BH has a number of examples (כִּי, אִם, פֶּן, etc.). However, in BH, whether a clause is coordinate or subordinate is often interpretive because of the high frequency of the *waw consecutive* in verbal coordination (see section 3.5). Thus, subordinate clauses are frequently unmarked grammatically because the conjunctions are often imprecise.[34]

### 4.3.1 אוֹ

*Alternative* – typically functions to provide an option between two or more substantives:

שְׁאַל־לְךָ אוֹת מֵעִם יְהוָה אֱלֹהֶיךָ הַעְמֵק הַעֲמֵק הַשְּׁאָלָה אוֹ הַגְבֵּהַּ
לְמָעְלָה

"Ask for a sign from YHWH your God, as deep as Sheol _or_ as high as heaven" (Isa 7:11), וְרַק הִיא יְחִידָה אֵין־לוֹ מִמֶּנּוּ בֵּן אוֹ־בַת, "She was an only child; except for her, he [Jephthah] had no son _or_ daughter" (Judg 11:34), אִם־עֶבֶד יִגַּח הַשּׁוֹר אוֹ אָמָה, "if an ox gore a male slave _or_ a female slave" (Exod 21:32).

### 4.3.2 אִם

*(a) Conditional/contingency* – introduces the protasis (the "if" statement) of a conditional statement: אִם־אֶמְצָא בִסְדֹם חֲמִשִּׁים צַדִּיקִם, "_if_ I find

---

33 At times אִם and כִּי may serve as coordinates.
34 Meyer 1992, 181–82; van der Merwe, Naudé, and Kroeze 1999, 57–58 and 294–305; and for comparison with epigraphic Hebrew, see Gogel 1998, 223–30.

in Sodom fifty righteous people" (Gen 18:26),
אִם־בִּדְרָכַי תֵּלֵךְ וְאִם אֶת־מִשְׁמַרְתִּי תִשְׁמֹר וְגַם־אַתָּה תָּדִין אֶת־בֵּיתִי,
"*If* you walk in my ways, and *if* you keep my require-
ments, then you will govern my house" (Zech 3:7),
בְּנִי אִם־חָכַם לִבֶּךָ יִשְׂמַח לִבִּי גַם־אָנִי, "My son, *if* your heart is
wise, my heart also will be glad" (Prov 23:15). This use is
negated by the particle לֹא, indicating a negative protasis:
אִם־לֹא חָפַצְתָּ בָּהּ, "*if* you are _not_ pleased with her" (Deut
21:14), אִם־לֹא יִמָּצֵא הַגַּנָּב וְנִקְרַב בַּעַל־הַבַּיִת אֶל־הָאֱלֹהִים, "*If*
the thief is _not_ caught, the master of the house shall appear
before the judges" (Exod 22:7 [Eng 22:8]).

**(b) *Concessive* –** אִם can function to indicate that an action that is expected to lead to another action does not:
אִם־יַעֲלוּ הַשָּׁמַיִם מִשָּׁם אוֹרִידֵם, "_though_ they go up to the heavens, I will bring them down from there" (Amos 9:2),
אִם־יַעֲמֹד מֹשֶׁה וּשְׁמוּאֵל לְפָנַי אֵין נַפְשִׁי אֶל־הָעָם הַזֶּה, "_Even if_
Moses and Samuel were before me, my heart would not
be with this people" (Jer 15:1).

**(c) *Alternative* –** In an interrogative clause, אִם when repeated functions as an alternative, marking off substantives
as options/alternates:

הֲתָבוֹא לְךָ שֶׁבַע שָׁנִים רָעָב בְּאַרְצֶךָ אִם־שְׁלֹשָׁה חֳדָשִׁים נֻסְךָ
לִפְנֵי־צָרֶיךָ וְהוּא רֹדְפֶךָ וְאִם־הֱיוֹת שְׁלֹשֶׁת יָמִים דֶּבֶר בְּאַרְצֶךָ

"Shall seven years of famine come to you in your land?
_Or_ will you flee three months before your foes while
they pursue you? _Or_ shall there be three days' pesti-
lence in your land?" (2 Sam 24:13), הֲלָנוּ אַתָּה אִם־לְצָרֵינוּ,
"Are you for us _or_ for our enemies?" (Josh 5:13),
הַלְּבֶן מֵאָה־שָׁנָה יִוָּלֵד וְאִם־שָׂרָה הֲבַת־תִּשְׁעִים שָׁנָה תֵּלֵד, "Can a
child be born to a man 100 years old, _or_ will Sarah, who
is 90 years old, give birth?" (Gen 17:17).

**(d) *Exceptive* –** Frequently with כִּי or בִּלְתִּי, אִם marks
an action that will not take place unless another action

is taken: לֹא אֲשַׁלֵּחֲךָ כִּי אִם־בֵּרַכְתָּנִי, "I will not let you go *unless* you bless me" (Gen 32:27 [Eng. 32:26]), הֲיִתֵּן כְּפִיר קוֹלוֹ מִמְּעֹנָתוֹ בִּלְתִּי אִם־לָכָד, "Does a young lion growl from his den *unless* he has made a capture" (Amos 3:4). Similarly, the exceptive use of אִם expresses a situation in which there are no other alternatives or possibilities, frequently to emphasize the situation at hand: אֵין זֹאת בִּלְתִּי אִם־חֶרֶב גִּדְעוֹן בֶּן־יוֹאָשׁ אִישׁ יִשְׂרָאֵל, "This is *nothing less* than the sword of Gideon, son of Joash, a man of Israel" (Judg 7:14), אֵין זֶה כִּי אִם־בֵּית אֱלֹהִים, "This is *nothing less* than the house of God" (Gen 28:17).

*(e) Maledictory* – Specifically in oath statements, אִם standing on its own functions to *negate an oath* emphatically, indicating that an action certainly will not take place: אִם־יִרְאוּ אֶת־הָאָרֶץ אֲשֶׁר נִשְׁבַּעְתִּי לַאֲבֹתָם, "[as I live] . . . *they will not see* the land which I swore to their ancestors" (Num 14:23), חַיֶּךָ וְחֵי נַפְשֶׁךָ אִם־אֶעֱשֶׂה אֶת־הַדָּבָר הַזֶּה, "By your life, and by the life of your soul, *I will not do* this thing!" (2 Sam 11:11), חַי־יְהוָה אִם־יוּמָת, "As YHWH lives, *he shall not* be put to death" (1 Sam 19:6).

*(f) Oath* – Contrasted with the *maledictory* use of אִם, it may be paired with כִּי or לֹא to introduce a positive oath, an action that one has committed oneself to take: נִשְׁבַּע יְהוָה צְבָאוֹת בְּנַפְשׁוֹ כִּי אִם־מִלֵּאתִיךְ אָדָם, "YHWH of hosts swears by himself, 'I will *surely* fill you with people'" (Jer 51:14),

אִם־לֹא הָאָרֶץ אֲשֶׁר דָּרְכָה רַגְלְךָ בָּהּ לְךָ תִהְיֶה לְנַחֲלָה וּלְבָנֶיךָ עַד־עוֹלָם

"*Surely* the land that your foot has walked upon will be an inheritance to you and your children to eternity" (Josh 14:9), אִם־לֹא יִסְחָבוּם צְעִירֵי הַצֹּאן אִם־לֹא יַשִּׁים עֲלֵיהֶם נְוֵהֶם, "*Surely* the little ones of the flock will be dragged away; *surely* he will make their pasture desolate because of them" (Jer 49:20).

*(g) Interrogatory* – אִם will often introduce a question: אִם־תִּתֵּן עֵרָבוֹן עַד שָׁלְחֶךָ, "*Will* you give a pledge until you send it?" (Gen 38:17), אִם מֵאֵת אֲדֹנִי הַמֶּלֶךְ נִהְיָה הַדָּבָר הַזֶּה, "*Has* this thing been done by my lord, the king?" (1 Kgs 1:27), אִם־יִתָּקַע שׁוֹפָר בְּעִיר וְעָם לֹא יֶחֱרָדוּ, "If a trumpet blows in the city, *will* not the people tremble?" (Amos 3:6).

## 4.3.3 ו

This conjunction functions on two levels, to conjoin nouns and to conjoin clauses. The *waw* conjoined to a finite verbal form can have unique functions (see section 3.5).

*(a) Adversative* – often introduces contrasting or antithetical ideas: נִחַמְתִּי כִּי עֲשִׂיתִם וְנֹחַ מָצָא חֵן בְּעֵינֵי יְהוָה, " 'I am sorry I have made them.' *But* Noah found favor in the eyes of YHWH" (Gen 6:7–8),

וּנְתַתִּיו לְגוֹי גָּדוֹל וְאֶת־בְּרִיתִי אָקִים אֶת־יִצְחָק

"and I will make him a great nation; *but* my covenant I will establish with Isaac" (Gen 17:20–21), רְאֵה נָא אָנֹכִי יוֹשֵׁב בְּבֵית אֲרָזִים וַאֲרוֹן הָאֱלֹהִים יֹשֵׁב בְּתוֹךְ הַיְרִיעָה, "See now, I live in a house of cedar, *but* the ark of God dwells within a tent" (2 Sam 7:2).

*(b) Conjunctive* – describes two or more interrelated concepts or situations that may otherwise not be related: קֹנֵה שָׁמַיִם וָאָרֶץ, "Maker of heaven *and* earth" (Gen 14:19), הִנְנִי גֹרֵשׁ מִפָּנֶיךָ אֶת־הָאֱמֹרִי וְהַכְּנַעֲנִי וְהַחִתִּי וְהַפְּרִזִּי וְהַחִוִּי וְהַיְבוּסִי, "See, I am going to drive out from before you the Amorite, *and* the Canaanite, *and* the Perizzite, *and* the Hittite, *and* the Jebusite" (Exod 34:11), וַיִּקַּח יוֹחָנָן בֶּן־קָרֵחַ וְכָל־שָׂרֵי הַחֲיָלִים אֵת כָּל־שְׁאֵרִית יְהוּדָה, "Johanan son of Kareah *and* all the commanders of the armies took the entire remnant of Judah" (Jer 43:5).

*(c) Alternative* – marks off alternatives or options: וְלֹא אוֹשִׁיעֵם בְּקֶשֶׁת וּבְחֶרֶב וּבְמִלְחָמָה בְּסוּסִים וּבְפָרָשִׁים, "I will not save them by bow *or* by sword *or* by war *or* by horses *or* by horsemen" (Hos 1:7), וְלֹא־יָדַע בְּשִׁכְבָהּ וּבְקוּמָהּ, "He did not know when she lay down *or* when she arose" (Gen 19:33), הִכָּה דָוִד אֶת־הָאָרֶץ וְלֹא יְחַיֶּה אִישׁ וְאִשָּׁה, "David attacked the land and he did not leave man *or* woman alive" (1 Sam 27:9).

When the conjunction is repeated with each alternative, it is typically rendered "whether...or": אָנֹכִי אֲחַטֶּנָּה מִיָּדִי תְּבַקְשֶׁנָּה גְּנֻבְתִי יוֹם וּגְנֻבְתִי לָיְלָה, "I bore the loss myself; from my hand you required it, *whether* stolen by day *or* stolen by night" (Gen 31:39).

*(d) Epexegetical* – introduces a clause or phrase that clarifies, expands, or paraphrases the clause that precedes it: אֲבָל אִשָּׁה־אַלְמָנָה אָנִי וַיָּמָת אִישִׁי, "Alas, I am a widow, *that is*, my husband died" (2 Sam 14:5), וְעַתָּה שְׁמַע יַעֲקֹב עַבְדִּי וְיִשְׂרָאֵל בָּחַרְתִּי בוֹ, "And now, listen, O Jacob my servant, [*that is*] Israel, whom I have chosen" (Isa 44:1), כֹּל אֲשֶׁר־דִּבֶּר יְהוָה נַעֲשֶׂה וְנִשְׁמָע, "All that YHWH has spoken, we will do, *that is*, we will obey" (Exod 24:7), וַיָּשֶׂם אֹתָם בִּכְלִי הָרֹעִים אֲשֶׁר־לוֹ וּבַיַּלְקוּט, "He put them in his shepherd's bag, *that is*, in the pouch" (1 Sam 17:40).

*(e) Circumstantial* – details the circumstances under which a certain action takes place (see section 5.2.11): וַיָּבֹא מַלְאַךְ הָאֱלֹהִים עוֹד אֶל־הָאִשָּׁה וְהִיא יוֹשֶׁבֶת בַּשָּׂדֶה, "so the messenger of God came again to the woman *while* she was sitting in the field" (Judg 13:9), הָבָה נִבְנֶה־לָּנוּ עִיר וּמִגְדָּל וְרֹאשׁוֹ בַשָּׁמַיִם, "Come, let us build ourselves a city and a tower, *with* its top in the heavens" (Gen 11:4).

*(f) Conditional* – introduces the apodosis of a conditional sentence: בְּבֹאָה רַגְלַיִךְ הָעִירָה וּמֵת הַיָּלֶד, "When your feet enter the city, *then* the child will die" (1 Kgs 14:12),

אִם־כֹּה יֹאמַר נְקֻדִּים יִהְיֶה שְׂכָרֶךָ וְיָלְדוּ כָל־הַצֹּאן נְקֻדִּים, "If he said 'The speckled shall be your wages,' *then* all the flock brought forth speckled" (Gen 31:8).

*(g) Hendiadys* – The *waw* conjunctive can function to con-join two or more words into a construction that refers to a single idea, or points to a single referent. Thus, the con-joined words take the place of a single word with mod-ifiers. This expression, called hendiadys,[35] can be con-structed with two or more nouns, or two or more verbs. *Nominal* hendiadys is a common label for the former. The latter construction, however, which is labeled here as *verbal* hendiadys, is sometimes categorized as an adverbial use of the finite verbal forms of certain roots.[36] Verbal hen-diadys, however, may also be considered a nuance of the verbal complement function of the infinitive construct (see section 3.4.1,a3).

(g.1) *Nominal hendiadys* – וְעַתָּה יַעַשׂ־יְהוָה עִמָּכֶם חֶסֶד וֶאֱמֶת, "Now, may YHWH show you *true faithfulness*" (2 Sam 2:6), הָאֵל הַנֶּאֱמָן שֹׁמֵר הַבְּרִית וְהַחֶסֶד, "The faithful God, who keeps his *covenant loyalty*" (Deut 7:9), וְהָאָרֶץ הָיְתָה תֹהוּ וָבֹהוּ, "The earth was a *formless void*" (Gen 1:2).

(g.2) *Verbal hendiadys* – one verb functioning adverbially to modify the idea of the other verb. The aspect of the verbs can be identical: וַתְּמַהֵר וַתֹּרֶד כַּדָּהּ, "She *quickly low-ered* her jar" (Gen 24:18), וַתְּמַהֵר וַתֵּרֶד מֵעַל הַחֲמוֹר, "She *quickly dismounted* from the donkey" (1 Sam 25:23), וַיֵּשְׁבוּ וַיִּבְכּוּ גַּם בְּנֵי יִשְׂרָאֵל, "Also, the people of Israel *wept again*" (Num 11:4); or the two verbal forms can also be of distinct aspect: וְאַתָּה תָשׁוּב וְשָׁמַעְתָּ בְּקוֹל יְהוָה, "And you shall *again obey* the voice of YHWH" (Deut 30:8). The root יסף in particular is often followed by an infinitive construct, functioning similarly to the verbal complement use of the

---

[35] The term "hendiadys" derives from a Latin modification of the Greek words *hen* ("one") *dia* ("through") and *dyoin* ("two").

[36] See Kautzsch 1910, 386; Joüon and Muraoka 1993, 650.

infinitive construct: וְלֹא־הֹסִיף עוֹד מֶלֶךְ מִצְרַיִם לָצֵאת מֵאַרְצוֹ, "The king of Egypt *did not come out of his land again*" (2 Kgs 24:7), לָכֵן לֹא־אוֹסִיף לְהוֹשִׁיעַ אֶתְכֶם, "Therefore, I will not *deliver you again*" (Judg 10:13).

## 4.3.4 כִּי

*(a) Causal* – This conjunction[37] forms a causal link between two clauses, introducing the reason an action or situation takes place, or providing the motivation for why something should be done: קֵץ כָּל־בָּשָׂר בָּא לְפָנַי כִּי־מָלְאָה הָאָרֶץ חָמָס מִפְּנֵיהֶם, "the end of all flesh has come before me *because* the earth is filled with violence because of them" (Gen 6:13), אֲהָהּ לַיּוֹם כִּי קָרוֹב יוֹם יְהוָה, "Alas for the day! *For* the day of YHWH is near" (Joel 1:15), בְּזֵעַת אַפֶּיךָ תֹּאכַל לֶחֶם עַד שׁוּבְךָ אֶל־הָאֲדָמָה כִּי מִמֶּנָּה לֻקָּחְתָּ, "By the sweat of your brow, you shall eat food until you return to the earth; *because* you were taken from it" (Gen 3:19), לֹא תַעֲלוּ וְלֹא־תִלָּחֲמוּ כִּי אֵינֶנִּי בְּקִרְבְּכֶם, "Do not go up, or fight, *because* I am not among you" (Deut 1:42).

*(b) Evidential*[38] – Although translated similarly to the *causal*, the evidential use of כִּי presents the evidence or motivation that lies behind a statement, rather than presenting the cause of an action or situation. Thus, the causal link is with the action of speech, not the contents of speech; the focus is not on what is spoken but on the reason the speaker is saying something. As such a link, כִּי provides the

---

[37] This particle כִּי is thought to have originated as a demonstrative particle (Kautzsch 1910, 305; Meyer 1992, 436; Brockleman 1956, 151). The various uses of the particle may be classified into two major groups: either some type of emphatic use (Muilenberg 1961, 135–60, with the most extensive treatment), or as a connective (Aejmelaeus 1986, 205). However, Muraoka states that the particle is basically demonstrative, with the emphatic nuance derived secondarily (1969, 132).

[38] Claasen 1983, 37–44; Aejmelaeus 1986, 203.

evidence for the whole or a specific part of a statement, a particular word in the statement, or even the emotional tone of the statement:

וַיֹּאמֶר דָּוִד אֶל־אַבְנֵר הֲלוֹא־אִישׁ אַתָּה וּמִי כָמוֹךָ בְּיִשְׂרָאֵל
וְלָמָּה לֹא שָׁמַרְתָּ אֶל־אֲדֹנֶיךָ הַמֶּלֶךְ כִּי־בָא אַחַד הָעָם
לְהַשְׁחִית אֶת־הַמֶּלֶךְ אֲדֹנֶיךָ

"David said to Abner, 'Are you not a man? Who is like you in Israel? Why did you not guard your lord, the king? _For_ one of the people came to kill the king, your lord.' " (1 Sam 26:15),

וַיֹּאמֶר נָתָן אֲדֹנִי הַמֶּלֶךְ אַתָּה אָמַרְתָּ אֲדֹנִיָּהוּ יִמְלֹךְ אַחֲרַי
וְהוּא יֵשֵׁב עַל־כִּסְאִי כִּי יָרַד הַיּוֹם וַיִּזְבַּח שׁוֹר וּמְרִיא־וְצֹאן לָרֹב

"Nathan said, 'My lord, the king. Did you say "Adonijah will rule after me, and he shall sit on my throne?" _For_ he went down today, and he sacrificed oxen, fatted cattle and sheep in abundance' " (1 Kgs 1:24–25).

*(c) Clarification* – introduces a subordinate clause that clarifies or explains the main clause:

זֶה־לְּךָ הָאוֹת כִּי אָנֹכִי שְׁלַחְתִּיךָ

"this will be the sign _that_ I have sent you" (Exod 3:12), הַמְעַט כִּי הֶעֱלִיתָנוּ מֵאֶרֶץ זָבַת חָלָב וּדְבַשׁ, "Is it not enough _that_ you brought us out from a land flowing with milk and honey?" (Num 16:13).

*(d) Result* – introduces clauses that express the outcome or consequence of the action or situation of the main clause: וְגַם־פֹּה לֹא־עָשִׂיתִי מְאוּמָה כִּי־שָׂמוּ אֹתִי בַּבּוֹר, "Even here, I have not done anything, _that_ they should put me into the dungeon" (Gen 40:15). This use of the particle is prevalent after questions: מָה רָאִיתָ כִּי עָשִׂיתָ אֶת־הַדָּבָר הַזֶּה, "What have you seen, _that_ you have done this thing?"

(Gen 20:10), מִי אָנֹכִי כִּי אֵלֵךְ אֶל־פַּרְעֹה, "Who am I *that* I should go to Pharaoh?" (Exod 3:11).

*(e) Temporal* – indicates that the time reference of a subordinate clause is contemporary with the situation of the main clause (see section 5.2.4):

וַיְהִי כִּי־הֵחֵל הָאָדָם לָרֹב עַל־פְּנֵי הָאֲדָמָה וּבָנוֹת יֻלְּדוּ לָהֶם וַיִּרְאוּ
בְנֵי־הָאֱלֹהִים אֶת־בְּנוֹת הָאָדָם כִּי טֹבֹת הֵנָּה

"*When* people began to multiply on the face of the earth and daughters were born to them, the sons of God saw that the daughters of humanity were beautiful" (Gen 6:1–2), כִּי אַתֶּם עֹבְרִים אֶת־הַיַּרְדֵּן אֶל־אֶרֶץ כְּנָעַן, "*When* you cross over the Jordan into the land of Canaan" (Num 33:51), וְהָיָה כִּי־תִקְרֶאנָה מִלְחָמָה וְנוֹסַף גַּם־הוּא עַל־שֹׂנְאֵינוּ, "*In the event* of war (literally: *when* war befalls), they will also join themselves to our enemies" (Exod 1:10).

When dealing with future situations, the temporal use is quite similar to the conditional use of כִּי. See (f), which follows.

*(f) Conditional* – introduces the protasis of conditional statements – the "if" statement: כִּי־תִמְצָא אִישׁ לֹא תְבָרְכֶנּוּ, "*If* you meet any man, do not greet him" (2 Kgs 4:29), כִּי תִקְנֶה עֶבֶד עִבְרִי שֵׁשׁ שָׁנִים יַעֲבֹד, "*If* you buy a Hebrew slave, he shall serve six years" (Exod 21:2), וְכִי־יִפְתַּח אִישׁ בּוֹר אוֹ כִּי־יִכְרֶה אִישׁ בֹּר וְלֹא יְכַסֶּנּוּ, "*If* a person opens a pit, or *if* a person digs a pit and does not cover it" (Exod 21:33), כִּי אָמַרְתִּי יֶשׁ־לִי תִקְוָה, "*If* I said, 'I have hope'" (Ruth 1:12).

The distinction between temporal and conditional is somewhat vague, especially when dealing with future temporal statements.[39] Consider: כִּי־יִשְׁאָלְךָ בִנְךָ מָחָר לֵאמֹר... וְאָמַרְתָּ לְבִנְךָ could be translated as "*If* your son asks you in time saying... then you

---

[39] Aejmelaeus 1986, 197.

shall answer your son" or "*When* your sons asks you in time
saying . . . then you shall answer your son" (Deut 6:20–21).

With the particles עַתָּה or אָז, כִּי introduces the apodosis – the "then" statement – of a conditional sentence:
כִּי לוּלֵא הִתְמַהְמָהְנוּ כִּי־עַתָּה שַׁבְנוּ זֶה פַעֲמָיִם, "For if we had not
delayed, [*then*] we could have returned twice" (Gen 43:10),
חַי הָאֱלֹהִים כִּי לוּלֵא כִּי דִּבַּרְתָּ כִּי אָז מֵהַבֹּקֶר נַעֲלָה הָעָם, "As God
lives, if you had not spoken, *then* the people would have
gone away in the morning" (2 Sam 2:27).

**(g) Adversative** – introduces an antithetical statement after
a negative clause. It often gives an alternative for the
negative statement: לֹא־תִקְרָא אֶת־שְׁמָהּ שָׂרָי כִּי שָׂרָה שְׁמָהּ,
"Do not call her name Sarai, *but* her name will be Sarah"
(Gen 17:15), לֹא־תִגַּע בּוֹ יָד כִּי־סָקוֹל יִסָּקֵל אוֹ־יָרֹה יִיָּרֶה,
"No hand shall touch him, *but* he shall surely
be stoned or shot through" (Exod 19:13),
לֹא־אֶקַּח אֶת־כָּל־הַמַּמְלָכָה מִיָּדוֹ כִּי נָשִׂיא אֲשִׁתֶנּוּ כֹּל יְמֵי חַיָּיו,
"I will not take the kingdom from his hand, *but* I will make
him ruler all the days of his life" (1 Kgs 11:34).

The *adversative* sense is also denoted by כִּי אִם,
again, noting an alternative to a negative statement:[40]
לֹא יִירָשְׁךָ זֶה כִּי־אִם אֲשֶׁר יֵצֵא מִמֵּעֶיךָ, "This man will not be
your heir, *but* one who will come forth from your
body . . ." (Gen 15:4), לֹא יַעֲקֹב יֵאָמֵר עוֹד שִׁמְךָ כִּי אִם־יִשְׂרָאֵל,
"Your name shall no longer be Jacob, *but rather* Israel" (Gen
32:29 [Eng. 32:28]).

**(h) Concessive** – introduces a clause that should, or is
expected to, lead to the action of the main clause
but, in fact, does not. Thus, the main clause occurs
in spite of the clause introduced by כִּי: כִּי־יִפֹּל לֹא־יוּטָל,

---

[40] The longer construction כִּי אִם is more common in denoting an adversative sense. The adversative force of this construction likely comes from
the adversative use of כִּי, which is further enhanced by a pleonastic use
of אִם (Schoors 1981, 251–52).

"*though* he falls, he will not stumble" (Ps 37:24), כִּי אָנַפְתָּ בִּי יָשֹׁב אַפְּךָ וּתְנַחֲמֵנִי, "*Although* you were angry with me, your anger turned away and you comforted me" (Isa 12:1), מֵאֹתוֹת הַשָּׁמַיִם אַל־תֵּחָתּוּ כִּי־יֵחַתּוּ הַגּוֹיִם מֵהֵמָּה, "Do not be terrified by the signs of heaven, *though* the nations are terrified by them" (Jer 10:2).

*(i) Asseverative* – emphasizes the clause it modifies. This use of כִּי may have originated in oath statements, to indicate an action that one will take:[41] חַי־יְהוָה כִּי בֶן־מָוֶת הָאִישׁ הָעֹשֶׂה זֹאת, "As Yhwh lives, *surely* the man who did this thing deserves to die" (2 Sam 12:5), כֹּה־יַעֲשֶׂה אֱלֹהִים וְכֹה יוֹסִף כִּי־מוֹת תָּמוּת יוֹנָתָן, "May God do this and more; *You shall surely die,* Jonathan" (1 Sam 14:44), חֵי פַרְעֹה כִּי מְרַגְּלִים אַתֶּם, "As Pharaoh lives, you are *surely* spies" (Gen 42:16).

The construction כִּי אִם highlights a negative oath, an action that one will not take, or an action/situation that one pledges to not allow:

וְאוּלָם חַי־יְהוָה אֱלֹהֵי יִשְׂרָאֵל . . . כִּי אִם־נוֹתַר לְנָבָל

"Nevertheless, as Yhwh, the God of Israel lives . . . *there would not have been* left to Nabal . . ." (1 Sam 25:34). On occasion, however, the construction כִּי אִם functions identically to the *asseverative* כִּי to indicate an action that one will take: חַי־יְהוָה כִּי־אִם־רַצְתִּי אַחֲרָיו וְלָקַחְתִּי מֵאִתּוֹ מְאוּמָה, "As Yhwh lives, *I will run* after him and take something from him" (2 Kgs 5:20), אִם־תַּעֲשׂוּן כָּזֹאת כִּי אִם־נִקַּמְתִּי בָכֶם, "Since you act like this, *I will surely take revenge* on you" (Judg 15:7).

The asseverative כִּי can function in other types of discourse as well, to place emphasis on the surety of a fact or situation: כִּי יֵבֹשׁוּ מֵאֵילִים אֲשֶׁר חֲמַדְתֶּם, "*surely* they will be ashamed of oaks that they have desired" (Isa 1:29), אִם לֹא תַאֲמִינוּ כִּי לֹא תֵאָמֵנוּ, "If you do not believe, *surely* you

---

[41] Williams 1967, 73.

will not last" (Isa 7:9), כִּי אִם־יֵשׁ אַחֲרִית "*Surely* there is a future" (Prov 23:18).

*(j) Perceptual* – With verbs of perception (seeing, hearing, believing, feeling, etc) כִּי can function to introduce a subordinate clause that indicates the object of perception: וַיַּרְא אֱלֹהִים כִּי־טוֹב, "God saw *that* [this] was good" (Gen 1:10), וַיְהִי כִּשְׁמֹעַ אִיזֶבֶל כִּי־סֻקַּל נָבוֹת וַיָּמֹת, "When Jezebel heard *that* Naboth was stoned and died" (1 Kgs 21:15), וִידַעְתֶּם כִּי אֲנִי יְהוָה אֱלֹהֵיכֶם, "You shall know *that* I am Yhwh, your God" (Exod 6:7).

*(k) Subject* – introduces clauses that function as a subject in a sentence: טוֹב כִּי־תִהְיֶה־לָּנוּ מֵעִיר לַעְזוֹר, "It is better *that you send us* help from the city" (2 Sam 18:3 *Qere*), אַל־יִחַר בְּעֵינֵי אֲדֹנִי כִּי לוֹא אוּכַל לָקוּם מִפָּנֶיךָ, "Let not my lord be angry *that I am not able to rise* before you" (Gen 31:35).

*(l) Recitative* – introduces direct speech, and is therefore usually left untranslated:

וַיֹּאמֶר חֲזָהאֵל כִּי מָה עַבְדְּךָ הַכֶּלֶב כִּי יַעֲשֶׂה הַדָּבָר הַגָּדוֹל הַזֶּה

"Hazael said <*that*>, 'What is your servant, a dog, that he should do this great thing?'" (2 Kgs 8:13),

כִּי כַּאֲשֶׁר נִשְׁבַּעְתִּי לָךְ בַּיהוָה אֱלֹהֵי יִשְׂרָאֵל לֵאמֹר כִּי־שְׁלֹמֹה בְנֵךְ יִמְלֹךְ אַחֲרַי

"Surely, as I swore to you by Yhwh, God of Israel, saying <*that*>, 'Solomon, your son, will be king after me'" (1 Kgs 1:30), כֵּן אֲמַרְתֶּם לֵאמֹר כִּי־פְּשָׁעֵינוּ וְחַטֹּאתֵינוּ עָלֵינוּ, "Thus, you have said <*that*>, 'Our trangressions and our sins are upon us'" (Ezek 33:10).

With the interrogative particle הֲ, כִּי can introduce a question posed by a speaker in context: וַיֹּאמֶר דָּוִד הֲכִי יֶשׁ־עוֹד אֲשֶׁר נוֹתַר לְבֵית שָׁאוּל, "David said

<*that*>, 'Is there anyone still left of the house of Saul?'"
(2 Sam 9:1), וַיֹּאמֶר הֲכִי קָרָא שְׁמוֹ יַעֲקֹב, "Then [Esau] said
<*that*>, 'Is he not rightly named Jacob?'" (Gen 27:36).

**(m) Exceptive** – indicates an action or situation that
will not take place unless accompanied or followed by another action/situation. The *exceptive* כִּי
is often translated "except" or "unless" in English:
וְלֹא יֹאכַל מִן־הַקֳּדָשִׁים כִּי אִם־רָחַץ בְּשָׂרוֹ בַּמָּיִם, "And
he will not eat from the holy [gifts] <u>unless</u>
he washes his body with water" (Lev 22:6),
אֵין־חֵפֶץ לַמֶּלֶךְ בְּמֹהַר כִּי בְּמֵאָה עָרְלוֹת פְּלִשְׁתִּים, "The king
does not desire any dowry, <u>except</u> for 100 foreskins of the
Philistines" (1 Sam 18:25).

After a general negative statement, כִּי אִם often introduces a specific situation that is op-
posed to, or reverses, the negative statement:[42]
לֹא־תִרְאֶה אֶת־פָּנַי כִּי אִם־לִפְנֵי הֱבִיאֲךָ אֵת מִיכַל, "You shall
not see my face, <u>unless</u> you bring Michal" (2 Sam 3:13),
נְהַג וָלֵךְ אַל־תַּעֲצָר־לִי לִרְכֹּב כִּי אִם־אָמַרְתִּי לָךְ, "Drive and go
forward; do not slow down the pace for me <u>unless</u> I tell
you" (2 Kgs 4:24).

**(n) Interrogative** – Occasionally, כִּי will function to introduce an interrogative clause: כִּי הָאָדָם עֵץ הַשָּׂדֶה, "Are
the trees of the field as human beings?" (Deut 20:19),
כִּי־הִצִּילוּ אֶת־שֹׁמְרוֹן מִיָּדִי, "Have they delivered Samaria from
my hand?" (2 Kgs 18:34).

## 4.3.5 פֶּן

**Consequential** – This conjunction most often indicates an
undesirable action or situation that arises from another ac-
tion as a consequence: לֹא תֹאכְלוּ מִמֶּנּוּ וְלֹא תִגְּעוּ בּוֹ פֶּן־תְּמֻתוּן,
"You shall not eat from it or touch it, <u>lest</u> you die"

---

[42] Schoors 1981, 251–52.

אַל־תַּשְׁמַע קוֹלְךָ עִמָּנוּ פֶּן־יִפְגְּעוּ בָכֶם אֲנָשִׁים מָרֵי נֶפֶשׁ (Gen 3:3), "Do not let your voice be heard among us, *or else* fierce men will attack you" (Judg 18:25), אַל־תּוֹכַח לֵץ פֶּן־יִשְׂנָאֶךָּ, "Do not reprove a scoffer, *lest* he hate you" (Prov 9:8).

## 4.4 Particles of Existence/Nonexistence

Hebrew uses the two words אַיִן and יֵשׁ to denote existence or nonexistence.[43]

### 4.4.1 אַיִן

*(a) Nonexistence* – denies the existence of a substantive, in which case it usually occurs in apposition with a preceding noun: אָדָם אַיִן לַעֲבֹד אֶת־הָאֲדָמָה, "*there was no* human to cultivate the ground" (Gen 2:5). However, it may also occur in the construct state with a following noun or pronoun: אֵין־יִרְאַת אֱלֹהִים בַּמָּקוֹם הַזֶּה, "*There is no* fear of God in this place" (Gen 20:11).

*(b) Nonpossession* – The particle is also used with the לְ preposition to show that the object of the preposition does not possess a substantive: אֵין לָהּ וָלָד, "*she had no* child" (Gen 11:30), וְאִם־אֵין לָאִישׁ גֹּאֵל, "But if *the man has no* next of kin" (Num 5:8).

*(c) Negative* – The particle can also negate verbal clauses when bound with a pronominal suffix. In this construction, the bound pronominal suffix is the subject of the verbal action that is being negated, usually a participle: אֵינֶנִּי נֹתֵן לָכֶם תֶּבֶן, "*I am not giving* you straw" (Exod 5:10), אֵינֶנִּי שֹׁמֵעַ, "*I will not listen*" (Isa 1:15).

---

[43] Joüon and Muraoka 1993, 576 and 604–05; Williams 1976, 67–68 and 79; van der Merwe, Naudé, and Kroeze 1999, 320–21; Seow 1995, 107–08.

## 4.4.2 יֵשׁ

*(a) Existence* – Antithetical to אַיִן, the particle יֵשׁ affirms the existence of a substantive. The particle can function in the same way as אַיִן in modifying a nominal clause: אָכֵן יֵשׁ יְהוָה בַּמָּקוֹם הַזֶּה, "Surely, YHWH *is* in this place" (Gen 28:16). With the pronominal suffixes, it indicates the subject of a verbless clause: אֶת־אֲשֶׁר יֶשְׁנוֹ פֹּה, "with *the one who is* here" (Deut 29:14 [Eng 29:15]).

*(b) Possession* – With the preposition לְ bound to a pronominal suffix, יֵשׁ expresses possession, with the pronominal suffix indicating the owner: מַה־יֶּשׁ־לָךְ, "What *do you have?*" (2 Kgs 4:2 *Qere*), יֶשׁ־לִי רָב, "*I have* enough" (Gen 33:9).

*(c) Predicate* – When bound to a pronominal suffix, יֵשׁ can function to express the subject of a participle. This usage is normally preceded by אִם to expresses intention or desire: אִם־יֶשְׁךָ מְשַׁלֵּחַ אֶת־אָחִינוּ אִתָּנוּ, "*If you will send* our brother with us" (Gen 43:4), וְעַתָּה אִם־יֶשְׁכֶם עֹשִׂים חֶסֶד, "Now then, *if you will deal* loyally" (Gen 24:49).

## 4.5 The Particles הִנֵּה and וְהִנֵּה

Though traditionally rendered in English as "Behold" or "Lo," neither הִנֵּה nor וְהִנֵּה is limited to a demonstrative function. In fact, the demonstrative nature of either particle is not even the primary aspect. Their primary function, rather, is as a "particle of interest,"[44] which calls special attention to an element of the context, either a single word or an entire statement. As the particle calls attention to an object, it also indicates a shift in perspective within a narrative. In essence, the particle introduces movement away from the narratival perspective to present vividly the perspective of a particular speaker or figure within the narrative. Consequently, הִנֵּה marks introductory or

---

[44] Waltke and O'Connor 1990, 300; Pratico and Van Pelt 2001, 148–49.

transitional signals within a dialogue, as the unique view of each speaker is laid out (see "*perception*" in section 4.5.2).[45] Furthermore, the particle has a strong "overtone of feeling"[46] based on its nature as an exclamation. Thus, there is no single rendering in English that adequately captures the force of הִנֵּה or וְהִנֵּה, since the specific use of either particle is dependent not only on textual context but also on the emotional mindset of the speaker and the other figures of the narrative as well.

### 4.5.1 הִנֵּה

The particle without the *waw* conjunction is unique in that it is usually used with the verb אָמַר.[47] Hence, it serves to introduce direct speech, much like the recitative function of the particle כִּי (see section 4.3.4,1). Within this use, there are a variety of nuances that the particle הִנֵּה can express:

*(a) Exclamatory* – functions quite frequently as a "presentative exclamation,"[48] emphasizing "immediacy" or "here-and-now-ness,"[49] often as a response to a summons. This exclamatory emphasis is often related to the presence of people or certain objects, calling attention to and focusing upon an object:[50] הִנְנִי שְׁלָחֵנִי, "*Here I am*, send me!" (Isa 6:8), הִנֵּה הָאֵשׁ וְהָעֵצִים וְאַיֵּה הַשֶּׂה לְעֹלָה, "*Here is* the fire and the wood, but where is the lamb for the sacrifice?" (Gen 22:7), וַיֹּאמֶר אֵלָיו אַבְרָהָם וַיֹּאמֶר הִנֵּנִי, "[God] said to him 'Abraham,' and [Abraham] said '*Here I am!*'" (Gen 22:1).

*(b) Immediacy* – Related to the exclamatory, הִנֵּה used with verbs or participles can point to the immediacy of the action of the verb or participle: הִנֵּה אָבִיךָ חֹלֶה, "Your father is

---

[45] Schneider 1989, 261–68.
[46] McCarthy 1980, 331.
[47] Zewi 1996, 21–37.
[48] Waltke and O'Connor 1990, 674.
[49] Lambdin 1971a, 168.
[50] Berlin 1983, 91. See also Andersen 1974, 94.

הִנֵּה אֲנָשִׁים בָּאוּ הֵנָּה הַלַּיְלָה מִבְּנֵי יִשְׂרָאֵל, <u>*now*</u> sick" (Gen 48:1), "Some men from the people of Israel have come here <u>*just*</u> tonight" (Josh 2:2).

### 4.5.2 וְהִנֵּה

The form of the particle with the conjunction occurs quite often with verbs of sight, or related contexts, typically introducing the object of perception.[51]

*(a) Immediate perception* – In some narrative situations, וְהִנֵּה points not to an immediate action but to the immediate perception of an action or the results of an action. Thus, it functions to indicate "suddenness in the presentation of perception," not a sense of immediacy or suddenness in the events of the narrative: וַיְהִי בַּחֲצִי הַלַּיְלָה וַיֶּחֱרַד הָאִישׁ וַיִּלָּפֵת וְהִנֵּה אִשָּׁה שֹׁכֶבֶת מַרְגְּלֹתָיו, "It happened in the middle of the night that the man was startled and bent forward; and <u>*behold*</u> there was a woman lying at his feet" (Ruth 3:8), וּבֹעַז עָלָה הַשַּׁעַר וַיֵּשֶׁב שָׁם וְהִנֵּה הַגֹּאֵל עֹבֵר, "Now Boaz went to the gate and sat there, <u>*and the kinsmen-redeemer was passing by*</u>" (Ruth 4:1).[52]

*(b) Perception* – With verbs of perception or within a perceptual situation, וְהִנֵּה will introduce a perception from a perspective that is distinct from the narrator or other figures in the narrative[53] and unique to the speaker: what may be termed the "participant perspective."[54] Unlike "immediate

---

[51] Zewi 1996, 37.

[52] Berlin 1983, 91. Berlin notes that in the two verses, the emphasis of suddenness is not placed on the action of Ruth lying down or the redeemer passing by. Rather, the emphasis is on the fact that, at a certain moment, Boaz noticed these actions occurring. Thus, the particle indicates "Boaz's perception as he becomes aware of Ruth's presence" and points out that "Boaz suddenly saw the *goel*, and not that the *goel* arrived immediately."

[53] Berlin 1983, 60.

[54] Andersen 1974, 94.

perception," this use of וְהִנֵּה refers to the unique perspective of the speaker as he or she perceives an action,
and not necessarily the immediate nature of the action.
Based on the emotionality of the particle, the object of
perception is often colored with a sense of excitement:
וָאָקֻם בַּבֹּקֶר לְהֵינִיק אֶת־בְּנִי וְהִנֵּה־מֵת, "I got up in the morning
to nurse my son and *[saw that] he was dead*" (1 Kgs 3:21),

וְלֹא־הֶאֱמַנְתִּי לַדְּבָרִים עַד אֲשֶׁר־בָּאתִי וַתִּרְאֶינָה עֵינַי וְהִנֵּה
לֹא־הֻגַּד־לִי הַחֵצִי

"I did not believe the reports until I came and my eyes had
seen *that the half was not told to me*" (1 Kgs 10:7).

*(c) Logical* – As it introduces perceptions, the particle also
has various *logical functions,* connecting two ideas together:
   (c.1) *Causal* – וְהִנֵּה אֵין־יוֹסֵף בַּבּוֹר וַיִּקְרַע אֶת־בְּגָדָיו, "*Because*
Joseph was not in the pit, he tore his clothes" (Gen 37:29),
וַיָּרָץ אֶל־תּוֹךְ הַקָּהָל וְהִנֵּה הֵחֵל הַנֶּגֶף בָּעָם, "Then [Aaron] ran
into the midst of the assembly *because* the plague had begun
among the people" (Num 17:12 [Eng. 16:47]).
   (c.2) *Occasion/circumstantial* –

וְהִנֵּה אֲנַחְנוּ מְאַלְּמִים אֲלֻמִּים בְּתוֹךְ הַשָּׂדֶה

"*While* we were binding sheaves in the field (Gen 37:7),
וַיָּבֹא אֶל־הָאִישׁ וְהִנֵּה עֹמֵד עַל־הַגְּמַלִּים עַל־הָעָיִן, "He went to the
man *while* he was standing by the camels at the spring"
(Gen 24:30).
   (c.3) *Conditional* –

וְרָאָהוּ הַכֹּהֵן בַּיּוֹם הַשְּׁבִיעִי וְהִנֵּה הַנֶּגַע עָמַד בְּעֵינָיו לֹא־פָשָׂה

"The priest will look at him on the seventh day, and *if,*
in his eyes, the infection has not changed" (Lev 13:5),
וְהִנֵּה נֵלֵךְ וּמַה־נָּבִיא לָאִישׁ, "*If* we go, what shall we take for
the man?" (1 Sam 9:7).
   (c.4) *Temporal* –

וְהִנֵּה אָנֹכִי בָא בְּקְצֵה הַמַּחֲנֶה וְהָיָה כַאֲשֶׁר־אֶעֱשֶׂה כֵּן תַּעֲשׂוּן

"*When* I arrive to the outskirts of town, do as I do" (Judg 7:17), וְיָרַדְתָּ לְפָנַי הַגִּלְגָּל וְהִנֵּה אָנֹכִי יֹרֵד אֵלֶיךָ, "Go down before me to Gilgal, and [*then*] I will go down to you" (1 Sam 10:8).

(c.5) *Result –* הֵן לִי לֹא נָתַתָּה זָרַע וְהִנֵּה בֶן־בֵּיתִי יוֹרֵשׁ אֹתִי, "You have given me no offspring, _so_ one born in my house is my heir" (Gen 15:3), כָּרְתָה בְרִיתְךָ אִתִּי וְהִנֵּה יָדִי עִמָּךְ לְהָסֵב אֵלֶיךָ אֶת־כָּל־יִשְׂרָאֵל, "Make your covenant with me, _so that_ my hand will be with you to bring to you all of Israel" (2 Sam 3:12).

(c.6) *Adversative –*

כִּי לֹא אֶחְמוֹל עוֹד עַל־יֹשְׁבֵי הָאָרֶץ נְאֻם־יְהוָה וְהִנֵּה אָנֹכִי מַמְצִיא אֶת־הָאָדָם אִישׁ בְּיַד־רֵעֵהוּ

" 'For I will no longer have pity on the inhabitants of the land,' declares YHWH, '_but rather_ I will cause the men to fall each into the hand of a neighbor' " (Zech 11:6),

וַיִּקְרָא אֲדֹנָי יְהוִה צְבָאוֹת בַּיּוֹם הַהוּא לִבְכִי וּלְמִסְפֵּד וּלְקָרְחָה וְלַחֲגֹר שָׂק וְהִנֵּה שָׂשׂוֹן וְשִׂמְחָה

"The lord, YHWH of hosts, called on that day to weeping and lamenting, to shaving the head and wearing sackcloth. _Instead_ there is rejoicing and merriment" (Isa 22:12–13).

# 5  Clauses and Sentences

Thus far in this book we have treated the syntax of individual words and phrases. By "phrases" we mean the function of individual words and the way they relate to each other in larger units to create noun phrases, verb phrases, adverbial phrases, and prepositional phrases. In most cases, a phrase is a series of words capable of serving the syntactical function of a single word. In this final section, we move beyond phrases to clauses and sentences.[1]

The very definitions of "clause" and "sentence" may be problematic, and so we begin by clarifying a few more terms. Put simply, a clause is a group of words containing a subject and only one predicate.[2] This distinguishes a clause from

---

[1] As elsewhere in this grammar, we have retained traditional terminology and explanations for most grammatical functions. However, the research of a growing number of scholars employing discourse analysis (or "discourse linguistics," also known in Europe as "text linguistics"; see Lowery 1995, 107) have highlighted the inadequacy of the traditional word-oriented and sentence-oriented study of BH grammar, emphasizing instead the need to include longer units of text in linguistic study (van der Merwe 1994, 14–15; Andersen 1974, 17–20). Selected studies have been fruitful (see especially Andersen 1970 and 1974, Miller 1996 and 1999, and to some degree the grammar of van der Merwe, Naudé, and Kroeze 1999), but after thirty years of research, this burgeoning discipline lacks consensus of methodology and terminology. See further the various articles in Bodine 1995 and Bergen 1994.

[2] Behind our brief and functional definitions remain unsettled debates among linguists. For rigorous definitions and explanations of how these

a phrase, which makes no specific grammatical predication. Having clarified clause and phrase, we need to qualify the statement with which we began this unit, "Thus far in this book we have treated the syntax of individual words and phrases." Exceptions to this statement exist in our treatment of the finite verbal forms (sections 3.2 and 3.3) and verbal sequences (section 3.5). Since Hebrew finite verbs contain implied subjects (embedded by means of pronominal morphemes), the subject and predicate of a clause are both contained in the verb, making it impossible to study verbal syntax without considering clause-level relationships.[3] Nonetheless, our study of BH syntax prior to this point in the book has been *primarily* focused on the phrase-level relationships of Hebrew nouns, verbs, and particles.[4] In section 5, we now turn to clausal and interclausal relationships.

A sentence is comprised of one or more clauses and is the largest grammatical structural unit, except for the discourse or the text itself. Thus, sentences combine to create texts, which may be further analyzed in terms of text-linguistic conventions of cohesion and rhetorical organization.[5] So the grammatical hierarchy moves from word to phrase to clause to sentence to discourse.[6]

---

issues relate specifically to the grammar of BH, see Andersen 1974, 21–28; Joüon and Muraoka 1993, 561–64; van der Merwe, Naudé, and Kroeze 1999, 59–65; Waltke and O'Connor 1990, 77–80.

[3] So, for example, כָּתַב in Joshua 8:32 is used in reference to the law of Moses, which *he wrote* in the presence of the Israelites. Since the subject "he" is implied in the verb, there is in the Hebrew syntax no noun phrase separate from the verb phrase "wrote in the presence of the Israelites." Thus, our treatment of the verbs necessarily went beyond the phrase level and considered the subjects with their verbs in clause-level relationships.

[4] Thus, until this point in the book, we have limited ourselves to a consideration of morphosyntactical relationships, as much as possible. "Morphosyntax" considers the way two words relate to each other, or in some cases, complex combinations of words in phrases (Richter 1978–80, 2:3–83, esp. 4 for Richter's definition of *Wortgruppe*, "phrase").

[5] Van der Merwe, Naudé, and Kroeze 1999, 21, 51–52, and 65–66.

[6] Or more fully, from morpheme (the smallest unit of meaningful speech) to word to phrase to clause to sentence to discourse.

Further definition may be needed to clarify the types of sentences possible in BH. A sentence with only one clause may be termed a "simple" sentence, which may be either nominal or verbal (see section 5.1). So, for example, the following nominal clause in Psalm 121:5 could be taken separately as a simple sentence: יְהוָה שֹׁמְרֶךָ, "Yʜwʜ (is) your keeper." Likewise, the verbal clause in Genesis 1:1 could be isolated as a simple sentence: בָּרָא אֱלֹהִים, "God created." A sentence with two or more clauses of equal syntactical status (or function) is a "compound" sentence.[7] Consider the following compound sentence from 1 Samuel 3:9: וַיֵּלֶךְ שְׁמוּאֵל וַיִּשְׁכַּב בִּמְקוֹמוֹ, "Then Samuel went and lay down in his place." The two clauses have the same subject, and are of equal syntactical status, albeit in the second clause, the subject is implied and the action is modified by a prepositional phrase. BH narrative uses the ubiquitous conjunction *waw* in a flexible way to link verbs in chains and sequences in such compound constructions (see section 3.5). A sentence with two or more clauses of unequal status is a "complex" sentence, in which one clause is subordinated to the other, the independent or main clause.

## 5.1 Nominal and Verbal Clauses

Clauses may be further classified as coordinate or subordinate.[8] The two categories included in this section are clauses that may be coordinated or juxtaposed in apposition with other clauses to create compound sentences. Thus, the *nominal* and *verbal* clauses are the most basic types of clauses. The

---

[7] Andersen is correct in stating that this traditional definition is inadequate for encompassing the realities of BH (1974, 24–28). But the traditional definition of a compound sentence is still useful for our purposes. The reader should also be aware that grammarians have used the designation "compound sentence" in very different ways, as reference to Kautzsch and Meyer will attest (Kautzsch 1910, 457–58; Meyer 1992, 355–57).

[8] Joüon and Muraoka 1993, 561; Andersen 1974, 24–27

various subordinate clauses possible in BH will be covered in section 5.2.[9]

### 5.1.1 *Nominal Clause*

BH has the ability to form a clause without the use of a finite verb.[10] The subject of such nominal clauses will be a noun or pronoun. Its predicate will be another noun, pronoun, prepositional phrase, adverb, or infinitive construct.[11]

Nominal clauses can be classified in two general categories. *Identification* clauses signify the nature or identity of the subject, while *description* clauses speak of the quality or attributes of the subject.[12] The former typically answers "who" or "what," while the latter describes what the subject is like. The expected word order of a nominal clause may be generally classified according to the type of nominal clause. Identification clauses, in general, are ordered subject-predicate and take a definite predicate, while description clauses are generally ordered predicate-subject and have an indefinite predicate. However, there are many exceptions to the ordering, depending on the presence of additional syntactical elements, an intended emphasis

---

[9] Joüon and Muraoka 1993, 561–86; Meyer 1992, 348–57; Kautzsch 1910, 450–57; Williams 1976, 96–99; Chisholm 1998, 113–14; van der Merwe, Naudé, and Kroeze 1999, 59–65 and 336–50; and for epigraphic Hebrew, see Gogel 1998, 273–92.

[10] Such verbless clauses were also present in the Canaanite dialect of the Amarna letters (Rainey 1996, 1:180).

[11] And so more accurately, this could be called a "verbless" clause, since the predicate may be nearly anything except a verb (as per Andersen 1970, 17–30). Recently it has been doubted whether nominal clauses should be considered a distinct clausal type in BH. Rather, it is argued, the copula הָיָה was assumed in such clauses, but was optional and so frequently omitted as unnecessary. In this view, the so-called nominal or verbless clause is simply a variety of the verbal clauses without the copula included (Sinclair 1999, 75).

[12] Andersen preferred to speak of "identification" and "classification" clauses (1970, 31–34).

on one of the elements, or, in some cases, the rhetorical function of the nominal clause.[13]

**(a) Noun as predicate** (see predicate nominative, section 2.1.2) – אַתָּה הָאִישׁ, "You *are the man*" (2 Sam 12:7), יְהוָה מֶלֶךְ, "Yhwh *is king*" (Ps 10:16). The predicate may be a proper noun: אֲנִי יְהוָה, "I *am Yhwh*" (Gen 15:7), אֲנִי יוֹסֵף, "I *am Joseph*" (Gen 45:3). Note the predicate-subject word order in *description* nominal clauses: נָבִיא הוּא, "he *is a prophet*" (Gen 20:7).

Sometimes, a *pleonastic* pronoun is situated between the subject and the predicate. The pronoun is redundant since it is not necessary grammatically to complete the predication (compare יְהוָה הָאֱלֹהִים, "Yhwh *is God*" [Josh 22:34] with יְהוָה הוּא הָאֱלֹהִים, "Yhwh *is God*" [1 Kgs 18:39]): עֵשָׂו הוּא אֱדוֹם, "Esau *is Edom*" (Gen 36:8).[14]

**(b) Adjective as predicate** (see section 2.5.2) – הִנֵּה אֲנַחְנוּ פֹה בִיהוּדָה יְרֵאִים, "Look, we *are afraid* here in Judah" (1 Sam 23:3), טוֹב חַדְּבָר, "The word *is good*" (1 Kgs 2:38), וְהַמַּיִם רָעִים, "The water *is bad*" (2 Kgs 2:19), וְהַנַּעֲרָה יָפָה עַד־מְאֹד, "The girl *was* very *beautiful*" (1 Kgs 1:4). The adjective regularly serves as predicate in clauses of description: הָרָה אָנֹכִי, "I *am pregnant*" (2 Sam 11:5), טָמֵא הוּא, "he *is unclean*" (Lev 13:11).

**(c) Participle as predicate** (see section 3.4.3, b) – עֹבְרִים אֲנַחְנוּ מִבֵּית־לֶחֶם יְהוּדָה עַד־יַרְכְּתֵי הַר־אֶפְרַיִם, "We *are passing* from Bethlehem of Judah to the remote part of the hill country of Ephraim" (Judg 19:18), יְהוָה שֹׁמְרֶךָ, "Yhwh *is your keeper*" (Ps 121:5), כִּי הִנֵּה־אָנֹכִי מֵקִים רֹעֶה, "For I am about to *raise up* a shepherd" (Zech 11:16), מַדּוּעַ פָּנֶיךָ רָעִים וְאַתָּה אֵינְךָ חוֹלֶה, "Why is your face sad, though you *are not sick*?" (Neh 2:2).

---

[13] See Waltke and O'Connor 1990, 130–35; Joüon and Muraoka 1993, 568–76; Kautzsch 1910, 454; Williams 1976, 98–99.

[14] Such pleonastic uses of the pronouns are apparently not intended to denote emphasis. See Muraoka 1985, 15.

With the passive participle, there is quite often a desiderative sense in the predication: בָּרוּךְ יְהוָה, "*Blessed is* Yhwh" or "May Yhwh *be blessed*" (Ruth 4:14), אֹרְרֶיךָ אָרוּר וּמְבָרֲכֶיךָ בָּרוּךְ, "*Cursed be* those who curse you, and *blessed be* those who bless you" (Gen 27:29).[15]

**(d) Prepositional phrase as predicate** – הָאֱלֹהִים בַּשָּׁמַיִם, "God is *in heaven*" (Eccl 5:1 [Eng 5:2]), קוֹל מִלְחָמָה בָּאָרֶץ, "The noise of battle *is in the land*" (Jer 50:22), לַיהוָה הוּא, "It *is Yhwh's*" (Lev 27:26), לֹא בָרַעַשׁ יְהוָה, "Yhwh *was not in the earthquake*" (1 Kgs 19:11), יְהוָה עִמְּךָ, "Yhwh *is with you*" (Judg 6:12).

### 5.1.2 *Verbal Clause*

The subject of a verbal clause will be a noun or pronoun, and its predicate will be a finite verb (i.e., perfect or imperfect aspect), or a nonfinite verb functioning as one.

Because the verbal clause is so prevalent in BH, we offer here a survey of its forms.

### (a) Subject of the verbal clause

(a.1) *Noun as subject* – The subject of a verbal clause is most often expressed by a noun: וַיְצַו יְהוֹשֻׁעַ אֶת־הַכֹּהֲנִים, "*Joshua* commanded the priests" (Josh 4:17), וַיִּכְתֹּב מֹשֶׁה אֵת כָּל־דִּבְרֵי יְהוָה, "*Moses* wrote down all the words of Yhwh" (Exod 24:4).

(a.2) *Pronoun as subject* – When an independent personal pronoun functions as the subject of a verb, there is generally a sense of prominence, since the subject is already inherent in the verbal form.

Specifically, the pronoun as subject can be *disjunctive,* expressing a strong contrasting or disjunctive sense, so that

---

[15] Joüon and Muraoka 1993, 566 and 576.

the subject of the verb is highlighted against another:

וַיָּשֶׂם אֶת־הַשְּׁפָחוֹת וְאֶת־יַלְדֵיהֶן רִאשֹׁנָה וְאֶת־לֵאָה וִילָדֶיהָ
אַחֲרֹנִים וְאֶת־רָחֵל וְאֶת־יוֹסֵף אַחֲרֹנִים וְהוּא עָבַר לִפְנֵיהֶם

"He put the maids and their children in front, and Leah and her children next, and Rachel and Joseph next. *But he* passed on before them . . ." (Gen 33:2–3).

The pronoun as subject can also be *emphatic,* highlighting the subject: הוּא יְשׁוּפְךָ רֹאשׁ וְאַתָּה תְּשׁוּפֶנּוּ עָקֵב, "*He* shall bruise your head, and *you shall bruise* his heel" (Gen 3:15), הוּא יַעֲבֹר לִפְנֵי הָעָם הַזֶּה, "*he shall go* across before this people" (Deut 3:28).[16]

With the first-person pronoun, the emphatic reference to the self can be *assertive,* connoting a sense of self-consciousness or assertiveness:[17] וַאֲנִי גְּמַלְתִּיךָ הָרָעָה, "*But I* have dealt wickedly with you" (1 Sam 24:18), אָנֹכִי אֵשֵׁב עַד שׁוּבֶךְ, "*I* will remain until you return" (Judg 6:18).

(a.3) *Indefinite subject* – There are situations in which the subject of a verb points to no person in particular, but to a general "someone," "one," or "anyone." There are several constructions that can express this indefinite[18] or vague[19] subject. First, the *third person masculine singular active verb,* either with a substantival participle as subject, or without a stated subject, often expresses an indefinite subject: עַל־כֵּן קָרָא שְׁמָהּ בָּבֶל, "Therefore *one calls* its name Babel" (Gen 11:9), כִּי־יִפֹּל הַנֹּפֵל מִמֶּנּוּ, "If *anyone falls* from it [your roof]" (Deut 22:8). Second, the *third person masculine singular passive verb* also expresses an indefinite subject: וְכִסָּה אֶת־עֵין הָאָרֶץ וְלֹא יוּכַל לִרְאֹת אֶת־הָאָרֶץ, "And they will cover the surface of the land so that *no one will be able to see* the land" (Exod 10:5), אָז הוּחַל לִקְרֹא בְּשֵׁם יְהוָה, "Then

---

[16] Muraoka 1985, 48.
[17] Joüon and Muraoka 1993, 539–40.
[18] Waltke and O'Connor 1990, 70.
[19] Joüon and Muraoka 1993, 578.

*people* began to call on the name of YHWH" (Gen 4:26). Third, the *third person masculine plural verb*, again either with a substantival participle as the subject, or an unstated subject, expresses an indefinite subject: מִן־הַבְּאֵר הַהִוא יַשְׁקוּ הָעֲדָרִים, "*They watered* the flock from that well" (Gen 29:2), שָׁמָּה קָבְרוּ אֶת־אַבְרָהָם וְאֵת שָׂרָה, "There *they buried* Abraham and Sarah" (Gen 49:31). Fourth, the *singular and plural participles* may also express an indefinite subject: לַבְּנִים אֹמְרִים לָנוּ עֲשׂוּ, "*They* keep saying to us 'Make bricks!'" (Exod 5:16), אֵלַי קֹרֵא מִשֵּׂעִיר, "*Someone* is calling me from Seir" (Isa 21:11). Finally, the anarthrous word אִישׁ may also serve as an indefinite subject of a finite verb: לִקְטוּ מִמֶּנּוּ אִישׁ לְפִי אָכְלוֹ, "Gather from it, *everyone*, as much as they should eat" (Exod 16:16), אִם־נָשַׁךְ הַנָּחָשׁ אֶת־אִישׁ וְהִבִּיט אֶל־נְחַשׁ הַנְּחֹשֶׁת וָחָי, "If the serpent bites *anyone*, and he looks to the bronze serpent, he will live" (Num 21:9).

## (b) Predication of the verbal clause

As noted, predication in the verbal clause is achieved by the finite verbs. The full treatment of the syntax of verbs is located in Chapter 3. This discussion will be limited to considering the construction of the verbal clause.

(b.1) *Word order* – The typical word order for a verbal clause is verb – subject – object (VSO): וַיֶּאֱהַב יִצְחָק אֶת־עֵשָׂו, "*Isaac loved Esau*" (Gen 25:28). Frequently, *temporal emphasis* will be marked by a temporal particle or adverbial phrase placed before the verb, describing the circumstances under which the predication of the verb takes place: בְּרֵאשִׁית בָּרָא אֱלֹהִים אֵת הַשָּׁמַיִם וְאֵת הָאָרֶץ, "*In the beginning*, God created heaven and earth" (Gen 1:1).

(b.2) The typical order of VSO will often be altered for several reasons. First, the subject can precede the verb to place *emphasis on the subject*: וְנֹחַ מָצָא חֵן בְּעֵינֵי יְהוָה, "*But Noah* found favor in the eyes of YHWH" (Gen 6:8); וַיהוָה הֵטִיל רוּחַ־גְּדוֹלָה אֶל־הַיָּם, "*YHWH* hurled a great wind

upon the sea" (Jonah 1:4).[20] Second, the subject will often precede the verb when there is a *change of subject* in
narratival flow:

וַיִּשָּׁבַע לוֹ וַיִּמְכֹּר אֶת־בְּכֹרָתוֹ לְיַעֲקֹב וְיַעֲקֹב נָתַן לְעֵשָׂו לֶחֶם
וּנְזִיד עֲדָשִׁים

"So he [Esau] swore to him, and sold his birthright
to Jacob. *Then Jacob* gave Esau bread and lentil stew"
(Gen 25:33–4).[21] Third, the object may also precede
the verb to place *emphasis on the object* of the verb:
אֶת־קֹלְךָ שָׁמַעְתִּי בַּגָּן, "*Your voice*, I heard in the garden" (Gen
3:10), אֶת־דִּמְכֶם לְנַפְשֹׁתֵיכֶם אֶדְרֹשׁ, "*Your lifeblood*, I will require" (Gen 9:5). Fourth, care must be taken with *poetic
texts* because word order in such texts is extremely variable:
כִּי־הוּא עַל־יַמִּים יְסָרָהּ, "For he has founded it upon the seas"
(Ps 24:2), עֹמְדוֹת הָיוּ רַגְלֵינוּ בִּשְׁעָרַיִךְ יְרוּשָׁלָ͏ִם, "Our feet are
standing within your gates, O Jerusalem!" (Ps 122:2). Fifth,
in answers to a question, the essential part of the *reply* usu-
ally comes first: וַיֹּאמְרוּ אֵלָיו אַיֵּה שָׂרָה אִשְׁתֶּךָ וַיֹּאמֶר הִנֵּה בָאֹהֶל,
"They said to him 'Where is Sarah, your wife?' He said,
'*She is in the tent*'" (Gen 18:9),

וַיֹּאמֶר חֲזָאֵל מַדּוּעַ אֲדֹנִי בֹכֶה וַיֹּאמֶר כִּי־יָדַעְתִּי אֵת
אֲשֶׁר־תַּעֲשֶׂה

"Hazael said 'Why is my lord weeping?' And he said,
'*Because I know* what you will do'" (2 Kgs 8:12). Finally,
*interrogative particles*, introducing both direct and indirect questions, will often come first in the verbal clause:
מִי הִגִּיד לְךָ כִּי עֵירֹם אָתָּה, "*Who* told you that you were
naked?" (Gen 3:11), עַל־מָה הִכִּיתָ אֶת־אֲתֹנְךָ, "*Why* have you
struck your donkey?" (Num 22:32).

---

[20] However, it is likely that only the redundant use of the pronoun when
a noun is subject marks real emphasis (5.1.2,a2; and see Andersen
1970, 24).

[21] Gesenius, however, notes that oftentimes when the subject precedes the
verb, it is not because of a shift in the narrative but because it is a description of the state of the subject within the narrative. (Kautzsch 1910, 455).

## 5.2 Subordinate Clauses

Subordinate clauses are dependent upon and modify an independent clause (or main clause) in a combination of two or more predications (see "complex" sentence at the beginning of this chapter). The following categories are helpful in considering the different types of subordination. Because BH makes no grammatical distinction between subordination and coordination, the reader should note carefully the variety of particles used to introduce them. However, it should also be kept in mind that most of these clauses can be introduced by a simple juxtaposition of clauses (asyndetically, or without conjunctions), or by the *waw* conjunctive.[22]

In general, there are two types of subordinate clauses: *complement* clauses and *supplement* clauses. Complement clauses are subordinate, but are closely linked to the main clause, and in fact cannot be omitted without changing the meaning of the main clause. Supplement clauses, on the other hand, are subordinate clauses that serve an adverbial function and could be omitted without changing the meaning of the main clause.[23] The first of these categories, the *substantival clause,* is a complement clause, and the rest are supplement clauses.[24]

### 5.2.1 *Substantival Clause*

BH can use either a nominal or verbal clause to serve as a noun substitute in nominative, genitive, or accusative

---

[22] The ubiquitous *waw* in BH narrative joins clauses paratactically (in coordination) or hypotactically (in subordination). Niccacci contends that many BH clauses are identified as subordinate due to contemporary conventions in European languages, even though the Hebrew syntax does not require subordination (Niccacci 1990, 128).

[23] Van der Merwe, Naudé, and Kroeze 1999, 64–65 and 367. A further distinction is that a speaker cannot perform a speech act in a supplement clause, but can in a complement clause.

[24] Joüon and Muraoka 1993, 589–645; Meyer 1992, 432–60; Waltke and O'Connor 1990, 632–46; Kautzsch 1910, 467–506; Williams 1976, 83–96; Chisholm 1998, 119–35; and for epigraphic Hebrew, see Gogel 1998, 277–91.

functions in relation to the main clause to which it is subordinate. As in our discussion of nouns (Chapter 2), the case names should not imply that BH marks these clauses morphologically as nominative, genitive, or accusative, only that the clauses function syntactically in these distinct roles.

*(a) Nominative* – substitutes for a noun in a nominative function, and is usually marked by the particles כִּי or אֲשֶׁר, or by an infinitive construct prefixed with the preposition לְ. Such a clause may serve as the subject of a main clause (see section 2.1.1): וַיֻּגַּד לְמֶלֶךְ מִצְרַיִם כִּי בָרַח הָעָם, "The king of Egypt was told that *the people had fled*" (Exod 14:5), or as a predicate nominative (section 2.1.2): זֶה אֲשֶׁר לֹא־תֹאכְלוּ, "This is that *which you shall not eat*" (Deut 14:12), or as a predicate adjective (sections 2.5.2 and 5.1.1,b): טוֹב אֲשֶׁר לֹא־תִדֹּר, "It is better that *you do not vow*" (Eccl 5:4). Such clauses also serve as the subject of interrogative sentences. The asyndetic (unmarked) nominative clause is rare.

*(b) Genitive* – substitutes for a noun in a genitive function (see section 2.2), following and modifying a noun or clause that precedes it. The relationship between the genitive clause and the element it modifies can be marked by a noun in construct followed by the genitive clause, or a simple juxtaposition of clauses: כָּל־יְמֵי הִתְהַלַּכְנוּ אִתָּם, "all of the days *we went about with them*" (1 Sam 25:15). The genitive clause may follow the relative particle אֲשֶׁר, as in the following: כָּל־יְמֵי אֲשֶׁר הַנֶּגַע בּוֹ יִטְמָא טָמֵא הוּא, "All the time that *he has an infection*, he is unclean" (Lev 13:46).

*(c) Accusative* – substitutes for a noun in an accusative function, indicating the object of a verb (section 2.3.1): וַיַּרְא יְהוָה כִּי רַבָּה רָעַת הָאָדָם, "Yʜwʜ saw that *the evil of humanity was great*" (Gen 6:5). An accusative acting as the object of a verb is frequently introduced by כִּי or

25:אֲשֶׁר וַיָּשֶׂם דָּנִיֵּאל עַל־לִבּוֹ אֲשֶׁר לֹא־יִתְגָּאָל, "But Daniel was resolved (literally: "placed upon his heart") that _he would not defile himself_" (Dan 1:8). The particle כִּי is especially common with verbs of perception, or in marking direct narration: וַתֵּרֶא הָאִשָּׁה כִּי טוֹב הָעֵץ, "The woman saw that _the tree was good_" (Gen 3:6), וַיֹּאמֶר כִּי אֶת־שֶׁבַע כְּבָשֹׂת תִּקַּח, "He said '_Take these seven ewe lambs_'" (Gen 21:30). Such clauses may also serve adverbially to modify the action of a verb (section 2.3.2): וַיַּרְא שָׁאוּל אֲשֶׁר־הוּא מַשְׂכִּיל מְאֹד, "Saul saw that _he was prospering greatly_" (1 Sam 18:15). The accusative function is the most frequent of the substantival uses.

### 5.2.2 *Conditional Clause*

Conditional sentences (expressing the "if...then..." relationship) are introduced by subordinate *conditional clauses* detailing the condition(s), that is, the "protasis." Several particles are used to introduce conditional clauses, including occasionally the simple *waw* conjunctive. At times the apodosis will be introduced by the simple *conditional waw* (section 4.3.3,f): וְרָאִיתִי מָה וְהִגַּדְתִּי לָךְ, "_If_ I see anything, then I will tell you_" (1 Sam 19:3), וְיֵשׁ יְהוָה עִמָּנוּ וְלָמָּה מְצָאַתְנוּ כָּל־זֹאת, "_If_ YHWH is with us, why then has all this befallen us?" (Judg 6:13).

The two primary types of conditional clauses are the real and unreal. The former points to an action or situation that either has been fulfilled in the past or has the potential of being fulfilled, while the latter is an action or situation that cannot be fulfilled, or stands contrary to what has occurred in the past.

**(a) Real conditional clauses** are most often introduced by the particles כִּי, אִם, or הֵן: אִם תִּהְיוּ כָמֹנוּ, "_If you become_ like us..." (Gen 34:15), כִּי־תִמְצָא אִישׁ לֹא תְבָרְכֶנּוּ, "_If you encounter a man_, do not greet him" (2 Kgs 4:29),

---

[25] At times even with the DDO, 1 Kgs 18:13.

מַה־נֹּאכַל בַּשָּׁנָה הַשְּׁבִיעִת הֵן לֹא נִזְרָע, "What shall we eat in the seventh year *if we cannot sow?*" (Lev 25:20).

On occasion, אֲשֶׁר can also function to indicate real conditional clauses:

אֶת־הַבְּרָכָה אֲשֶׁר תִּשְׁמְעוּ אֶל־מִצְוֹת יְהוָה אֱלֹהֵיכֶם

"the blessing [will obtain], *if you listen to the commands of YHWH, your God*" (Deut 11:27).

A negative real conditional clause can be introduced by אִם־לֹא: וְהָיָה אִם־לֹא חָפַצְתָּ בָּהּ, "*If you are not pleased* with her..." (Deut 21:14).

**(b) Unreal conditional clauses** are primarily marked by the particle לוּ, and the related particle לוּלֵא: לוּלֵא הִתְמַהְמָהְנוּ, "*if we had not delayed*" (Gen 43:10,)

לוּ הַחֲיִתֶם אוֹתָם לֹא הָרַגְתִּי אֶתְכֶם

"*if you had let them live*, I would not kill you" (Judg 8:19). The particle כִּי can also function in this manner.

### 5.2.3 *Final Clause*

BH does not always make a sharp distinction between final and result clauses, which taken together may also be called "telic clauses."[26] A primary means of introducing final clauses is with the infinitive construct prefixed with the לְ preposition: וַיַּעֲלֶה אַחְאָב לֶאֱכֹל וְלִשְׁתּוֹת, "so Ahab *went up to eat and to drink*" (1 Kgs 18:42, a final clause), לָמָּה לֹא מָצָתִי חֵן בְּעֵינֶיךָ לָשׂוּם אֶת־מַשָּׂא כָּל־הָעָם הַזֶּה עָלָי, "why have I not found favor in your eyes, *that you laid the burden* of all this people on me?" (Num 11:11, a result clause).

**(a) Final clauses** – express the purpose or motivation for the action or situation of the main clause. They are often introduced by the particle אֲשֶׁר. The particles לְמַעַן or בַּעֲבוּר also function in this manner,

---

[26] Joüon and Muraoka 1993, 633–35; Williams 1967, 86.

often with the particle אֲשֶׁר, but not necessarily so: וְאַשְׁמִעֵם אֶת־דְּבָרַי אֲשֶׁר יִלְמְדוּן לְיִרְאָה אֹתִי, "I will make them hear my words, *so that they may learn to fear me*" (Deut 4:10), לְמַעַן יַאֲמִינוּ כִּי־נִרְאָה אֵלֶיךָ יְהוָה, "*so that they might believe* that YHWH appeared to you" (Exod 4:5).

Purpose can also be expressed by an imperative with a simple prefixed *waw* conjunctive:

מָה אֶעֱשֶׂה לָכֶם וּבַמָּה אֲכַפֵּר וּבָרְכוּ אֶת־נַחֲלַת יְהוָה

"What can I do for you, and how can I make atonement *that you will bless the inheritance of YHWH?*" (2 Sam 21:3).

*(b) Result clauses* – express the end result or consequence of the action or situation of the main clause. Like final clauses, result clauses are introduced by אֲשֶׁר. The particle לְמַעַן, governing a finite or infinite verb, also functions to introduce result clauses:[27] וַיִּקְרָא אַבְרָהָם שֵׁם־הַמָּקוֹם הַהוּא יְהוָה יִרְאֶה אֲשֶׁר יֵאָמֵר הַיּוֹם, "Abraham called the name of that place 'YHWH will provide,' *so that it is said to this day* ..." (Gen 22:14).

Often, if the main clause is a question, the result clause is marked by כִּי: מָה־אֱנוֹשׁ כִּי־תִזְכְּרֶנּוּ, "What is man *that you remember him?*" (Ps 8:5),

הַאֱלֹהִים אָנִי לְהָמִית וּלְהַחֲיוֹת כִּי־זֶה שֹׁלֵחַ אֵלַי לֶאֱסֹף אִישׁ מִצָּרַעְתּוֹ

"Am I God, to kill and to make alive, *that this man is sending* word to me to cure a man of his leprosy?" (2 Kgs 5:7).

*(c) Negative final/result clauses* – serve as the negative of either the final or result clause, and are introduced with אֲשֶׁר לֹא: אֲשֶׁר לֹא יִשְׁמְעוּ אִישׁ שְׂפַת רֵעֵהוּ, "*so that they will not understand each other*" (Gen 11:7, a negative final clause), אֲשֶׁר לֹא־יֹאמְרוּ זֹאת אִיזָבֶל, "*so that no one will say* 'This is Jezebel'" (2 Kgs 9:37, a negative result clause).

[27] Waltke and O'Connor 1990, 638.

The particles פֶּן, לְבִלְתִּי, and לְמַעַן לֹא function to mark a negative final clause: בְּלִבִּי צָפַנְתִּי אִמְרָתֶךָ לְמַעַן לֹא אֶחֱטָא־לָךְ, "I have hidden your word in my heart, *so that I will not sin against you*" (Ps 119:11, a negative final clause).

### 5.2.4 *Temporal Clause*

The subordinate *temporal clause* expresses the time frame of an action or situation, and how it relates to the idea of the main clause. A primary means of expressing temporal clauses is the infinitive with the prepositions בְּ, כְּ, אַחַר, אַחֲרֵי, or מִן; but other prepositions are used as well. As demonstrated by the variety of temporal clauses that follow, so the infinitive can express a simultaneous, preceding, or succeeding action (see section 3.4.1,b): בֶּן־שְׁלֹשִׁים שָׁנָה דָוִד בְּמָלְכוֹ, "David was about thirty years old *when he began to reign*" (2 Sam 5:4), בָּעֶרֶב כְּבוֹא הַשֶּׁמֶשׁ, "in the evening, *when the sun sets*" (Deut 16:6), אַחֲרֵי הַכֹּתוֹ אֵת סִיחֹן, "*after he had defeated* Sihon" (Deut 1:4), וַיִּמָּלֵא שִׁבְעַת יָמִים אַחֲרֵי הַכּוֹת־יְהוָה אֶת־הַיְאֹר, "seven days passed *after* YHWH *had struck* the Nile" (Exod 7:25).

In addition to the infinitive, there are also other means by which a temporal clause is expressed.

**(a) Contemporary action or situation** – Introduced by כַּאֲשֶׁר or כִּי, a subordinate clause can describe an action or situation that is contemporary with the main clause: וַיְהִי כַּאֲשֶׁר כִּלָּה לְהַקְרִיב אֶת־הַמִּנְחָה וַיְשַׁלַּח אֶת־הָעָם, "*When he [Ehud] presented the tribute,* he sent the people away" (Judg 3:18), וַיְהִי כַּאֲשֶׁר הִקְרִיב לָבוֹא מִצְרָיְמָה, "*When he* "[*Abraham*] *came* near to Egypt" (Gen 12:11).

**(b) Later or succeeding situation** – Introduced by עַד, which is also used in the compound forms עַד אֲשֶׁר, עַד אֲשֶׁר אִם, עַד אִם, or עַד כִּי the *temporal* clause may express action that is *later* than the action of the main clause. The particle טֶרֶם, also found prefixed with the preposition

בְּ, also expresses a later situation. The idea of succeeding action is also expressed by the *wayyiqtol* pattern, as well as the conjunction לִפְנֵי and the adverb בָּרִאשֹׁנָה. It should be noted that the translation of the various particles ranges from "until" and "before" to "after." What is critical to note, however, is that the subordinate clause refers to a situation that comes temporally after the main clause, regardless of how the particles are translated in English: תָּמִים אַתָּה בִּדְרָכֶיךָ מִיּוֹם הִבָּרְאָךְ עַד־נִמְצָא עַוְלָתָה בָּךְ, "You were blameless in your ways from the day you were created, *until iniquity was found in you*" (Ezek 28:15), וְלֹא־הֶאֱמַנְתִּי לַדְּבָרִים עַד אֲשֶׁר־בָּאתִי וַתִּרְאֶינָה עֵינַי, "I did not believe things *until I came and my eyes saw*" (1 Kgs 10:7), וַיְהִי כַּאֲשֶׁר כִּלּוּ הַגְּמַלִּים לִשְׁתּוֹת וַיִּקַּח הָאִישׁ נֶזֶם זָהָב, "When the camels had finished drinking, *the man took* a gold ring" (Gen 24:22), וַיָּלִינוּ שָׁם טֶרֶם יַעֲבֹרוּ, "They camped there *before they crossed over*" (Josh 3:1).

The construction אַחַר הַדְּבָרִים is often used in narrative to indicate a later situation:

אַחַר הַדְּבָרִים הָאֵלֶּה הָיָה דְבַר־יְהוָה אֶל־אַבְרָם

*After these things*, the word of Yʜwʜ came to Abram" (Gen 15:1).

*(c) Preceding situation* – shows a situation that occurred before the action of the main clause and is introduced most often by אַחַר/אַחֲרֵי, which can be used with אֲשֶׁר. Less frequently, the particle מֵאָז is also used in this manner. Again, it is important to note that the subordinate clause refers to a situation coming before the main clause: "... in בְּאַרְבַּע עֶשְׂרֵה שָׁנָה אַחַר אֲשֶׁר הֻכְּתָה הָעִיר the fourteenth year *after the city was captured*" (Ezek 40:1), אַחַר הַדָּבָר הַזֶּה לֹא־שָׁב יָרָבְעָם מִדַּרְכּוֹ הָרָעָה, "*After this event*, Jeroboam did not turn from his evil ways" (1 Kgs 13:33),

וַיְהִי בָרָד וְאֵשׁ מִתְלַקַּחַת בְּתוֹךְ הַבָּרָד כָּבֵד מְאֹד אֲשֶׁר
לֹא־הָיָה כָמֹהוּ בְּכָל־אֶרֶץ מִצְרַיִם מֵאָז הָיְתָה לְגוֹי

"So there was hail and fire flashing continually in the midst of the hail, very severe, such as had not been in all the land of Egypt *since it became a nation*" (Exod 9:24).

Often, the *waw* conjunctive plus subject (noun or pronoun) plus perfect denotes present perfect or pluperfect in English (only context dictates which is intended):[28] וַיָּשָׁב אַהֲרֹן אֶל־מֹשֶׁה אֶל־פֶּתַח אֹהֶל מוֹעֵד וְהַמַּגֵּפָה נֶעֱצָרָה, "Aaron returned to Moses at the entrance of the tent of meeting; now the plague *had been checked*" (Num 17:15 [Eng. 16:50]),), הַבֹּקֶר הָיָה וְרוּחַ הַקָּדִים נָשָׂא אֶת־הָאַרְבֶּה, "When it was morning, the east wind *had (already) brought* the locusts" (Exod 10:13).

## 5.2.5 *Causal Clause*

The subordinate *causal* clause shows the reason or basis for the action or situation of the main clause. BH has a variety of causal clauses that are introduced by a simple *waw* conjunctive,[29] an infinitive clause (typically an infinitive construct with the לְ preposition), a verbal clause (with perfect plus *waw* consecutive), or the particles כִּי and אֲשֶׁר, although Joüon notes that the latter particle often shows weak causation.[30] Both כִּי and אֲשֶׁר can also be used in conjunction with יַעַן, which can be used alone as well. The preposition עַל can also be used to denote a causal clause, either alone or in conjunction with כִּי or אֲשֶׁר. The preposition is also used in the formulaic statement עַל־דְּבַר אֲשֶׁר.[31] There are also many less frequent combinations of particles and prepositions that are used to introduce causal clauses.

---

[28] So *waw* + S(ubject) + perfect = anterior action or situation. Zevit has demonstrated the clarity with which authors of BH could thus mark anterior action, that is, action that began prior to the action of the main clause (Zevit 1998, 15–37, and see Joüon and Muraoka 1993, 624).

[29] Kautzsch 1910, 492.

[30] Joüon and Muraoka 1993, 638.

[31] Waltke and O'Connor 1990, 640.

Examples: כִּי עָשִׂיתָ זֹּאת אָרוּר אַתָּה, "*Because* you did this, you are cursed" (Gen 3:14), יַעַן אֲמָרְכֶם אֶת־הַדָּבָר הַזֶּה, "*because* you speak this word" (Jer 23:38),

וְגֵר לֹא תִלְחָץ וְאַתֶּם יְדַעְתֶּם אֶת־נֶפֶשׁ הַגֵּר

"You shall not oppress a stranger, *since* you know the life of a stranger" (Exod 23:9).

*(a)* Joüon notes that the particle עֵקֶב, which is sometimes with אֲשֶׁר, has a special causal nuance, expressing "in recompense for the fact" of some action, or in a negative manner, "in punishment for the fact":[32] וְהִתְבָּרְכוּ בְזַרְעֲךָ כֹּל גּוֹיֵי הָאָרֶץ עֵקֶב אֲשֶׁר שָׁמַעְתָּ בְּקֹלִי, "By your seed all the nations of the earth will be blessed, *because* you obeyed my voice" (Gen 22:18), כֵּן תֹּאבֵדוּן עֵקֶב לֹא תִשְׁמְעוּן בְּקוֹל יְהוָה אֱלֹהֵיכֶם, "... so you shall perish *because* you have not listened to the voice of YHWH your God" (Deut 8:20).

*(b)* The preposition מִן can also function to indicate cause: נְעָלֵינוּ בָּלוּ מֵרֹב הַדֶּרֶךְ מְאֹד, "Our sandals are worn out *because* of our long journey" (Josh 9:13), לֹא־יָכֹל עוֹד לְהָשִׁיב אֶת־אַבְנֵר דָּבָר מִיִּרְאָתוֹ אֹתוֹ, "He could no longer speak a word to Abner, *because* he was afraid of him" (2 Sam 3:11).

### 5.2.6 *Comparative Clause*

*(a)* A subordinate clause will often function to make a comparison with the action or situation of the main clause. The situation that is the standard of comparison is usually stated in the main clause, or apodosis. The compared situation is typically denoted by the subordinate clause, the protasis. The most common construction for the comparative clauses is כַּאֲשֶׁר plus protasis, followed by כֵּן plus apodosis: וַיְהִי כַּאֲשֶׁר פָּתַר־לָנוּ כֵּן הָיָה, "And *just as* he interpreted for us,

---

[32] Joüon and Muraoka 1993, 639.

*so* it happened" (Gen 41:13). The reverse order, where the apodosis comes first, also occurs: כֵּן תַּעֲשֶׂה כַּאֲשֶׁר דִּבַּרְתָּ, "*So* do, *just as* you have spoken" (Gen 18:5).

*(b)* The comparative relationship between clauses is also denoted by the particles כְּ and כֵּן, where the former governs the main clause, typically a verbal or infinitival clause,[33] and the latter governs the subordinate clause:

כְּעֵינֵי עֲבָדִים אֶל־יַד אֲדוֹנֵיהֶם כְּעֵינֵי שִׁפְחָה אֶל־יַד גְּבִרְתָּהּ
כֵּן עֵינֵינוּ אֶל־יְהוָה

"*Just as* the eyes of the servants [look] to the hand of their masters; *just as* the eyes of the maidservant [look] to the hand of her mistress; *so* our eyes [look] to YHWH" (Ps 123:2).

The subordinate clause of the comparative relationship can also be introduced by the preposition כְּ: כִּי כָמוֹךָ כְּפַרְעֹה, "for *you are like Pharaoh*" (Gen 44:18), כָּכֶם כַּגֵּר יִהְיֶה לִפְנֵי יְהוָה "*As you are, so is the alien* before YHWH" (Num 15:15).

### 5.2.7 *Exceptive Clause*

This subordinate clause functions to present an exception to the idea, action, or situation that is presented in the main clause. The particle אִם, used either alone or with the particles בִּלְתִּי (which also functions alone) or כִּי and אֶפֶס כִּי, as well as אַךְ and רַק, introduce these clauses (see sections 4.2.2 on אַךְ, 4.2.9 on כִּי, 4.2.15 on רַק): לֹא אֲשַׁלֵּחֲךָ כִּי אִם־בֵּרַכְתָּנִי, "I will not release you, *unless you bless me!*" (Gen 32:27 [Eng 32:26]),

גַּם־יְהוָה הֶעֱבִיר חַטָּאתְךָ לֹא תָמוּת אֶפֶס כִּי־נִאֵץ נִאַצְתָּ
אֶת־אֹיְבֵי יְהוָה בַּדָּבָר הַזֶּה

---

33 Waltke and O'Connor 1990, 641.

"Yhwh has taken away your sin; you will not die. *However,* because by this deed you have given occasion to the enemies of Yhwh to blaspheme ..." (2 Sam 12:13–14).

### 5.2.8 *Restrictive Clause*

This clause places a limitation on the idea or action of the main clause. These clauses are most often introduced by the particles אֶפֶס כִּי, אַךְ, or רַק (see section 4.2.2,a on אַךְ, 4.2.15,a on רַק):

וְהִשְׁמַדְתִּי אֹתָהּ מֵעַל פְּנֵי הָאֲדָמָה אֶפֶס כִּי לֹא הַשְׁמֵיד אַשְׁמִיד אֶת־בֵּית יַעֲקֹב

"I will destroy it from the face of the earth, *but* I will not completely destroy the house of Jacob" (Amos 9:8), לַחְמֵנוּ נֹאכֵל וְשִׂמְלָתֵנוּ נִלְבָּשׁ רַק יִקָּרֵא שִׁמְךָ עָלֵינוּ, "We will eat our own bread, and wear our own clothes; *only* let us be called by your name (Isa 4:1), הָלֹךְ אֵלֵךְ עִמָּךְ אֶפֶס כִּי לֹא תִהְיֶה תִּפְאַרְתְּךָ, "I will surely go with you; *nevertheless,* the honor shall not be yours" (Judg 4:9).

### 5.2.9 *Intensive Clause*

This subordinate clause expands and adds to the idea of the main clause. The primary markers of these clauses are גַּם and אַף (see sections 4.2.4,b on אַף, 4.2.5,b on גַּם): וַתִּקַּח מִפִּרְיוֹ וַתֹּאכַל וַתִּתֵּן גַּם־לְאִישָׁהּ עִמָּהּ וַיֹּאכַל, "She took from its fruit and ate, and she *gave also* to her husband with her, and he ate" (Gen 3:6); אַף־אֲנִי בַּחֲלוֹמִי, "*I also saw* in my dream" (Gen 40:16).

### 5.2.10 *Adversative Clause*

This subordinate clause presents an antithesis to the idea of the main clause. The relationship between those clauses can be marked by לֹא, כִּי (which is

also used with אִם), or the particles אוּלָם and אֲבָל:
גַּם־הוּא יִהְיֶה־לְעָם וְגַם־הוּא יִגְדָּל וְאוּלָם אָחִיו הַקָּטֹן יִגְדַּל מִמֶּנּוּ,
"He also will become a people, and he, too, will be great.
*But, his younger brother shall be greater than he*" (Gen 48:19),
וַיֹּאמֶר לֹא כִּי אֲנִי שַׂר־צְבָא־יְהוָה עַתָּה בָאתִי, "He said 'No.
*Rather, I come now* as the captain of the army of YHWH'"
(Josh 5:14).

The *waw* conjunction can also perform this function:
וְלֹא־יִקָּרֵא עוֹד אֶת־שִׁמְךָ אַבְרָם וְהָיָה שִׁמְךָ אַבְרָהָם, "No longer
will your name be Abram, *but* it will be Abraham" (Gen
17:5), אַל־תָּלֶן הַלַּיְלָה בְּעַרְבוֹת הַמִּדְבָּר וְגַם עָבוֹר תַּעֲבוֹר, "Do
not spend the night at the fords of the wilderness, *but* by
all means, cross over" (2 Sam 17:16).

### 5.2.11 *Circumstantial Clause*

This subordinate clause describes the circumstances under which the action or situation of the main clause
takes place. Frequently, the simple conjunction וֹ functions
to introduce a circumstantial clause (see section 4.3.3,e):
מִגְדָּל וְרֹאשׁוֹ בַשָּׁמַיִם, "a tower *with its top in the sky*" (Gen
11:4), כֹּה הִרְאַנִי וְהִנֵּה אֲדֹנָי נִצָּב עַל־חוֹמַת אֲנָךְ וּבְיָדוֹ אֲנָךְ,
"Thus he showed me – the lord was standing on
a vertical wall *with a plumb line in his hand*" (Amos
7:7).

Quite often, the circumstantial clause is juxtaposed to the main clause with no connecting particle:
וַיֵּט אָהֳלֹה בֵּית־אֵל מִיָּם, "He pitched his tent, *with Bethel on
the west*" (Gen 12:8), וַיִּתְקָעֵם בְּלֵב אַבְשָׁלוֹם עוֹדֶנּוּ חַי, "and he
thrust them through Absalom's heart *while he was still alive*"
(2 Sam 18:14).

As illustrated, the predicate of a circumstantial
clause that is concomitant with the situation of the
main clause is expressed by nouns, adjectives, or
prepositional phrases. The participle serves this same
function: וַיָּבֹא אֱלִישָׁע דַּמֶּשֶׂק וּבֶן־הֲדַד מֶלֶךְ־אֲרָם חֹלֶה, "Elisha

came to Damascus *while Ben-Hadad, King of Aram was ill*"
(2 Kgs 8:7),

וַיֵּרָא אֵלָיו יְהוָה בְּאֵלֹנֵי מַמְרֵא וְהוּא יֹשֵׁב פֶּתַח־הָאֹהֶל כְּחֹם
הַיּוֹם

"Now Y<small>HWH</small> appeared to him by the oaks of Mamre,
*while he was sitting* at the tent door in the heat of the day"
(Gen 18:1).

Finite verbal forms are used to express circumstances that are either in the past or the future.[34]
A perfect verb as the predicate of the circumstantial
clause expresses anterior action (see section 3.5.4,c):
אַל־תְּאַחֲרוּ אֹתִי וַיהוָה הִצְלִיחַ דַּרְכִּי, "Do not delay me,
since Y<small>HWH</small> *has prospered* my way" (Gen 24:56),
וַיִּשְׁבּוּ אֶת־הַנָּשִׁים אֲשֶׁר־בָּהּ מִקָּטֹן וְעַד־גָּדוֹל לֹא הֵמִיתוּ אִישׁ,"They
took captive the women who were in [the city], both small
and great, *without killing anyone*" (1 Sam 30:2).

An imperfect verb as the predicate expresses future circumstances:

הַמְכַסֶּה אֲנִי מֵאַבְרָהָם אֲשֶׁר אֲנִי עֹשֶׂה וְאַבְרָהָם הָיוֹ יִהְיֶה
לְגוֹי גָּדוֹל וְעָצוּם

"Shall I hide from Abraham what I am about to do, *since
he will become* a great and mighty nation?" (Gen 18:17–18),
אֶעְבְּרָה בְאַרְצֶךָ בַּדֶּרֶךְ בַּדֶּרֶךְ אֵלֵךְ לֹא אָסוּר יָמִין וּשְׂמֹאול, "Let
me pass through your land; I will travel only on the highway;
*I will not turn* to the right or to the left" (Deut 2:27).

### 5.2.12 *Concessive Clause*

This subordinate clause denotes "causal contrast";[35]
that is, it presents an action or situation that would

---

[34] Williams 1976, 83. Gesenius further notes that circumstantial clauses employing a verb particularize the action of the main clause, or provide a
reason for the action of the main clause (Kautzsch 1910, 490).

[35] Joüon and Muraoka 1993, 641.

seemingly lead to, or be expected to cause, the action or situation of the main clause, but, in fact, does
not. The clause can be asyndetic, that is, without any
markers, by juxtaposition, or it can take a simple *waw*
conjunctive: הִנֵּה־נָא הוֹאַלְתִּי לְדַבֵּר אֶל־אֲדֹנָי וְאָנֹכִי עָפָר וָאֵפֶר,
"Certainly, now, I have ventured to speak to the lord,
*although* I am dust and ashes" (Gen 18:27). The particles כִּי,
עַל, or גַּם כִּי also express the idea of "although," while the
particles אִם and כִּי express the notion of "even though" (see
sections 4.3.2,b and 4.3.4,h): גַּם כִּי־תַרְבּוּ תְפִלָּה אֵינֶנִּי שֹׁמֵעַ,
"*Even though* you multiply prayers, I will not listen"
(Isa 1:15), וְלֹא־נָחָם אֱלֹהִים דֶּרֶךְ אֶרֶץ פְּלִשְׁתִּים כִּי קָרוֹב הוּא,
"God did not lead them by the way of the
Philistines, *even though* it was near" (Exod 13:17),
כִּי אִם־תְּכַבְּסִי בַּנֶּתֶר וְתַרְבִּי־לָךְ בֹּרִית נִכְתָּם עֲוֹנֵךְ לְפָנַי, "*Although*
you wash yourselves with lye and use much soap, the stain
of your iniquity is before me" (Jer 2:22).

### 5.2.13 *Relative Clause*

This clause stands subordinate to a main clause and
attributes a quality, state, or verbal idea to the main clause.
This group can be further divided into *limiting* and *nonlimiting* relative clauses.[36] A *limiting* relative clause functions
to make a distinction between more than one member
of a group or class: הַמַּיִם אֲשֶׁר מֵעַל לָרָקִיעַ, "The waters
*which were above the firmament*" (Gen 1:7). A *nonlimiting*
relative clause simply marks a general attribute of the
antecedent without setting it off against other members of
its "class":[37] וְעַתָּה אָרוּר אָתָּה מִן־הָאֲדָמָה אֲשֶׁר פָּצְתָה אֶת־פִּיהָ,

---

[36] Gesenius prefers the categories "complete" and "incomplete" relative
clauses, the former used for "the nearer definition of a noun," and the
latter, relative clauses that are not dependent on a noun (Kautzsch 1910,
485).
[37] Joüon and Muraoka 1993, 592.

"And now, you are cursed from the ground *which has opened its mouth*" (Gen 4:11). **(a)** The most frequent indicator of the relative clause is the particle אֲשֶׁר. In poetry, or in later texts, the prefix -שֶׁ identifies the relative clause. Within more archaic poetry, the particles זוּ, זוֹ, or זֶה are used. Occasionally, the attributive use of the participle can also mark a relative clause. Examples: אַתָּה וְכָל־הָעָם הַזֶּה אֶל־הָאָרֶץ אֲשֶׁר אָנֹכִי נֹתֵן לָהֶם, "You and all this people, to the land *which I am giving to them*" (Josh 1:2), הַיָּמִים אֲשֶׁר מָלַךְ דָּוִד עַל־יִשְׂרָאֵל, "The days *that David reigned over Israel*" (1 Kgs 2:11), בְּרֶשֶׁת־זוּ טָמָנוּ, "In the net *in which they hid*" (Ps 9:16), מַה־שֶּׁהָיָה הוּא שֶׁיִּהְיֶה, "That *which has been done* is that *which will be*" (Eccl 1:9). The relative clause can also be asyndetic: בְּאֶרֶץ לֹא לָהֶם, "In a land *that is not theirs*" (Gen 15:13).

**(b)** With certain relative clauses, in particular those pointing to a geographical location, a resumptive pronoun, referring to the antecedent of the relative pronoun, occurs, but is best left untranslated:[38] הַמָּקוֹם אֲשֶׁר אַתָּה עוֹמֵד עָלָיו אַדְמַת־קֹדֶשׁ הוּא, "The place *which you are standing upon* is holy ground [literally: The place which you are standing upon it, it is holy ground]" (Exod 3:5), גּוֹי אֲשֶׁר לֹא־תִשְׁמַע לְשֹׁנוֹ, "A nation *whose* language you will not understand [literally: a nation, whose its language you will not understand]" (Deut 28:49), יִוָּדַע הַנָּבִיא אֲשֶׁר־שְׁלָחוֹ יְהוָה בֶּאֱמֶת, "The prophet will be known as the prophet *whom* YHWH has truly sent [literally: The prophet will be known as the prophet whom YHWH has truly sent him]" (Jer 28:9).

**(c) *Paronomasia*** – The repetition of a word both in the main clause and the relative clause can be used to express

---

[38] Waltke and O'Connor 1990, 333–35; Joüon and Muraoka 1993, 595–600; Kautzsch 1910, 444–46.

a sense of indeterminateness:[39] הוֹלֵךְ אֲנִי אֲשֶׁר־עַל הוֹלֵךְ,
". . . while I go *wherever I will go*" (2 Sam 15:20),
וַיִּתְהַלְּכוּ בַּאֲשֶׁר יִתְהַלָּכוּ, "They went *wherever* they could go"
(1 Sam 23:13), וְחַנֹּתִי אֶת־אֲשֶׁר אָחֹן וְרִחַמְתִּי אֶת־אֲשֶׁר אֲרַחֵם, "I
will be gracious to *whomever I will* [literally: to whom I will
be gracious] and I will show compassion on *whomever I will*
[literally: to whom I will show compassion]" (Exod
33:19).

### 5.2.14 *Disjunctive Clause*

This subordinate clause represents an idea that is alternative to, or stands apart from, the idea of the main clause.
Typically, the conjunction אוֹ denotes the idea of "or":
הַגִּידוּ לִי וְאֶפְנֶה עַל־יָמִין אוֹ עַל־שְׂמֹאל, "Let me know, that I
may turn to the right *or* to the left" (Gen 24:49). The
idea of "or" can also be expressed by the *waw* conjunc-
tive: וְלֹא אוֹשִׁיעֵם בְּקֶשֶׁת וּבְחֶרֶב וּבְמִלְחָמָה בְּסוּסִים וּבְפָרָשִׁים, "I
will not save them by bow *or* by sword *or* by war *or* by horses
*or* by horsemen" (Hos 1:7). The notion of "either . . . or"
or "whether . . . or" can be expressed by consecutive *waw*
conjunctions: וְגֹנֵב אִישׁ וּמְכָרוֹ וְנִמְצָא בְיָדוֹ מוֹת יוּמָת, "He who
kidnaps a man, *whether he sells him or* he is found in his
possession . . . " (Exod 21:16). The notion of "whether . . .
or" is also expressed by consecutive אִם particles:

אִם־בִּמְקוֹם אֲשֶׁר יִהְיֶה־שָּׁם אֲדֹנִי הַמֶּלֶךְ אִם־לְמָוֶת
אִם־לְחַיִּים כִּי־שָׁם יִהְיֶה עַבְדֶּךָ

"Wherever my lord the king may be, *whether for death or for
life*, there your servant will be" (2 Sam 15:21).

### 5.3 Additional Sentence Types

At the beginning of this chapter, we provided working definitions for "simple," "compound," and "complex" sentences, as

---

[39] Joüon and Muraoka 1993, 599.

well as the slippery term "sentence" itself. In what follows, we offer an overview of other important sentence types in BH.

### 5.3.1 *Interrogative Sentences*

An interrogative clause, in its most basic sense, poses a direct question, which can be pointed to the reader or confined within the narrative. This question can be genuine, or it can be rhetorical, in which case it is not expected to be answered. Interrogative sentences are often distinguished only by intonation, as they are not marked with any morphological tags: וַיֹּאמֶר שָׁלֹם בּוֹאֶךָ, "And [Samuel] said, '*Do you come peacefully?*'" (1 Sam 16:4). However, the following are particles for marking interrogatives.

*(a)* Interrogative clauses may be marked by the particle הֲ to indicate direct questions: אַל־תִּירָאוּ כִּי הֲתַחַת אֱלֹהִים אָנִי, "Do not fear, *for am I in the place of God?*" (Gen 50:19), הֲשָׁלוֹם לַנַּעַר לְאַבְשָׁלוֹם, "*Is it well* with the young man Absalom?" (2 Sam 18:32).

*(b)* In the case of a disjunctive question, "X or Y?" the particle אִם will introduce the second option: הֲלָנוּ אַתָּה אִם־לְצָרֵינוּ, "Are you with us *or with our enemies?*" (Josh 5:13).

*(c)* In addition to the particle הֲ, there is a group of interrogative pronouns that introduce specific types of questions, including אָן, אֵי, אֵיךְ, מַה, מִי, etc.:

מֶה חֳרִי הָאַף הַגָּדוֹל הַזֶּה

"*Why* this great anger?" (Deut 29:23 [Eng. 29:24]), מִי הִגִּיד לְךָ כִּי עֵירֹם אָתָּה, "*Who* told you that you were naked?" (Gen 3:11), אֵיךְ תֹּאמַר אֲהַבְתִּיךְ, "*How* can you say 'I love you?'" (Judg 16:15), אֵי הֶבֶל אָחִיךְ, "*Where* is Abel, your brother?" (Gen 4:9).

*(d)* The particle אֵפוֹא often follows an interrogative to give an additional emphasis to the question: מִי־אֵפוֹא הוּא הַצָּד־צַיִד, "*Who was it, then,* who hunted game?" (Gen 27:33).

These interrogative markers can also mark *exclamatory clauses*: הֲנִגְלֹה נִגְלֵיתִי אֶל־בֵּית אָבִיךָ, "*I certainly revealed myself* to the house of your fathers" (1 Sam 2:27), אֵיךְ נָפְלוּ גִבֹּרִים בְּתוֹךְ הַמִּלְחָמָה, "*How the mighty have fallen* in the midst of the battle!" (2 Sam 1:25), מַה־טֹּבוּ אֹהָלֶיךָ יַעֲקֹב, "*How beautiful* are your tents, O Jacob!" (Num 24:5). Additionally, a *substantive* can function as an exclamation. This use is not marked by morphology, and so is context sensitive: וַיֹּאמֶר אֶל־אָבִיו רֹאשִׁי רֹאשִׁי, "He said to his father, '*My head! My head!*'" (2 Kgs 4:19).

Interrogative clauses can also function to denote *indirect questions,* which report or refer to the question of another speaker, although that first question need not be explicitly stated. Because indirect questions logically refer to another's speech, they are not meant to be answered. These clauses are introduced in the same manner as direct questions: לֹא יָדַעְתִּי מֵאַיִן הֵמָּה, "I do not know *where they are from*" (Josh 2:4), לֹא יָדַעְנוּ מִי־שָׂם כַּסְפֵּנוּ בְּאַמְתְּחֹתֵינוּ, "we do not know *who put our money in our sacks*" (Gen 43:22), שְׁאַל מָה אֶעֱשֶׂה־לָּךְ, "Ask *what I should do* for you" (2 Kgs 2:9).

## 5.3.2 *Oath Sentences*

A maledictory oath, or curse, is often introduced by the formulaic statement – "May God add to this and more...." The content of the oath itself, the apodosis, is marked by אִם if the oath statement is negative, expressing an action that one will not take, whereas אִם לֹא and כִּי function to introduce positive statements, actions that one will take.

Examples:

כֹּה יַעֲשֶׂה יְהוָה לִי וְכֹה יֹסִיף כִּי הַמָּוֶת יַפְרִיד בֵּינִי וּבֵינֵךְ

"Thus may Yʜwʜ do to me and more *if anything but death part you and me* [that is, Nothing but death will part you and me.]" (Ruth 1:17),

כֹּה יַעֲשֶׂה־לִי אֱלֹהִים וְכֹה יֹסִיף כִּי אִם־לִפְנֵי בוֹא־הַשֶּׁמֶשׁ אֶטְעַם־לֶחֶם אוֹ כָל־מְאוּמָה

"Thus may God do to me and more also *if I taste bread or anything else before the sun goes down* [that is, I will not taste bread or anything else...]" (2 Sam 3:35).

The protasis of an oath is also introduced by several constructions involving the adjective חַי or חֵי and either the self (אֲנֹכִי/אֲנִי) or an authority figure, such as Pharaoh, but more frequently, the divine (יְהוָה or אֱלֹהִים). The apodoses of these oaths are introduced by the same particles as already noted – אִם for negative statements and אִם לֹא or כִּי for positive statements: חַי־יְהוָה כִּי בְנֵי־מָוֶת אַתֶּם, "As Yʜwʜ lives, *all of you must surely die!*" (1 Sam 26:16), חֵי פַרְעֹה כִּי מְרַגְּלִים אַתֶּם, "By the life of Pharaoh, *you are surely spies!*" (Gen 42:16).

### 5.3.3 *Wish Sentences*

Desiderative clauses express a strong wish or desire. Often, the expression of a wish can take on the character of a question or exclamation.

*(a)* The most common means of expressing a desire in BH is through the use of the volitional verbs (see section 3.3): יְהִי אוֹר, "*Let there be* light" (Gen 1:3), הִפָּרֶד נָא מֵעָלָי, "*Please separate* from me" (Gen 13:9). Occasionally, an optative clause introduced by a finite verb is marked with אִם or לוּ: וַיֹּאמֶר אַבְרָהָם אֶל־הָאֱלֹהִים לוּ יִשְׁמָעֵאל יִחְיֶה לְפָנֶיךָ "Abraham said to God, '*O that Ishmael might live* before you!" (Gen 17:18), לוּ־מַתְנוּ בְּאֶרֶץ מִצְרַיִם, "*Would that we died* in the land of Egypt!" (Num 14:2).

*(b)* The expression of a wish can often resemble a question. Thus, the interrogative particles, in particular מִי, can be used to introduce a strong wish or desire: מִי־יְשִׂמֵנִי שֹׁפֵט בָּאָרֶץ, "*O that someone would appoint* me judge in the land" (2 Sam 15:4). The construction מִי יִתֵּן is a notable peculiarity in BH expressing an optative sense, sometimes with the sense of "God grant!":[40] וּמִי יִתֵּן אֶת־הָעָם הַזֶּה בְּיָדִי, "*Would that* this people were under my authority!" (Judg 9:29), וּמִי יִתֵּן כָּל־עַם יְהוָה נְבִיאִים, "*Would that* all Yhwh's people were prophets!" (Num 11:29).

*(c)* The expression of a wish can also be constructed with a participle or a prepositional phrase acting as the predicate in the clause: אֹרְרֶיךָ אָרוּר וּמְבָרֲכֶיךָ בָּרוּךְ, "*Cursed be* those who curse you and *blessed be* those who bless you" (Gen 27:29), שָׁלוֹם לָכֶם, "*Peace to you*" or "*May you have peace*" (Gen 43:23).

*(d)* Similar to the statements of oath are *asseverative clauses*, which also express a strong assertion. This statement may be an oath, in which case the asseverative clause functions as an elliptical oath statement. However, the clause can simply be a reinforcement or affirmation of a fact. In addition to the particles already noted, רַק, אָכֵן, אַךְ, אָמְנָה, אָמְנָם, אֲבָל, and הִנֵּה are all used to mark affirmation: רַק אֵין־יִרְאַת אֱלֹהִים בַּמָּקוֹם הַזֶּה, "*Surely* there is no fear of God in this place" (Gen 20:11), אֲבָל אֲשֵׁמִים אֲנַחְנוּ עַל־אָחִינוּ, "*Surely* we are guilty concerning our brother" (Gen 42:21), אָכֵן יֵשׁ יְהוָה בַּמָּקוֹם הַזֶּה, "*Surely* Yhwh is in this place" (Gen 28:16), הִנֵּה מִשְׁמַנֵּי הָאָרֶץ יִהְיֶה מוֹשָׁבֶךָ, "Your dwelling will *certainly* be away from the fertility of the land" (Gen 27:39).

---

[40] Joüon and Muraoka 1993, 616.

### 5.3.4 *Existential Sentences*

There are two main ways in which the existence of a thing or person is expressed in BH.

*(a)* For *past or future time*, a form of the verb הָיָה expresses existence: הַנָּחָשׁ הָיָה עָרוּם מִכֹּל חַיַּת הַשָּׂדֶה, "The serpent *was* more crafty than any other animal of the field" (Gen 3:1), אִישׁ הָיָה בְאֶרֶץ־עוּץ, "There *was* a man in the land of Uz" (Job 1:1), כֹּה יִהְיֶה זַרְעֶךָ, "So *shall* your descendants *be*" (Gen 15:5).

*(b)* For *present time*, the verb הָיָה is not used. Rather, the particle of existence יֵשׁ is used (see section 4.4.2). This particle is not negated, but rather, the absence of something in present time is expressed by the particle אַיִן (section 4.4.1): אָכֵן יֵשׁ יְהוָה בַּמָּקוֹם הַזֶּה, "Surely, Yнwн *is* in this place" (Gen 28:16), אָדָם אַיִן לַעֲבֹד אֶת־הָאֲדָמָה, "*There was no* human to cultivate the ground" (Gen 2:5).

### 5.3.5 *Negative Sentences*

*(a)* Typically, verbal clauses are negated by לֹא, although אַל is used with the imperfect as a functional equivalent to a negated imperative or the other volitional verbs (see sections 4.2.3, 4.2.11): לְאָדָם לֹא־מָצָא עֵזֶר כְּנֶגְדּוֹ, "for Adam, *there was not found* a suitable helper" (Gen 2:20), אַל־תִּירָא מִפְּנֵיהֶם, "*Do not be afraid* of them" (Josh 11:6).

*(b)* Nominal clauses are typically negated by אַיִן, although לֹא can also negate nominal clauses: אֵין לָהּ וָלָד, "She *had no* child" (Gen 11:30), לֹא־טוֹב הֱיוֹת הָאָדָם לְבַדּוֹ, "It is *not good* for the man to be alone" (Gen 2:18).

*(c)* Specifically for negation of infinitives construct, לְבִלְתִּי is used: לְבִלְתִּי סוּר־מִמֶּנּוּ יָמִין וּשְׂמֹאול, "So that you *might not turn* from it to the right or to the left" (Josh 23:6), הִשָּׁמֶר לְךָ פֶּן־תִּשְׁכַּח אֶת־יְהוָה אֱלֹהֶיךָ לְבִלְתִּי שְׁמֹר מִצְוֹתָיו, "Take

care that you do not forget Yнwн your God *by not keeping* his commandments" (Deut 8:11).

### 5.3.6 *Elliptical Clauses and Sentences*

At times, BH omits certain parts of speech from clauses. Close attention to context generally reveals the omitted element(s), and ambiguity is seldom a result.

*(a)* Substantives are often omitted in *comparisons,* particularly in the clause presenting the compared situation: מְשַׁוֶּה רַגְלַי כָּאַיָּלוֹת, "He makes my feet like *hinds [feet]*" (2 Sam 22:34 *Qere*), וַתָּרֶם כִּרְאֵים קַרְנִי, "You have exalted my horn like *[that of] the wild ox*" (Ps 92:11).

*(b)* Pronouns are often omitted when their antecedents are clear from the context, primarily in two situations: as the *subject of nonfinite verbs*: בַּהֲפֹךְ אֶת־הֶעָרִים אֲשֶׁר־יָשַׁב בָּהֵן לוֹט, "*When he overthrew* the cities in which Lot lived" (Gen 19:29), עֹמֵד עַל־הַגְּמַלִּים עַל־הָעָיִן, "*He was standing* by the camels at the well" (Gen 24:30); and when functioning as the *object of the verb*: וַיָּבֵא אֶל־הָאָדָם, "He brought *them* to the man" (Gen 2:19).

*(c)* Certain expressions of quantitative measure, such as "day," "month," or "year" are omitted after numerals: אַךְ בֶּעָשׂוֹר לַחֹדֶשׁ הַשְּׁבִיעִי, "On exactly the *tenth [day]* of the seventh month" (Lev 23:27),

וְלֹא אָנֹכִי שֹׁקֵל עַל־כַּפַּי אֶלֶף כָּסֶף

"Even if I should receive a *thousand [pieces]* of silver" (2 Sam 18:12 *Qere*).

*(d)* Ellipsis also occurs frequently with negatives: אַל בְּנֹתַי, "*No*, my daughters (Ruth 1:13), הֲיֵשׁ יְהוָה בְּקִרְבֵּנוּ אִם־אָיִן, "Is Yнwн in our midst or *not [in our midst]*?" (Exod 17:7).

# APPENDIX I: *Stem Chart*

| | | Horizontal Axis – "Type" | | |
|---|---|---|---|---|
| | | Simple | Factitive-Causative | Causative |
| Vertical Axis – "Voice" | Active | קַל<br>**QAL** (G) | פִּעֵל<br>**PIEL** (D) | הִפְעִיל<br>**HIPHIL** (H) |
| | Passive | נִפְעַל<br>**NIPHAL** (N) | פֻּעַל<br>**PUAL** (Dp) | הָפְעַל<br>**HOPHAL** (Hp) |
| | Reflexive | נִפְעַל<br>**NIPHAL** (N) | הִתְפַּעֵל<br>**HITHPAEL** (HtD) | Ø |

*Sources:* Joüon and Muraoka 1993, 124; Greenberg 1965, 42; Goshen-Gottstein 1969, 70–91, esp. 74–75; Harper 1888, 71; and Waltke and O'Connor 1990, 353–54.

# APPENDIX II: *Expanded Stem Chart*

| Axis of Causation – Voice of the Undersubject | | |
|---|---|---|
| No Causation | Brings about a *State* | Causes an *Action* |
| No Generated Predication | Generates a **Nominal** Predication | Generates **Verbal** Predication |
| No Undersubject | Patiency Nuance | Agency Nuance |

| | | No Causation | Brings about a *State* | Causes an *Action* |
|---|---|---|---|---|
| **Axis of Voice** – Voice of the Primary Subject | Active | **QAL** **Stative** ......▶ | **PIEL** **Factitive** 1 makes 2 *be* x Outcome describable by *adjectival* clause | **HIPHIL** ▶ **2 Place Ingressive** 1 makes 2 *become* x **1 Place Internal** 1 makes *self* do/become x |
| | | **Fientive** ➤ Intransitive ➤ Transitive ......▶ | ......▶ **Resultative** 1 makes 2 *be* x-ed Outcome describable by *participle* clause | ▶ **2 Place Causative** 1 makes 2 *do* x ▶ **3 Place Causative** 1 makes 2 *do* x to 3 |
| | Passive | **(Qal Passive)** **NIPHAL** | **PUAL** Passive of Piel | **HOPHAL** Passive of Hiphil |
| | Middle | **NIPHAL** Middle Adjectival Reflexive-Reciprocal | **HITHPAEL** Reflexive-Reciprocal of Piel Also later Passive | **HISHTAPHEL** only in הִשְׁתַּחֲוָה |

*Source:* Based on Waltke and O'Connor 1990 (343–61), and with the help of Lawson G Stone.

# Glossary

**Ablative**   Expresses a relationship of separation, or movement away from a substantive. 4.1.10; 4.1.13; 4.1.14

**Absolute Noun**   The basic, lexical form of a noun in Hebrew; can function as a nominative, dative, or accusative.

**Accompaniment**   Expresses addition to a noun, or to a verbal action or situation. 4.1.4; 4.1.5; 4.1.16; 4.1.17

**Accusative**   The noun case that marks the direct object, the recipient of action, of a verb. Example: "I hit *the ball.*" 2.3

**Active Voice**   Construction of a verbal clause in which the subject performs an action. Example: "He cut the grass." See Passive Voice. 3.1.1.

**Addition**   See Accompaniment. 4.1.2; 4.1.16; 4.2.4; 4.2.5

**Advantage**   Specifically here, an action or situation that is meant for the benefit of another. 4.1.2; 4.1.7; 4.1.10

**Adverb**   A word that modifies a verb or adjective, but also other adverbs (item adverbs) and, in many cases, entire clauses (clausal adverbs); typically expresses how an action or situation takes place. 4.2

**Adversative**   Expresses opposition or antithesis. 4.1.5; 4.1.16; 4.3.3; 4.3.3; 4.5.2

**Agency Nuance**   With Hiphil or Hophal causatives, indicates that the secondary subject takes action toward a third object; the secondary subject is effected to take action toward a third object. See Patiency Nuance. 3.1; 3.1.3; 3.1.6

**Agent**   The one who performs the action of a verb. 3.1.2; 3.5.4; 4.1.10; 4.1.13

**Agreement**   Expresses similarity. 4.1.9

**Alternative**   Expresses a choice between two or more options. 4.3.1; 4.3.2; 4.3.3

**Anaphoric**   A syntactical element, typically a pronoun, used to refer to something or someone that has been mentioned earlier in the text.

**Anarthous**  See Indefinite.

**Aorist**  Greek verbal tense, generally referring to past time, that focuses on the completed nature of a verb, rather than its duration. 3.2.1

**Apodosis**  The main clause of a conditional statement; the "then" statement. 3.5.2; 4.2.1; 4.2.10; 4.3.3; 4.3.4; 5.2.6; 5.3.2

**Apposition**  Construction in which two nouns are juxtaposed, refer to the same element, and have the same grammatical function; the second noun (the apposition) typically modifies the first noun (the leadword). 2.4

**Aspect**  From the German *Aspekt;* the manner in which the action or situation of a verb relates to time, in terms of completeness or lack of, in Hebrew and other Semitic languages. 3.2

**Assertive**  Expresses a notion of confidence or boldness. 5.1.2

**Asseverative**  Expresses emphasis or surety. 4.2.2; 4.2.4; 4.2.15; 4.3.4; 5.3.3

**Asyndetic**  A string of words, phrases, or clauses that are not connected by a conjunction that is expected. 5.2.1,a; 5.2.12; 5.2.13,a

**Attributive**  Construction that functions to describe a quality or attribute. 2.2; 2.2.5; 2.3.1,c 2.4.2; 2.5.1; 3.4.3,a; 5.2.13,a

**Benediction**  A blessing spoken by one, meant to bless another. 3.3.1,c

**Biblical Hebrew**  The language of the Hebrew Bible/Old Testament; contrast with Epigraphic Hebrew, which focuses on extra-biblical inscriptions; or Rabbinic Hebrew, which focuses on Hebrew texts written after the Bible.

**Cardinal Number**  A number used in counting, to indicate the quantity of objects. 2.7.1

**Case**  The function of a noun within a sentence; see Accusative, Dative, Genitive, Nominative. 2.0

**Causal**  Expressing the cause of an action or situation. 2.2.7; 4.1.2,g; 4.1.5,f; 4.1.8; 4.1.10,d; 4.1.11,b; 4.1.13,e; 4.1.14,c; 4.1.16,d; 4.2.10,b; 4.3.4,a, b; 4.5.3,c1; 5.2.5

**Causation**  Refers either to the act or process of causing an action/idea to take place. 2.3.1,e; 3.1; 3.1.3; 3.1.6

**Causative**  A verbal notion that expresses the subject of the verb causing another (the secondary subject) to take some action. 2.3.1,d; 3.1.3; 3.1.4; 3.1.5; 3.1.6; 3.1.7

**Circumstantial**  Refers to the conditions under which, or the manner in which, an action is performed. 4.3.3,e; 4.5.2,c2; 5.2.11

**Clause**  A group of words with a subject and only one predicate, forming the basic unit of predication; can be verbal or verbless, dependent or independent. See Nominal Clause, Verbal Clause, Subordinate Clause, Independent Clause. 5.1

**Cognate Accusative**   Construction in which the verb and its object are derived from the same root. Example: "I *dreamt* a *dream.*" 2.3.1,c

**Cohortative**   An expression of strong wish or desire directed to the first person, the self. 3.3.3

**Comitative**   See Accompaniment.

**Comparative**   A relationship in which the quality or quantity of two or more nouns is compared. 2.5.4; 4.1.13,g; 4.2.4,c; 4.2.10,a; 5.2.6

**Complement Accusative**   An object that is used with certain intransitive verbs, which are modified to function as transitive verbs. 2.3.1,d

**Complete Passive**   A passive voice construction in which the agent of the verb is specified. Most English passive constructions are complete passives, whereas most Hebrew passive constructions are incomplete passives. Example: "The book was written *by the author.*" See Incomplete Passive, Passive voice. 3.1.2,a

**Complex Sentence**   A sentence in which two or more clauses are joined together, and in which one clause is subordinate to another. 5.0

**Concessive**   Expresses an action or situation that is expected, or may lead to another action but, in fact, does not. 4.2.5,c; 4.3.2,b; 4.3.4,h; 5.2.12

**Conditional**   An action or situation that may or may not occur, dependent on the completion, or incompletion, of another action. Real conditions are those that can potentially be fulfilled, whereas unreal conditions are those that cannot or will not be fulfilled. 5.2.2

**Conjugation**   Different forms of the verb that make it specific for person, gender, and number, as well as aspect and type of action. 3.0

**Conjunction**   A particle that joins two or more words, or clauses, together. 4.3

**Consequential**   Expresses the potential or actual consequences of an action/situation. 3.5.1,b; 3.5.2,b; 3.5.3,b; 4.3.5

**Construct Chain**   A phrase with a construct noun followed by an absolute noun, expressing a genitive relationship between the two nouns. 2.3

**Construct Noun**   A form of the noun in Hebrew that functions to form genitive relationships. 2.3

**Contingent**   An action or idea that is dependent on another action/idea. 3.2.2,d

**Coordinate**   Expresses some notion of equality, either in stature, rank, or quality. 5.1

**Coordinate Conjunction**   A conjunction that joins nouns or clauses that have identical grammatical functions. 4.3

**Coordinate Relationship**   A linkage of two or more verbs, in which the leading, or governing, verb influences the aspect and mode of the linked verb. 3.5

**Coordinating Adverb**   An adverb that functions to show coordination between two clauses. 4.2

**Correspondence**   Expresses a complete equality in identity and quality between two substantives. 4.1.9,b

**Customary**   Describes action occurring in past or present time with regular repetition. 3.2.2,b

**Dative**   Case that marks the indirect object of a verb – often the recipient in verbs of speaking or giving. Example: "I threw the ball *to my dog*." 4.1.10,e

**Declarative**   An expression of assessment, judgment, or evaluation. 3.1.3,d; 3.1.6,c; 4.1.2,c

**Declensions**   Different forms placed on nouns or adjectives that give them specific function and reference according to gender and number.

**Definiteness (or Determination)**   A noun having the definite article; refers to a specific or known person, place, or thing. 2.6

**Degree**   With the preposition עַד, expresses a large quantity or an extreme quality. 4.1.15,d

**Demonstrative**   A substantive that points to, or highlights, other substantives. Also labeled "deictic." Example: "He wrote *this* book." 2.5.1; 2.6.6; 4.2.8,b

**Denominative**   A verbal form that is derived from a noun. Recall that in Hebrew, the verbal form is primary, while nominal forms are derived from the verbal form. 3.1.3,b; 3.1.5,d; 3.1.6,d

**Desiderative**   Expresses a wish or desire. 5.3.2

**Determination**   See Definiteness. 2.6

**Direct Object**   The recipient of verbal action. Example: "He kicked *the ball*." 2.3.1

**Disjunctive**   Establishes a contrast between words or clauses. 5.2.14; 5.3.1,b

**Distributive**   Reference to each and every member of a group. 2.7.1,d

**Double Accusative**   The use of two accusatives, or direct objects, with factitive or causative verbs; one receives action from the main subject, while the other receives action from the secondary subject. See Agency Nuance, Patiency Nuance, Secondary Subject. 2.3.1,e1

**Duration/Durative**   Expresses progressive, continuous action. 3.4.2,b; 3.4.3,b

**Duty**   An action that one is compelled to take. 4.1.16,b

**Elliptical**   Describes a clause from which certain parts of speech have been omitted. 5.3.5

**Emotive**   With the preposition עַל, indicates an expression of emotion. 4.1.16,i

**Epexegetical**   Providing an additional explanation or clarification. 2.2.6; 3.5.1,d; 4.3.3,d

**Essence** Specifically with the בְּ preposition, marks the predicate of a clause. 4.1.5,h

**Estimative** Expresses judgment or assessment of the value, worth, significance, or status of a substantive. 4.1.10,k; 4.1.13,d

**Ethical Dative** Action that is on behalf of another; action that is meant to benefit another. 4.1.10,e1

**Euphonic** A particle or part of speech that has no syntactical function, but is added for an audible effect. 3.3.2.

**Evidential** Expresses the evidence or motivation for speech; does not focus on what is said, but the reason for speaking. 4.3.4,b

**Exceptive** Taking out or omitting something from a situation. 4.3.2,d; 4.3.4,m; 5.2.7

**Exclamatory/Exclamation** A sharp or sudden utterance; a sudden expression of emotion. 4.5; 5.3.1; 5.3.3

**Exhortation** Speech or language intended to encourage. 3.3.3,c

**Existential** Expresses the existence or presence of a substantive. 4.4; 5.3.4

**Experience** Expressed by a verb, a state of mind, such as "love," "hate," "fear." 3.2.1,c

**Explicative** A substantive that typically precedes the subject, and explains what is contained in the subject. 2.2.12; 2.4.5

**Factitive** A verbal form that expresses the causing of a state. 3.1.3,a

**Fientive** A verb that describes an action or change of state. 3.1.1,a

**Final Clauses** Subordinate clauses that express the purpose or motivation behind the idea of the main clause. 5.2.3

**Finite** A verb that is inflected for aspect, person, gender, and number; can stand as a predicate in independent clauses.

**Frequentative** Describes action that is repeated, either over time or space. See Iterative, Pluralic. 3.1.3,c

**Generic** Refers to a class or group of similar or identical substantives, rather than a specific individual or type. 2.6.5

**Genitive** A relationship between nouns, often denoting attribute or possession, but other relationships as well; usually noted in English by the particle "of." 2.2

**Gentilic** A noun that refers to a single member of a collective group, typically an ethnic or national group. 2.6.3.

**Governing Verb** The first verb in a coordinate relationship within a narrative text; typically influences the aspect and usage of linked verbs that follow. 3.5

*Hapax Legomenon* From Greek for "read once," an expression, word, or form that is used only once in a text.

**Hendiadys** Expression of a singular idea by two independent words. 4.3.3,g

**Immediacy**   Expresses action that takes place with little or no loss of time; emphasis on the "present," relative to the narrative. 4.5.1,a

**Imminence**   An action or situation that is impending (taking place soon, relative to the context). 3.4.1,f

**Imperative**   An expression of will directed to another; expressing a command, entreaty, or wish to another party. 3.3.2

**Incomplete Passive**   A passive voice construction in which the agent of the verb is not expressed. Example: "*The book was written.*" See Complete Passive. 3.1.2,a

**Indefinite**   Describes a noun without the definite article; typically refers to a general or generic, rather than specific, individual. 2.6

**Indefinite Subject**   An unspecified agent of a verb, usually expressed in English by "someone" or "anyone" 5.1.2,a3

**Independent Clause**   A clause that can stand on its own, with complete meaning. 5.2

**Indeterminate**   see Indefinite. 2.6

**Indicative**   A verbal form that expresses actions or states objective facts. 3.2.2

**Indirect Object**   A noun representing the secondary goal of the action of the verb. See Dative.

**Indirect Questions**   Phrases that report or refer to a question from another; the first question need not be explicitly stated. Example: "She knows *where the cat is hiding.*" 5.1.2,b2; 5.3.1

**Infinitive**   A verbal form, functioning as a verbal noun, that is, not limited to person, gender, or number. 3.4.1; 3.4.2

**Inflexion**   A morphological change in words that marks distinctions such as case, gender, number, tense, person, mood, or voice. 2.0

**Ingressive**   Expresses entry into a state. 3.1.2; 3.1.6,d

**Instrumental**   Identifies a person, place, or thing used as a means, agent, or tool with which an action is performed. 4.1.5,c

**Intensive**   Adding force or emphasis; specifically with Piel verb forms, expressing a repeated or enhanced action. 3.1.3,c; 4.2.12; 5.2.9

**Interest**   Action that is meant for the benefit of another; with the preposition עַל, indicates the one for which an emotion is intended. See Ethical Dative, Advantage. 4.1.16,i

**Internal Accusative**   An abstract noun that is identical to the action expressed by the verb. Example: "He will live *life.*" See Cognate Accusative. 2.3.1,c

**Interrogative**   Expresses a question; often introduced by interrogative particles, which introduce questions. 4.3.4,n; 5.3.1

**Intransitive Verb**   A verb that does not have a direct object.

**Iterative**   Expresses repetition of an action over time. 3.1.3,c

**Jussive**   Expresses a command or wish predominantly to the third but to the second person as well. 3.3.1

**Juxtaposition**  Position of two parts of speech directly next to each other; the position of being directly next to another.

**Leadword**  The first noun in an appositional construction; typically modified by the second noun, termed the apposition. 2.4

**Linked Verb**  A verb in a coordinate relationship that is typically influenced by, and successive to, the governing verb. 3.5

**Locative**  Expresses the location of a noun or clause at a point in time or point in space. 4.1.10,b; 4.1.12,a; 4.1.15,a; 4.1.16,a; 4.1.17,d; 4.1.18,b; 4.2.7; 4.2.8,b; 4.2.16,a

**Logical**  Expresses the expected consequence or result of an action or situation. 3.3.2; 3.5; 4.2.1,b; 4.2.14,b; 4.5.3,c

**Maledictory**  An oath statement that express a curse or ill will. 5.3.2

**Manner**  The fashion, custom, or procedure of an action. 2.3.2,c; 3.4.2,c; 4.1.1,b; 4.1.5,i; 4.1.10,j; 4.1.16,e; 4.2.8,a; 4.2.10,a; 4.2.13,a; 4.2.17

**Material**  The matter with which some other thing is created or formed. 2.2.10; 2.3.2,f; 2.4.3; 4.1.5,c; 4.1.13,c

**Means**  Points to a substantive by or with which an action is performed. 2.2.9

**Measure**  Expresses the quantity of a substantive. 2.2.11; 2.4.4; 2.7.1,a

**Merism**  A construction involving two polar nouns to express the totality between those two poles. Example: "night and day," referring to totality of time, not just the two periods of "night" and "day." 4.2.7, n.29

**Middle Voice**  Verbal construct in which the subject and the object are identical, but without the emphasis on the subject acting upon itself, as with the reflexive. 3.1.2,b

**Modal**  A verbal form that expresses a strong wish or desire. 3.3

**Mood**  A verbal inflexion that expresses the factuality of the verb, either real, as with indicative verbs, or unreal, as with volitional or modal verbs.

**Morpheme**  The smallest meaningful unit of language; typically refers to a single "word" or particle, which is formed by a group of phonemes.

**Morphology**  The study of the formation of parts of speech.

**Naming**  With the definite article, the indication that a common noun is to be viewed as a proper noun. 2.6.3

**Narrative**  Presentation of events or theme as a story.

**Nominal Clause**  A unit of predication that does not include a finite verb; a predication formed by two substantives. 5.1.1

**Nominative**  A noun case that typically marks the subject of the verb. 2.1

**Normative**  Expresses classification of a substantive according to a standard; oftentimes, will express division of a larger group according to smaller divisions. 4.1.10,i

**Northwest Semitic**  Group of languages, including Aramaic, Ugaritic, and Phoenician, to which Hebrew belongs.

**Oath**  A solemn commitment to the truth of one's words; a commitment to take, or not to take, a certain action. 5.3.2

**Object** see Direct Object; Indirect Object.

**Obligation** An action that should or should not be done, according to societal, cultural, or historical traditions. 3.2.2,d3

**Optative** Expresses a strong wish or desire. 5.3.3

**Ordinal Number** A number designating the place of order occupied by an item in a sequence. 2.7.2

**Paronomasia** A word play; figure of speech that involves a play on words, often with words that sound similar; within relative clauses, paranomasia often functions to express indefiniteness. 5.2.13,c

**Participle** A part of speech having the characteristic of both verb and adjective. 3.4.3

**Particle** A unit of speech with a connective or limiting function – articles, prepositions, conjunctions, adverbs; or as utterances – interjections and exclamations.

**Partitive** A portion or part of a larger group. 4.1.13,e

**Passive Voice** Construction in which the subject of the verb receives the action of the verb. Example: "The building *was built* by the contractor." 3.1.2,a

**Patiency Nuance** With factitive verbs, indication that the secondary subject does not have a role in the action of the verb; the secondary subject is affected, only, and does not take other action. See Agency Nuance. 3.1.3

**Perceptual** Marking the object of perception; identifying the thing that is perceived. 4.1.2,d; 4.3.4,j; 4.5.2,b

**Performative** Describes an action that is completed by speech or utterance. Example: "Your name will no longer be Abram, but Abraham." 3.2.1,f

**Permissive** Describes an action that is agreeable to the object, and allowed to occur by the subject. 3.1.6,e

**Personal Complement** Marker of the indirect object of a verb. 4.1.17,c

**Perspective** The specific view or perception of a speaker within the narrative.

**Phoneme** A unit of letters in a language that functions to produce a single, distinctive sound in that language.

**Phonology** The study of the sounds of a language.

**Phrase** A group of words that can syntactically function as one word. 5.0

**Pleonasm/Pleonastic** An expression that employs unnecessary words; a redundant expression. 5.1.1,a

**Pluralic** Describes action that is intensified over space. 3.1.3,c

**Possession** Expresses that a person, place, or thing belongs to another. 4.1.4,b; 4.1.10,f; 4.1.12,a; 4.4.1,b; 4.4.2,b

**Postpositive** The location of a part of speech after a specified position; a postpositive infinitive, for example, comes after the finite verb it modifies. An infinitive absolute that comes before the finite verb would be *prepositive*. 3.4.2,b

**Predicate** A substantive or verb that makes an assertion about the subject of a sentence. 2.1.2; 2.5.2; 3.4.3,b; 4.4.2,c; 5

**Predicate Adjective** An adjective that makes an assertion about the substantive it modifies. 2.5.2

**Preposition** A part of speech that expresses various spatial, temporal, logical, or comparative relationships between nouns or clauses. 4.1

**Preterite** Verbal form referring specifically to indicative action in the past. 3.2.2

**Privative** Expresses removal or extraction. 4.1.13,f

**Prohibition** An act of restraining; a command meant to restrain or stop an action. 4.2.3; 4.2.11

**Promise** With imperatives, an assurance that the addressed party will take some action in the future. 3.3.2,c

**Protasis** The introductory clause of a conditional statement – the "if" clause. 5.3.2; 5.2.2; 5.2.6

**Purpose** An expression of the reason or rationale behind an action. 2.2.8; 3.4.1,c; 3.5.5,b; 4.1.10,d; 4.1.11,a

**Quasi-Active** Describes verbs that are normally passive, but used with identical subject and object. See Middle Voice. 3.1.2,b

**Quasi-Datival** Describes constructions that indicate the indirect object of verbs. 4.1.10,e

**Rank** With the preposition עַל, indicates one's position or responsibility. 4.1.16,c

**Reciprocal** Describes action in which two or more parties both affect each other; action that is mutual. 3.1.2,c; 3.1.5,b.

**Recitative** With the preposition כִּי, introduces the contents of direct speech; functionally, marks a direct quotation. 4.3.4,1

**Referential** With the definite article, refers to a person, place, or thing that has been previously mentioned in the narrative. 2.6.1

**Reflexive** Describes action that is directed to the self; hence, the subject and the object of the verb are identical. 3.1.2,c; 3.1.5,a

**Relative Clause** A dependent clause that modifies the main clause. 5.2.13

**Resolve** Expression of self-determination. 3.3.3,a

**Restrictive** Expressing a limitation, exception, or restriction of an action or idea. 4.1.17,e; 4.2.2,a; 4.2.15,a; 5.2.8.

**Result** The end/outcome of an action. 2.2.9; 3.4.1,d; 4.3.4,d; 4.5.2,c5

**Resultative** With Piel verbs, describes the bringing about of the outcome of an action designated by the verbal root. 3.1.3

**Result Clause** A subordinate clause that expresses the end result of the idea of the main clause. 5.2.3,b

**Rhetorical**   Specifically with the particle כְּ, expresses a comparison established between two clauses, with the second clause typically indicating some persuasion. 4.3.4,c

**Rhetorical Question**   A question with no expected answer. 4.3.4,c; 5.3.1

**Secondary Subject**   With causative or factitive verbs, the substantive in which an action, state, or change of state is brought about by the main subject of the verb; also referred to as "under subject." 3.1

**Sentence**   A grammatical unit comprised of one or more clauses. See Simple Sentence and Complex Sentence. 5; 5.3

**Simple Sentence**   A sentence consisting of only one clause. See Complex Sentence. 5; 5.3

**Simultaneous**   Describes action that occurs, or a state that exists, at the same time as another. 3.4.1,b1; 3.4.1,b2; 3.4.2,c; 5.2.4

**Solitary**   With the definite article, identifies common nouns that refer to a singular entity, and hence, are on their way to becoming proper nouns. 2.6.4

**Source**   The point of origin, or the initiator of action. 4.1.13,a

**Spatial**   Expresses how a noun is related to space. 4.1.1,a; 4.1.2,f; 4.1.3; 4.1.4,d; 4.1.5,a; 4.1.6; 4.1.7,a; 4.1.10,a; 4.1.14,b; 4.1.16,a

**Species**   Classification of a substantive with others according to their type, group, or quality. 2.4.1

**Specification**   A clarification or explanation of verbal action or situation; an expression that specifically points out a substantive. 2.2.6; 2.3.2,e; 3.4.1,g; 3.5.1,d; 4.1.2,g; 4.1.5,e; 4.1.10,h

**Stative Verb**   A verb that expresses a state, rather than an action or change of state; usually, in English, this function is completed through predicate adjectives. 3.1.1,b

**Stem (or Derived Stem)**   A vowel pattern applied to a Hebrew verbal root, which functions to specify type of action. 3.1

**Subject**   The agent who or that performs the action of a verb. 2.1.1

**Subjunctive**   A verbal form that expresses nonfactual actions or situations, such as wishes, expectations, possible actions, and conditional actions. 3.2.2

**Subordinate Clause**   A clause that is associated with, and modifies the meaning of, an independent clause. 5.2

**Subordinate Conjunction**   A conjunction that joins a subordinate clause to a main, independent clause. 4.3

**Substantive**   A word or a group of words functioning as a noun.

**Substitution**   The replacement of one substantive for another. 4.1.18,d

**Succession**   In coordinate relationships, the primary relationship formed between governed and linked verbs denoting an action or situation that follows, either temporally or logically, another action or situation. 3.5

**Superlative**   The highest degree of an adjective. Example: "*tallest.*" 2.2.13; 2.5.4,b; 4.1.10,k

**Syntax**   The organization of grammatical parts of speech to form meaningful units, such as phrases or clauses.

**Telic**   Expresses a goal, or movement toward a goal; with subordinate clauses, typically expresses the result of an action, or the motive behind an action.

**Temporal**   Expresses a substantive's relationship to time; with clauses, can express how the time of a subordinate clause relates to the time of the main clause. 3.4.1,b; 3.5.1,a; 3.5.2,a; 3.5.5,a; 4.1.1,b; 4.1.5,b; 4.1.6; 4.1.9,c; 4.1.10,c; 4.1.12,b; 4.1.13,b; 4.1.15,b; 4.2.1,a; 4.2.7; 4.2.14,a; 4.3.4,e; 4.5.2,c4; 5.2.4.

**Tense**   Distinction in the form of a verb to express the time or duration of action. Note that in BH, verbs are not strictly marked for tense; rather, their relationship to time is noted by aspect.

**Terminative**   Expressing movement, with special emphasis on the completed goal of that movement. 4.1.2,a; 4.1.5,a; 4.1.10,a; 4.1.16,a; 4.2.16,b

**Transitive**   A fientive verb with an identified direct object. 3.1.1,a

**Verbal Clause**   A clause in which the predicate is formed by a finite verb. 5.1.2

**Verbal Complement**   An infinitive that functions to complete the meaning of certain verbs. Example: "I know how *to play* the piano." 3.4.1,a3

**Vocative**   Grammatical case that marks direct address. 2.1.3; 2.6.2

**Voice**   Verbal inflection that indicates the relationship of the subject of the verb to the action of the verb. In English, voice is established, typically, by word order, whereas in BH, it is established by the derived stems. See Active Voice, Passive Voice. 3

**Volitional**   Describes a verbal form that expresses a choice or decision to which one has committed or will commit. 3.5.2,c

# Sources Consulted

All abbreviations may be found in Patrick H. Alexander et al., eds., *The SBL Handbook of Style for Ancient Near Eastern, Biblical, and Early Christian Studies*. Peabody, Mass.: Hendrickson, 1999, 121–152.

Aejmelaeus, Anneli. 1986. "Function and Interpretation of כִּי in Biblical Hebrew." *Journal of Biblical Literature* 105:193–209.

Andersen, Francis I. 1970. *The Hebrew Verbless Clause in the Pentateuch.* Journal of Biblical Literature Monograph Series 14. Nashville, Tenn.: Published for the Society of Biblical Literature by Abingdon Press.

———. 1974. *The Sentence in Biblical Hebrew.* Janua Linguarum, Series Practica 231. The Hague: Mouton.

Andersen, Francis I., and A. Dean Forbes. 1983. " 'Prose Particle' Counts of the Hebrew Bible." Pages 165–83 in *The Word of the Lord Shall Go Forth.* Edited by Carol L. Meyers and M. O'Connor. Winona Lake, Ind.: Eisenbrauns.

Bauer, Hans, and Pontus Leander. 1991. *Historische Grammatik der hebräischen Sprache des Alten Testamentes.* Halle: Niemeyer, 1918–22. Reprint, Hildesheim: Olms.

Ben Zvi, Ehud, Maxine Hancock, and Richard Beinert. 1993. *Readings in Biblical Hebrew: An Intermediate Textbook.* New Haven, Conn.: Yale University Press.

Bergen, Robert D., ed. 1994. *Biblical Hebrew and Discourse Linguistics.* Winona Lake, Ind.: Eisenbrauns for the Summer Institute of Linguistics.

Bergsträsser, Gotthelf. 1962. *Hebräische Grammatik mit Benutzung der von E. Kautzsch bearbeiteten 28. Auflage von Wilhelm Gesenius' hebräischer Grammatik.* 2 vols. Leipzig: Hinrichs, 1918/1929. Reprint, Hildesheim: Olms.

———. 1983. *Introduction to the Semitic Languages.* Translated and supplemented by Peter T. Daniels. Winona Lake, Ind.: Eisenbrauns.

Berlin, Adele. 1983. *Poetics and Interpretation of Biblical Narrative.* Sheffield, Eng.: Almond Press.

Beyer, Klaus. 1969. *Althebräische Grammatik: Laut- und Formenlehre.* Göttingen: Vandenhoeck und Ruprecht.

Blau, Joshua. 1976. *A Grammar of Biblical Hebrew.* Ponta Linguarum Orientalium NS XII. Wiesbaden: Otto Harrassowitz.

Bodine, Walter R., ed. 1995. *Discourse Analysis of Biblical Literature: What It Is and What It Offers.* SemeiaSt. Atlanta: Scholars Press.

Brockelmann, Carl. 1956. *Hebräische Syntax.* Neukirchen: Neukirchener Verlag.

Chisholm, Robert B., Jr. 1998. *From Exegesis to Exposition: A Practical Guide to Using Biblical Hebrew.* Grand Rapids, Mich.: Baker.

Claassen, W. T. 1983. "Speaker-Oriented Functions of KI in Biblical Hebrew." *Journal of Northwest Semitic Languages* 11:29–46.

Comrie, Bernard. 1976. *Aspect: An Introduction to the Study of Verbal Aspect and Related Problems.* Cambridge Textbooks in Linguistics. Cambridge: Cambridge University Press.

Crawford, Timothy G. 1992. *Blessing and Curse in Syro-Palestinian Inscriptions of the Iron Age.* New York: Peter Lang.

Dobson, John H. 1999. *Learn Biblical Hebrew.* Dallas, Tex.: SIL International.

Emerton, J. A. 1994. "New Evidence for Use of Waw Consecutive in Aramaic." *Vetus Testamentum* 44:255–58.

⸻. 2000a. "Two Issues in the Interpretation of the Tel Dan Inscription." *Vetus Testamentum* 50:29–37.

⸻. 2000b. "The Hebrew Language." Pages 171–99 in *Text in Context: Essays by Members of the Society for Old Testament Studies.* Edited by A. D. H. Mayes. New York: Oxford University Press.

Endo, Yoshinobu. 1996. *The Verbal System of Classical Hebrew in the Joseph Story: An Approach from Discourse Analysis.* SSN 32; Assen: van Gorcum.

Fassberg, Steven E. 1999. "The Lengthened Imperative קָטְלָה in Biblical Hebrew." *Hebrew Studies* 40:7–13.

⸻. 2001. "The Movement from *Qal* to *Pi"el* in Hebrew and the Disappearance of the *Qal* Internal Passive." *Hebrew Studies* 42:243–55.

Garr, W. Randall. 1985. *Dialect Geography of Syria-Palestine, 1000–586 B.C.E.* Philadelphia: University of Pennsylvania.

Goetze, Albrecht. 1942. "The So-Called Intensive of the Semitic Languages." *Journal of the American Oriental Society* 62:1–8.

Gogel, Sandra Landis. 1998. *A Grammar of Epigraphic Hebrew.* SBLRBS 23. Atlanta: Scholars.

Goshen-Gottstein, M. H. 1969. "The System of Verbal Stems in the Classical Semitic Langauges." Pages 70–91 in *Proceedings of the*

*International Conference on Semitic Studies Held in Jerusalem, 19–23 July 1965.* Jerusalem: Israel Academy of Sciences and Humanities.

Greenberg, Moshe. 1965. *Introduction to Hebrew.* Englewood Cliffs, N.J.: Prentice-Hall.

Harper, William R. 1888. *Elements of Hebrew by an Inductive Method.* 8th ed. New York: Charles Scribner's Sons.

Harris, Zellig S. 1939. *Development of the Canaanite Dialects.* American Oriental Series 16. New Haven, Conn.: American Oriental Society.

Hetzron, Robert. 1969. "The Evidence for Perfect *\*Yaqtul* and Jussive *\*Yaqt'ul* in Proto-Semitic." *Journal of Semitic Studies* 14:1–21.

Horsnell, Malcolm J. A. 1999. *A Review and Reference Grammar for Biblical Hebrew.* Hamilton, Ont.: McMaster University.

Hostetter, Edwin C. 2000. *An Elementary Grammar of Biblical Hebrew.* Biblical Languages: Hebrew, 1. Sheffield, Eng.: Sheffield Academic Press.

Huehnergard, John. 1987. "'Stative,' Predicative Form, Pseudo-Verb." *Journal of Near Eastern Studies* 46:215–32.

———. 1988. "The Early Hebrew Prefix-Conjugations." *Hebrew Studies* 29:19–23.

Jenni, Ernst. 1968. *Das hebräische Pi'el: Syntaktisch-semasiologische Untersuchung einer Verbalform im Alten Testament.* Zurich: EVZ.

———. 1981. *Lehrbuch der hebräischen Sprache des Alten Testaments.* Basel: Helbing und Lichtenhahn.

———. 1992. *Die hebräischen Präpositionen, I: Die Präposition Beth.* Stuttgart: Kohlhammer.

Johnson, Bo. 1979. *Hebräisches Perfekt und Imperfekt mit vorangehendem wᵉ.* Lund: Gleerup.

Joosten, J. 1998. "The Functions of the Semitic D Stem: Biblical Hebrew Materials for a Comparative-Historical Approach. *Or* 67:202–30.

Joüon, Paul, and Takamitsu Muraoka. 1993. *A Grammar of Biblical Hebrew.* 2 vols. Subsidia biblica 14/1–2. Rome: Editrice Pontificio Istituto Biblico.

Kaufman, Stephen A. 1996. "Semitics: Directions and Re-Directions." Pages 273–82 in *The Study of the Ancient Near East in the Twenty-First Century: The William Foxwell Albright Centennial Conference.* Edited by Jerrold S. Cooper and Glenn M. Schwarz. Winona Lake, Ind.: Eisenbrauns.

Kautzsch, Emil, ed. 1910. *Gesenius' Hebrew Grammar.* Translated and revised by A. E. Cowley. 2d English ed. Oxford: Clarendon.

Kelley, Page H. 1992. *Biblical Hebrew: An Introductory Grammar.* Grand Rapids, Mich.: Eerdmans.

Kelley, Page H., Terry L. Burden, and Timothy G. Crawford. 1994. *A Handbook to Biblical Hebrew: An Introductory Grammar.* Grand Rapids, Mich.: Eerdmans.

Kittel, Bonnie Pedrotte, Vicki Hoffer, and Rebecca Abts Wright. 1989. *Biblical Hebrew: A Text and Workbook*. New Haven/London: Yale University Press.

Kouwenberg, N. J. C. 1997. *Gemination in the Akkadian Verb*. Studia Semitica Neerlandia. Assen: Netherlands: Van Gorcum.

Krašovec, Jože. 1977. *Der Merismus im Biblisch-Hebräischen und Nordwestsemitischen*. BibOr 33. Rome: Editrice Pontificio Istituto Biblico.

————. 1983. "Merism – Polar Expression in Biblical Hebrew." *Biblica* 64:231–39.

Kroeze, Jan H. 2001. "Alternatives for the Nominative in Biblical Hebrew." *Journal of Semitic Studies* 46:33–50.

Lambdin, Thomas O. 1969. "Review of Ernst Jenni, *Das hebräische Pi'el: Syntaktisch-semasiologische Untersuchung einer Verbalform im Alten Testament*." *Catholic Biblical Quarterly* 42: 388–89.

————. 1971a. *Introduction to Biblical Hebrew*. New York: Charles Scribner's.

————. 1971b. "The Junctural Origin of the West Semitic Definite Article." Pages 315–33 in *Near Eastern Studies in Honor of William Foxwell Albright*. Edited by Hans Goedicke. Baltimore: The Johns Hopkins Press.

Landes, George M. 2001. *Building Your Biblical Hebrew Vocabulary: Learning Words by Frequency*. Atlanta: Scholars Press.

Lowery, Kirk E. 1995. "The Theoretical Foundations of Hebrew Discourse Grammar." Pages 103–30 in *Discourse Analysis of Biblical Literature: What It Is and What It Offers*. Edited by Walter R. Bodine. SemeiaSt. Atlanta: Scholars Press.

Martin, James D. 1993. *Davidson's Introductory Hebrew Grammar*. 27th ed. Edinburgh: T & T Clark.

McCarthy, Walter. 1980. "The Uses of $w^e$ *hinneh* in Biblical Hebrew." *Biblica* 61:330–42.

McFall, Leslie. 1982. *The Enigma of the Hebrew Verbal System*. Sheffield, Eng.: Almond Press.

Meier, Samuel A. 1992. *Speaking of Speaking: Marking Direct Discourse in the Hebrew Bible*. VTSup 46. Leiden: E. J. Brill.

Meyer, Rudolf. 1992. *Hebräische Grammatik*. Berlin: Walter de Gruyter. [English trans: *Hebrew Grammar*. 3d ed. Translated by P. T. Daniels. Winona Lake, Ind.: Eisenbrauns.]

Miller, Cynthia L. 1994. "Introducing Direct Discourse in Biblical Hebrew Narrative." Pages 199–241 in *Biblical Hebrew and Discourse Linguistics*. Edited by R. D. Bergen. Winona Lake, Ind.: Eisenbrauns for the Summer Institute of Linguistics.

————. 1996. *The Representation of Speech in Biblical Hebrew Narrative: A Linguistic Analysis*. HSM 55. Atlanta: Scholars Press.

————. 1999. *The Verbless Clause in Biblical Hebrew: Linguistic Approaches*. Linguistic Studies in Ancient West Semitic 1. Winona Lake, Ind.: Eisenbrauns.

Moscati, Sabatino, ed. 1980. *An Introduction to the Comparative Grammar of the Semitic Languages: Phonology and Morphology.* 3d ed. Porta Linguarum Orientalium 6. Wiesbaden: Harrassowitz.

Muilenberg, James. 1961. "The Linguistic and Rhetorical Usages of the Particle כ in the Old Testament." *Hebrew Union College Annual* 32:135–60.

Muraoka, T. 1978. "On the So-Called *Dativus Ethicus* in Hebrew." *Journal of Theological Studies* 29:495–98.

1985. *Emphatic Words and Structures in Biblical Hebrew.* Jerusalem and Leiden: Magnes Press, The Hebrew University, E. J. Brill.

Niccacci, A. 1990. *The Syntax of the Verb in Classical Hebrew Prose.* JSOTSup 86. Sheffield, Eng.: JSOT Press.

Polzin, Robert. 1976. *Late Biblical Hebrew: Toward an Historical Typology of Biblical Hebrew Prose.* HSM 12. Missoula, Mont.: Scholars.

Pratico, Gary D., and Miles V. Van Pelt. 2001. *Basics of Biblical Hebrew Grammar.* Grand Rapids, Mich.: Zondervan.

Rainey, Anson F. 1986. "The Ancient Hebrew Prefix Conjugation in Light of Amarnah Canaanite." *Hebrew Studies* 27:4–19.

1988. "Further Remarks on the Hebrew Verbal System." *Hebrew Studies* 29:35–42.

1996. *Canaanite in the Amarna Tablets: A Linguistic Analysis of the Mixed Dialect Used by the Scribes from Canaan.* 4 vols. Handbuch der Orientalistik 25/1–4. Leiden: Brill.

Revell, E. J. 1989. "The System of the Verb in Standard Biblical Prose." *Hebrew Union College Annual* 60:1–37.

Richter, Wolfgang. 1978–80. *Grundlagen einer althebräischen Grammatik.* 3 vols. St. Ottilien: EOS Verlag.

Rocine, B. M. 2000. *Learning Biblical Hebrew: A New Approach Using Discourse Analysis.* Macon, Ga.: Smyth and Helwys.

Rooker, Mark F. 1990. *Biblical Hebrew in Transition: The Language of the Book of Ezekiel.* JSOTSup 90. Sheffield, Eng.: JSOT Press.

Ross, Allen P. 2001. *Introducing Biblical Hebrew.* Grand Rapids, Mich.: Baker.

Rubinstein, Eliezer. 1952. "A Finite Verb Continued by an Infinitive Absolute in Hebrew." *Vetus Testamentum* 2:262–67.

1998. *Syntax and Semantics: Studies in Biblical and Modern Hebrew.* Texts and Studies in the Hebrew Language and Related Subjects, 9. Tel Aviv: The Chaim Rosenberg School of Jewish Studies.

Sáenz-Badillos, Angel. 1993. *A History of the Hebrew Language.* Translated by John Elwolde. Cambridge: Cambridge University Press.

Schneider, Wolfgang. 1989. *Grammatik des Biblischen Hebräisch.* Munich: Claudius Verlag.

Schoors. A. 1981. "The Particle כִּי." Pages 240–76 in *Remembering All the Way*. Oudtestamentische Studiën 21. Edited by B. Albrektson. Leiden: Brill.

Segal, M. H. 1927. *A Grammar of Mishnaic Hebrew.* Oxford: Clarendon.

Segert, Stanislav. 1984. *A Basic Grammar of the Ugaritic Language.* Berkeley: University of California Press.

Seow, C. L. 1995. *A Grammar for Biblical Hebrew.* 2d ed. Nashville, Tenn.: Abingdon.

Shulman, Ahouva. 2001. "Imperative and Second Person Indicative Forms in Biblical Hebrew Prose." *Hebrew Studies* 42:271–87.

Sinclair, Cameron. 1999. "Are Nominal Clauses a Distinct Clausal Type?" Pages 51–75 in *The Verbless Clause in Biblical Hebrew: Linguistic Approaches.* Edited by Cynthia L. Miller. Linguistic Studies in Ancient West Semitic 1. Winona Lake, Ind.: Eisenbrauns.

Smith, Mark S. 1991. *The Origins and Development of the Waw-Consecutive: Northwest Semitic Evidence from Ugarit to Qumran.* HSS 39. Atlanta, Ga.: Scholars Press.

Thomas, D. Winton. 1954. "A Consideration of Some Unusual Ways of Expressing the Superlative in Hebrew." *Vetus Testamentum* 3:209–24.

Van der Merwe, Christo H. J. 1994. "Discourse Linguistics and Biblical Hebrew Linguistics." Pages 13–49 in *Biblical Hebrew and Discourse Linguistics.* Edited by R. D. Bergen. Winona Lake, Ind.: Eisenbrauns for the Summer Institute of Linguistics.

Van der Merwe, Christo H. J., Jackie A. Naudé, and Jan H. Kroeze. 1999. *A Biblical Hebrew Reference Grammar.* Biblical Languages: Hebrew 3. Sheffield, Eng.: Sheffield Academic Press.

Waltke, Bruce K., and M. O'Connor. 1990. *An Introduction to Biblical Hebrew Syntax.* Winona Lake, Ind.: Eisenbrauns.

Weingreen, J. 1959. *A Practical Grammar for Classical Hebrew.* 2d ed. Oxford: Clarendon Press.

Westermann, Claus. 1991. *Basic Forms of Prophetic Speech.* Translated by H. C. White. Louisville, Ky.: Westminster/John Knox.

Williams, Ronald J. 1976. *Hebrew Syntax: An Outline.* 2d ed. Toronto: University of Toronto.

Zevit, Ziony. 1988. "Talking Funny in Biblical Henglish and Solving a Problem of the *yaqtul* Past Tense." *Hebrew Studies* 29: 25–33.

——— 1998. *The Anterior Construction in Classical Hebrew.* SBLMS 50. Atlanta: Scholars Press.

Zewi, Tamar. 1996. "The Particles הִנֵּה and וְהִנֵּה in Biblical Hebrew." *Hebrew Studies* 37:21–37.

# Subject Index

Page numbers in **bold italics** refer to discussions that define the subject.

# Scripture Index

Brackets indicate English references where English versification differs from the MT.

216